This volume, derived from a workshop on the 'Interrelationship between Macroeconomic Policies and Rural Development' held at the ILO in December 1989, assesses the changing role of agriculture in economic development against the background of world economic crisis and the response to it through the structural adjustment programmes. Following an introductory chapter which sets the scene, the four studies in the first part of the book deal with the effects of world economic crisis on agrarian development at the global level, as well as in the three major developing regions of the world: Africa, Asia and Latin America. The second part consists of two studies which are concerned with the longer-term issues in relation to agricultural change and economic development. This volume will help to generate fresh perspectives on the role of agriculture in economic development during the crucial decade of the 1990s.

Economic crisis and Third World agriculture

The ILO's World Employment Programme (WEP) aims to assist and encourage member States to adopt and implement active policies and projects designed to promote full, productive and freely chosen employment and to reduce poverty. Through its action-oriented research, technical advisory services, national projects and the work of its four regional employment teams in Africa, Asia and Latin America, the WEP pays special attention to the longer-term development problems of rural areas where the vast majority of poor and underemployed people still live, and to the rapidly growing urban informal sector.

At the same time, in response to the economic crises and the growth in open unemployment of the 1980s, the WEP has entered into an ongoing dialogue with the social partners and other international agencies on the social dimensions of adjustment, and is devoting a major part of its policy analysis and advice to achieving greater equity in structural adjustment programmes. Employment and poverty monitoring, direct employment creation and income generation for vulnerable groups, linkages between macro-economic and micro-economic interventions, technological change and labour market problems and policies are among the areas covered.

Through these overall activities, the ILO has been able to help national decision-makers to reshape their policies and plans with the aim of eradicating mass poverty and promoting productive employment.

This publication is the outcome of a WEP project.

Economic crisis and Third World agriculture

EDITED BY

AJIT SINGH
Queens' College, Cambridge

AND

HAMID TABATABAI
International Labour Office, Geneva

A study prepared for the International
Labour Office within the framework of
the World Employment Programme

 CAMBRIDGE
UNIVERSITY PRESS

Published by the Press Syndicate of the University of Cambridge
The Pitt Building, Trumpington Street, Cambridge CB2 1RP
40 West 20th Street, New York, NY 10011–4211, USA
10 Stamford Road, Oakleigh, Melbourne 3166, Australia

First published 1993

Printed in Great Britain at the University Press, Cambridge

A catalogue record for this book is available from the British Library

Library of Congress cataloguing in publication data

ISBN 0 521 44101 3 hardback

SE

Contents

Figures

Tables

Preface

SAMIR RADWAN

Chief, Policies and Programmes for Development Branch, Employment and Development Department

The role of agriculture in economic development is a recurrent subject in economic literature. Classical economists, particularly David Ricardo, have underlined the role of food supply as a crucial factor in determining economic growth. More recently, Simon Kuznets has described the process of structural transformation as one characterised by a transition from an economy dominated by agriculture to one that is predominantly urban, industrial and service-oriented. Following in Kuznets' tradition, various writers, especially Arthur Lewis, have analysed the mechanisms through which such transformation takes place. It is within this broader perspective that the present volume may be read. The volume acquires an added significance particularly as it attempts to address the issue of the role of agriculture in economic development at a time of economic crisis. The volume tries to explore the two-way relationship where agriculture affects the crisis and is affected by it.

The present volume, a study prepared for the International Labour Office within the framework of the World Employment Programme, is part of ongoing research on rural development at the ILO. The main objective of this research has been to contribute to the design of strategies which combine growth with distributional equity and poverty alleviation. Given this context, the research has focussed on the following issues: (a) the magnitude, nature and causes of rural poverty and the policy options available for its alleviation; (b) institutional aspects of agricultural development, especially agrarian structures and reforms; (c) the functioning of rural labour markets; (d) women in rural development; (e) participatory organisations of the rural poor; and (f) development strategies, agriculture and macroeconomic policies.

In December 1989 the ILO organised a workshop on the 'Interrelationship between Macroeconomic Policies and Rural Development' in Geneva. The workshop brought together some of the prominent researchers working in the area of rural development from around the world. Its twin objectives were: (a) to assess the research on rural development carried out at the ILO over the past fifteen years and financed mainly by the Swedish Agency for Research and Economic Cooperation with Developing Countries (SAREC); and (b) to discuss the possible future orientations of work in this area at the ILO.

Some fifteen background papers were prepared for the workshop to help focus the discussions. They attempted to provide analytical summaries of the research results in specific areas and to identify some emerging issues. They thus provided a basis for evaluating the past research and also for developing ideas for future research.

Six of the studies were subsequently revised in the light of the discussions at the workshop and are brought together in this volume along with an introductory chapter by the editors. These studies address the changing role of agriculture in the economic development of Third World countries in the 1990s and beyond in the light of the new international economic environment following the widespread economic crises of the 1980s and the structural transformation that has taken place as a result of rapid economic growth in many developing countries over the past three to four decades. This new context calls for a re-examination of its implications for the development of agriculture itself and its interactions with the rest of the economy. The introductory chapter attempts to identify the relevant issues from both short-term and long-term perspectives. Part I of the book following the Introduction is mainly concerned with the analysis of recent experiences in different developing regions and Part II with the long-term role of agriculture from the standpoint of theory as well as practice.

It is hoped that this volume provides a contribution to the present debate on structural adjustment and development.

Acknowledgements

We are indebted to many persons and institutions, and a word of thanks is in order. Earlier versions of the manuscript or parts thereof were reviewed by a number of colleagues. Our gratitude goes to Messrs Rolph van der Hoeven and Wouter van Ginneken of the ILO, Professor Hans Singer of the Institute of Development Studies, University of Sussex, Professor John Weeks of the School of Oriental and African Studies, University of London, and to two anonymous referees appointed by Cambridge University Press. Their comments and suggestions have been of great help in finalising the manuscript. Special thanks go to Ms Rosa del Rosario and Ms Cheryl Wright for typing successive versions of the manuscript with care and good humour.

We are particularly grateful to the Swedish Agency for Research and Economic Cooperation with Developing Countries (SAREC) for their financial support.

The ILO's World Employment Programme

The ILO's World Employment Programme (WEP) aims to assist and encourage member States to adopt and implement active policies and projects designed to promote full, productive and freely chosen employment and to reduce poverty. Through its action-oriented research, technical advisory services, national projects and the work of its four regional employment teams in Africa, Asia and Latin America, the WEP pays special attention to the longer-term development problems of rural areas where the vast majority of poor and underemployed people still live, and to the rapidly growing urban informal sector.

At the same time, in response to the economic crises and the growth in open unemployment of the 1980s, the WEP has entered into an ongoing dialogue with the social partners and other international agencies on the social dimensions of adjustment, and is devoting a major part of its policy analysis and advice to achieving greater equity in structural adjustment programmes. Employment and poverty monitoring, direct employment creation and income generation for vulnerable groups, linkages between macroeconomic and microeconomic interventions, technological change and labour market problems and policies are among the areas covered.

Through these overall activities, the ILO has been able to help national decision-makers to reshape their policies and plans with the aim of eradicating mass poverty and promoting productive employment.

This publication is the outcome of a WEP project.

The designations employed in ILO publications, which are in conformity with United Nations practice, and the presentation of material therein do not imply the expression of any opinion whatsoever on the part of the International Labour Office concerning the legal status of any country, area or territory or of its authorities, or concerning the delimitation of its frontiers. The responsibility for opinions expressed in studies and other contributions rests solely with their authors, and publication does not constitute an endorsement by the International Labour Office of the opinions expressed in them.

Reference to names of firms and commercial products and processes does not imply their endorsement by the International Labour Office, and any failure to mention a particular firm, commercial product or process is not a sign of disapproval.

1 Introduction

AJIT SINGH AND HAMID TABATABAI

Prior to the modern stage of economic development, the bulk of economic activity in most societies is normally concentrated in agriculture. Economists have therefore long recognised the importance of this sector for initiating and sustaining economic growth. Traditionally, following Kuznets' (1965) classic analysis, agriculture's contribution to economic development has been thought to lie in the following areas: (a) providing surplus labour to industry and to other sectors of the economy; (b) supplying food to the non-agricultural labour force and agricultural raw materials to industry; (c) providing savings and capital resources for the development of industry and other economic sectors; (d) earning foreign exchange needed for industrialisation, infrastructural and other investment projects; and (e) providing a market and demand for the goods and services produced by the non-agricultural sectors.[1] Kuznets also argued that a rise in productivity in agriculture is a pre-condition for economic growth and structural change since only then can agriculture generate a surplus and be in a position to fulfil its developmental tasks.[2]

However, in the closing decade of this century and beyond there is a different analytical and policy agenda concerning the role of agriculture in economic development. This new agenda arises from two different sets of factors. The first is of a recent vintage and concerns the international economic environment. The decade of the 1980s was characterised, in both time and space, by an extended crisis with serious adverse consequences for the Third World. These consequences are likely to be prolonged not only because the international economy may for long not experience another 'golden age' of growth as in the third quarter of this century, but also because of the way in which the crisis itself has been and is being managed, at both international and national levels. The second set of factors relates to the long-term transformation of many developing economies which experienced prior to the 1980s, and some even during the 1980s, relatively sustained growth for a period of two or three decades. The consequent structural changes have often been profound and their implications for future development strategies need to be examined. This Introduction discusses each of these two sets of factors in turn to identify their implications for the development of agriculture itself as well as for the interactions of agriculture with the rest of the economy. The final section previews the six studies included in the volume.

The order of discussion is as follows. We begin by outlining the chief features of the Third World's economic crisis in the 1980s, particularly its severe regional impact in Latin America and Africa, and setting out the broad issues it raises in relation to the role of agriculture. From a global perspective, an analytically important question is whether the behaviour of the agrarian economy in the economic slowdown of the 1980s in developing countries was similar to what happened to the agricultural sector during the Great Depression of the 1930s. This subject is not merely of historical or intellectual interest; since, as we shall see below, it leads to the important issue of the aggregate supply response of agriculture to price changes, it also has a direct bearing on the contemporary policy debate. The subsequent subsections comment on various aspects of this debate, which arises essentially from an important consequence of the economic crisis of the 1980s – the fact that a large number of countries became balance-of-payments-constrained, especially in the two most affected developing continents of Latin America and Africa. These countries were therefore obliged to implement stabilisation and adjustment measures, often under the aegis of the Bretton Woods institutions. Since, for many, agriculture accounts for a large share of export earnings, it must necessarily play a key role in any stabilisation and adjustment programme. However, the specific adjustment measures adopted by governments tend to have major implications not only for agricultural exports but also for the development of the agrarian economy as a whole, as well as for inflation, rural and urban poverty and income distribution.

Although stabilisation policies normally have a short-term focus, they inevitably also have repercussions for long-term structural change and development of the economy. Such long-term issues with respect to agriculture include the vital questions of employment and of absorption of the rapidly expanding rural and urban labour forces in developing countries as well as of intersectoral resource flows. They also draw their impetus in the current context from other considerations, including the last four decades of experience of economic development together with developments in the theoretical and empirical literature on the subject. These long-term questions concerning the role of agriculture are examined in the second section.

The final section introduces individually the papers included in this volume.[3] The papers do not address all the issues raised in this Introduction, but deal only with a subset. Many of the remaining questions are subjects of present, and it is to be hoped future, research at the ILO and elsewhere.

Third World agriculture in a crisis environment: analytical and policy issues

The economic crisis of the 1980s

In an influential study in the mid-1970s, the ILO estimated that developing countries would need a long-term economic growth rate of 7 to 8 per cent per annum, accompanied by substantial income redistribution policies, if they were to meet the basic needs of the poorest people in their societies by the end of the century (ILO, 1976, p. 42). In view of such pressing needs, and partly also in the light of the generally successful record of the developing countries during the previous two decades, the United Nations General Assembly in its December 1980 resolution on the International Development Strategy for the Third United Nations Development Decade stated that 'the average annual rate of growth of gross domestic product for developing countries as a whole during the decade [of the 1980s] should be 7 per cent'.[4] Such rates of growth imply a sustained annual rise of about 4–5 per cent in *per capita* terms.

However, as World Bank (1992) data show, the actual experience of the 1980s for a large number of developing countries, particularly in Latin America and sub-Saharan Africa, has been greatly at variance with this ambition. In 1965–73, the period before the first oil shock, the developing countries as a whole (i.e., the hundred or so low- and middle-income economies in the World Bank definition) managed to achieve a rate of growth of GNP *per capita* of 4.3 per cent per annum, despite the fact that their population was increasing at a rate of 2.5 per cent per annum. For the poor majority of the world, this was by any standard a fast rate of material development as it implied a doubling of *per capita* GNP every sixteen–seventeen years; it was also in line with the rate required to meet the basic needs of the poorest in these countries by the year 2000.

Mainly through borrowings, Third World nations by and large also managed to weather the first oil shock and other fluctuations in the world economy in the 1970s reasonably well. They were able to achieve an overall rate of growth of GNP *per capita* of 2.6 per cent per annum during 1973–80. During 1980–90, however, this growth rate declined to 1.5 per cent despite the fact that since 1973 the population in developing countries grew at the lower rate of 2.0 per cent per annum. More significantly, for the African and Latin American countries, the 1980s was a disastrous decade: these countries have experienced a sizeable *fall* in their *per capita* GNP. Not surprisingly, this decline has been accompanied by large reductions in real wages and employment in a wide range of countries on the two continents.

The World Bank data also point to another important fact: the sharply contrasting experience of the Asian countries in the 1980s relative to those in Africa and Latin America.[5] Notwithstanding the world economic crisis, both South and East Asian countries increased their trend rates of growth of GNP *per capita* in the 1980s. They also achieved significant increases in employment and appear to have by and large fulfilled the United Nations as well as the ILO targets for the decade.

Apart from the obvious question of why Asian countries have performed so much better than African and Latin American countries, these global developments raise several more specific issues in relation to the role of agriculture which are of special relevance for the present volume. First, what has been the relative experience of the agrarian economy in the three developing continents during this turbulent decade? Second, has the world economic crisis affected all the main economic sectors equally or has the impact on agriculture been different from that on other sectors (e.g., manufacturing)? Third, to what extent, if any, did the past performance of agriculture itself contribute to the overall economic decline of Latin American and African countries during the last decade? These and related issues are dealt with at some length in Part I of this volume, notably in chapter 2.

Agriculture during the Great Depression

In relation to the impact of the global economic crisis on Third World agriculture in the 1980s, the experience of the agrarian economy during the Great Depression of the 1930s is both relevant and instructive. There is a large and distinguished literature on the subject with respect to the United States which is well worth recalling in the present context.

An outstanding fact about the Great Depression in the United States was its highly differentiated sectoral impact. Agricultural production in the Depression years was much less affected, if at all, than manufacturing or other economic sectors. Between 1929 and 1932, agricultural prices in the United States fell by more than half in absolute terms and by nearly 40 per cent in relative terms. Yet agricultural production, if anything, rose during this period, as did the planted area. In contrast, manufacturing production fell by nearly 50 per cent over the same period.[6] Moreover, the fall in agricultural output in 1933 can be ascribed mainly to the influence of weather in the Great Plains (Galbraith and Black, 1938; Johnson, 1950).

Available evidence (Binswanger, 1990) also indicates that the labour input into agriculture during the Depression years hardly changed at all. By contrast, Johnson (1950) notes that between 1929 and 1933 employment in manufacturing as a whole fell by 30–35 per cent and in certain types of manufacturing (automobiles, for example) by more than 40 per cent. Hours worked fell by even more.

Two other aspects of the experience of United States agriculture in the Great Depression are noteworthy. First, there was a sharp fall in agricultural wage rates which was not matched in manufacturing. Between 1929 and 1933 wages in agriculture were halved while in manufacturing hourly earnings of production workers fell by only a fifth, from 56.6 cents in 1929 to 44.2 cents in 1933 (Johnson, 1950, p. 546). Second, although land and labour inputs into agriculture did not fall, there was a sharp reduction in farmers' use of fertilisers – by nearly 50 per cent. This evidently did not have much effect on agricultural production.[7]

The strikingly different responses of agriculture and manufacturing in the Great Depression attracted much attention from economists at the time, not least from theorists of the trade cycle.[8] Harrod (1936) suggested that because of the non-capitalist mode of production in agriculture farmers have a backward-bending supply curve of labour and, consequently, agricultural production is expected to be maintained in a depression. As both Galbraith and Black (1938) and Johnson (1950) have pointed out, however, this is not a satisfactory explanation for the behaviour of US agriculture in the 1930s. It was by then highly commercialised; only a relatively small number of farmers were engaged in subsistence or 'non-capitalistic' agriculture in the Harrodian sense and they accounted for perhaps less than 10 per cent of US farm output. Harrod's explanation is likely to be more relevant in the context of present-day developing countries, where subsistence agriculture accounts for a considerably higher proportion of output than in the United States in the 1930s.

A number of other theories have also been put forward to account for the differences in behaviour of agriculture and industry during the Depression, including the nature of the market structure in the two sectors. However, the consensus today seems to be that it is the supply-side conditions – costs and techniques – that differ between agriculture and manufacturing. As a consequence, in a cyclical downturn or depression, the supply curves of land, labour and capital in agriculture tend to be far more inelastic than in manufacturing. Although individual crops respond to changes in relative prices quickly and in the expected direction, the aggregate supply response of agriculture tends to be very slow in the short to medium term.

It is interesting to consider whether the 1980s' slowdown in economic activity has had a similar relative effect on agriculture and industrial production in the Third World as did the 1930s' Depression in the United States and, if so, whether similar causal factors have been in operation. Moreover, as we shall see below, the question of the supply response of agriculture to price changes is a central issue in current controversies with respect to structural adjustment programmes in the Third World.

Stabilisation and structural adjustment programmes

An overwhelming consequence of the slowdown in the world economy and trade and the extraordinary rise in real interest rates that resulted from the dramatic change in the United States monetary policy following the second oil shock of 1979 was that a large number of Third World nations, particularly those in Africa and Latin America, experienced severe foreign exchange constraints. They were obliged to go to the International Monetary Fund (IMF) and the World Bank for balance-of-payments support and economic assistance. However, such support was forthcoming only if countries adopted the Fund/Bank prescriptions for economic adjustment in the short run as well as in the medium and the long term (the so-called structural adjustment programme). Between 1980 and 1985, there were on average 47 countries with IMF programmes in any year – a far larger number than ever before (Cornia, 1987, p. 49).

The Bretton Woods institutions have a definite approach to adjustment which finds best expression in the actual stabilisation and structural adjustment programmes they implemented in various parts of the Third World (Avramovic, 1988; Taylor, 1988). Thus, in the short term, the IMF's adjustment programmes for many developing countries have invariably included the following elements: (a) a large devaluation of the domestic currency; (b) a reduction of the public sector borrowing requirement by reducing or eliminating consumer subsidies and many other social expenditures; (c) an increase in interest rates to raise domestic savings; and (d) a reduction of the money supply.

In addition to these short-term financial measures the Fund, often in association with the World Bank, also proposes other major policy changes to affect resource allocation, income distribution and the system of incentives, which they believe will bear fruit in the medium to long term and thus help correct the structural imbalances of the economy. In particular, developing countries are generally asked to adopt policy measures which (for example, in African countries) favour the production of export crops over food for domestic consumption or manufacturing; private sector economic activity over public, parastatal or cooperative production; and the allocation of resources by market forces (for example, by 'liberalising' controls on prices or imports) rather than directly by the government.

As Singh (1986a) has noted, in view of the enormous unfavourable changes in world economic conditions which occurred in the 1980s, many of which are likely to persist in the foreseeable future, the developing countries are today faced not only with short-term liquidity or balance-of-payments problems but also with the necessity of long-term structural adjustment. Many countries are in fundamental structural disequilibrium in the sense that their economies are unable to generate enough exports to pay for the imports required to maintain *per capita* income at a constant level, let alone to ensure a steady rise in living standards. The correction of this disequilibrium requires major changes in the structure of national production, both agricultural and industrial.

Therefore, although most economists would acknowledge the need for structural adjustment, there is much disagreement with the objectives and methods of structural adjustment as pursued by the Bretton Woods institutions (see World Bank, 1988 and 1990, for a more recent, nuanced, position of the Bank). Since agriculture in most developing countries accounts for more than half of export earnings and employs a large proportion of the labour force, its treatment in Fund/Bank programmes is of critical importance in the policy debate about structural adjustment. A number of important questions are at issue here, in relation to short- and long-term adjustment as well as to the global repercussions of adjustment programmes.

Supply response of agriculture

In view of the significance of agriculture for exports as well as for domestic food supply and hence for inflation, the success or failure of the orthodox adjustment programmes hinges to a crucial degree on the supply response of agriculture to adjustment measures. These measures essentially attempt to increase the relative prices and profitability of agricultural and other tradeable goods through, for example, currency devaluations, reduced export taxes and lower input prices (brought about by a reduction or elimination of domestic industrial protection). To put it in more popular terms, the basic purpose of the exercise is to 'get the prices right' and to eliminate the alleged 'urban bias' with which developing countries typically are thought to be afflicted.

There is a wide range of studies from all parts of the Third World showing that production of individual agricultural crops responds quickly and positively to relative price increases, the long-run response being larger than in the short run (see, for example, Askari and Cummings, 1976 and 1977; Bond, 1983). But even if individual crops respond quickly by a shift of resources from one use to another, this does not mean that the supply elasticity of agriculture as a whole is also high in the short term. In his review of the literature on this issue, Binswanger (1990) reports that for the United States, several developing countries, and a cross-section of developed and developing countries, the estimates of the aggregate supply elasticity of agriculture ranged from 0.05 to 0.25 in the short run.[9]

The analytical reasons for these results were presaged earlier in our analysis of the experience of United States agriculture during the Great Depression. As Binswanger puts it:

the price elasticity of all agriculture is very low in the short run. The problem is that the main factors of agricultural production – land, capital, and labor – are fixed in the short run.

Unlike individual crops, aggregate agricultural output can grow only if more resources are devoted to agriculture or if technology changes. The literature shows convincingly that the long-run response of agriculture is large: higher prices will slow migration out of rural areas and increase investment in agriculture. But these responses take time to develop fully – as much as ten to twenty years. They also depend greatly on public investments in roads, markets, irrigation, infrastructure, education, and health. (Binswanger, 1990, p. 232)

The focus of most adjustment programmes, however, is more specifically on increasing agricultural *exports*. Balassa (1986) has reported a large response of agricultural exports to changes in relative prices brought about by devaluation. For the period 1965–82 he found that, for the developing countries as a whole, the elasticity of the ratio of agricultural exports to agricultural output with respect to the real exchange rate was 0.68; for *net* agricultural exports, the corresponding elasticity was as high as 4.96 (cited in Binswanger, 1990, p. 240). In sub-Saharan African countries these elasticities were in general much greater than those in the developing countries as a whole. On the face of it, therefore, these results may suggest that Fund/Bank policy measures achieve their basic objective of an improvement in a country's balance-of-payments position.

This, however, would be a hasty conclusion; there is evidence that an expansion of export production may take place at the expense of domestic production, or that agricultural exports may increase while domestic food production and consumption do not rise and may even fall. Binswanger (1990, p. 241) notes that, in Mexico's adjustment in 1984–88, net agricultural exports rose rapidly after the devaluation of 1985 but neither aggregate output nor food consumption increased. If *per capita* food consumption or production falls, quite apart from any distributional or equity considerations, this may jeopardise the whole of the adjustment programme by fuelling inflation and political strife. Such an outcome can be avoided by policy measures which increase overall agricultural production. But this can only happen over a longer timespan with increased investments to improve infrastructure and technology in agriculture – investments which are often threatened when governments have to reduce fiscal spending greatly as part of the Fund/Bank adjustment programmes.

Impact on rural poverty

What has been the impact of the changes in world economic conditions in the 1980s on rural poverty in the Third World? There is no simple relationship between these variables; rather there is a complex chain of causation which links the deceleration in world economic growth, as well as other changes in international economic forces, with possible variations in rural and urban poverty in the developing countries. An examination of these causal links raises a number of conceptual issues which are outlined below.

The first link in this causal chain concerns the relationship between the world economic crisis, overall economic growth and agricultural development in the developing countries. The next is the relationship between the last two variables and rural poverty. There is a large body of literature which suggests that there is no necessary 'trickle-down' effect of either overall economic growth or of agricultural expansion – neither of these need automatically benefit the poorest people.[10] But is this a symmetrical relationship? Would not reduced GDP or agricultural growth (resulting from the world economic crisis) necessarily harm the poor?

More importantly, a significant link in the causal chain is provided by the adjustment measures which countries adopt in response to externally induced economic disequilibria. These adjustment measures – whether of the IMF variety or not – often include changes to a country's monetary, fiscal, exchange-rate or commercial policies. Such policy changes inevitably have significant implications for income distribution and poverty, both rural and urban.

There is a large measure of controversy concerning the consequences for poverty and income distribution of IMF/World Bank economic adjustment programmes in developing countries. There is a sizeable body of opinion, and not only in the Third World, which decries the adverse distributional implications of these programmes, particularly for the poor. However, the Bretton Woods institutions argue that many of their preferred policies lead to an improvement rather than a worsening of income distribution or a deterioration in the condition of the poor. They suggest that, since the essential purpose of the policy measures is to switch resources from non-trading towards export sectors, for a typical commodity-exporting developing country this involves provision of greater incentives for agriculture at the expense of urban industry and other economic activity.

That is, it reduces 'urban bias'. Since urban incomes and living standards are higher than those in rural areas, such a resource switch must lead to a reduction in income inequality and rural poverty.[11]

This is clearly a serious and, on the face of it, a plausible argument which requires careful examination. Let us consider it briefly in relation to the specific question of devaluation which is often the centrepiece of IMF stabilisation programmes. It is essential to the logic of an 'effective devaluation' that there should be a cut in real wages by making all imported goods (and their substitutes) more expensive in relation to workers' income. If successfully implemented, a typical IMF programme has two extremely important short-term effects on the economy: (i) it leads to a cut in overall compensation and real wages; and (ii) it leads to a redistribution of income away from those who produce for the domestic market to those who are involved in production of exports or import substitutes.

The seeds of inflation and indeed of political destabilisation lie in these selfsame effects of devaluation. As Kaldor points out:

The main objection to this approach is that it assumes devaluation is capable of changing critical price and wage relationships that are the outcome of complex political forces and that could not be changed by domestic fiscal and monetary policies. But it is more likely that a large-scale devaluation will end up by reproducing much the same initial price relationships at the cost of a great deal of additional inflation. (Kaldor, 1983, p. 35)

Leaving aside the question of inflation for the moment, whether even an effective devaluation will improve income distribution in a developing country will depend on the nature of the existing income distribution between rural and urban areas and, more importantly, on the rural income distribution itself. Rural areas do not just produce commodities for export; they also produce food and subsistence agriculture, most of which is non-traded. Often the export sector is small in employment terms in relation to the total size of the agricultural economy. In such circumstances a devaluation will increase income inequality in the rural areas, and may also do so overall.

In short, the effects of devaluation and of the consequent changes in internal relative prices on income distribution depend very much on the structure of the economy. In some circumstances income distribution might improve but, for the reasons outlined above, there can be no presumption that it will do so in a typical developing country, let alone in all countries. Even if it reduces income inequality in a given country, it may nevertheless worsen the plight of the poorer sections of the community because of its other effects. In particular, large devaluations, as noted previously, invariably lead to inflation. There is a large body of literature which shows that 'inflation' by itself is a major determinant of rural poverty because it reduces the purchasing power of the rural landless poor.[12] Moreover, apart from devaluation, IMF programmes often involve cuts in food subsidies and increases in producer prices. These are likely to lead to a greater than average rise in food prices which, unless accompanied by other compensating measures, will have particularly serious consequences for the urban and the rural landless poor.

Apart from its consequences for inflation, a typical IMF adjustment programme can have a major impact on the rural poor through changes in fiscal policy. To the extent that the required reductions in the public sector borrowing requirement are achieved by imposing regressive indirect taxes (e.g., increasing value-added tax) and cuts in social expenditure on health, education, etc., the effect on the poor will be adverse. On the other hand, officially, an avowed purpose of IMF stabilisation programmes is to make possible 'efficient, non-inflationary economic growth' in the developing countries. In so far as this objective is actually met in practice, the poor may be expected to gain even in the absence of 'trickle-down', because of reduced inflation and increased fiscal spending made possible by renewed economic growth.

Longer-term and global implications of adjustment programmes for agriculture

However, apart from questions concerning the methods of achieving economic adjustment, there are also important issues which relate to the long-term implications of Fund/Bank programmes and the role of agriculture in that context. As seen earlier, for short-term stabilisation and balance-of-payments reasons, in these programmes agriculture is promoted relative to industry and, within agriculture, export crops are promoted relative to food crops. A central question here is whether this is the right kind of structural change from the point of view of *long-term development* in the developing countries. In the foreseeable future the world economy is more likely to grow at its slower post-1973 trend rate than it did in the 'golden age' period of 1950–73 (see Glyn *et al.*, 1990; Singh, 1990). This will mean that, among other things, world trade is likely to expand at a slower pace than it did in the golden age. It is also likely to mean that the adverse terms of trade experienced by the developing countries during the 1980s may not be reversed. In such circumstances, it is to say the least arguable that, whatever its short-term merits, from a long-term standpoint the Bretton Woods institutions are promoting the wrong kind of structural change in the developing countries.

Moreover, this Fund/Bank sponsored pattern of structural adjustment has extremely important global repercussions. With an exogenous increase in the supply of agricultural commodities, which have a low income and price elasticity of demand, prices may fall. This would negate gains which the developing countries would obtain from increased commodity production.[13] There are indications that to some degree this process is already taking place. One relevant piece of evidence is the fact that, despite a long and sustained expansion in the economies of industrial countries in the 1980s (since the trough of 1982), agricultural commodity prices generally remained weak. On the basis of past economic relationships, one would have expected such a prolonged OECD economic expansion to have led to much higher commodity prices and more favourable terms of trade for the developing countries. This has not occurred; the reverse has happened instead.[14]

Not only have commodity prices been low in the 1980s but there is evidence that they have also been subject to greater *fluctuations* than before. Keynes (1974) had argued long ago, in the now famous United Kingdom Treasury Memorandum of 1942, that fluctuations in commodity prices are inefficient from the point of view of the world economy as a whole. In a later, important contribution, Kaldor (1976) showed that the *advanced* countries are harmed both by too high a level of commodity prices (which leads to inflation because of the nature of the labour market institutions in these countries) as well as by too *low* a level of these prices (as this results in lower demand for the North's products in the South).[15] Nevertheless, there is an enormous prejudice among economic policymakers in the North and orthodox economists against market intervention and in particular against international commodity agreements (ICAs). In a notable contribution, Maizels (1988) has carefully examined all the standard arguments against the ICAs and found them wanting. He concludes that most of these arguments are based on untenable assumptions or are otherwise invalid or of limited applicability. Nevertheless, in view of the conflicting analyses in this area and because of its potential global importance for both rich and poor countries, the issue of international commodity agreements must continue to remain high on the policy research agenda.

The question of commodity price fluctuations raises other important issues – both at global and at national policy level. First, what are the reasons for the increased fluctuations? Apart from the weather and the volatility associated with food production technology in advanced countries, it has been argued by Mellor (1987, p. 49) that 'the most important factor in increased price variability is the withdrawal of the United States from providing world price stability as a by-product of its domestic farm income support programs'.[16] On the other hand, the World Bank (1986) and many orthodox economists suggest that liberalisation of domestic and international markets for agricultural products in the advanced countries will *reduce* commodity price instability. As these alternative theories have rather different policy implications, there is clearly need for further work in this area.

Second, from the point of view of economic policy within developing countries themselves, a very important issue is to what extent, if any, they should protect domestic agriculture from international price fluctuations. In view of the magnitude of these fluctuations, unless there is overt government intervention with provision of a floor of stable domestic prices, agricultural investment by individual farmers may be much less than otherwise.

Agriculture and development: the long-term issues

Structural changes and the role of agriculture

Apart from the international economic crisis and the need for stabilisation and adjustment in a large number of countries, impetus for current reassessments of the role of agriculture in economic development comes from long-term factors. As noted earlier, notwithstanding the economic problems of the developing countries in the 1980s, many of them have achieved an impressive degree of economic growth during the last 30 years.

Sustained growth brought about significant changes in the structure of developing economies, particularly as regards the importance of agriculture. The contribution of agriculture to GDP in developing economies halved, from 32 to 15 per cent, over the period from 1960 to 1989 (UNCTAD, 1992, p. 446). All the regional groups of countries experienced much the same decline, at least until 1980, in the share of agriculture in total output.[17] However, even though agriculture's share in the labour force has also declined, this sector still engages three-fifths of the Third World's labour force (FAO, 1986). A comparison of the two shares, furthermore, suggests that, until 1980, not only was labour productivity in agriculture much lower than in all non-agricultural sectors combined, but the difference in productivity levels was widening over time. In the 1980s, the pace of structural change decelerated as the share of agriculture in GDP declined more slowly than in the past or actually rose in some regions. FAO (1986) estimates, however, indicate that agriculture's share in labour force continued to fall in all regions in the 1980s at much the same rate as before. This may suggest that the migration of labour from agriculture to other sectors does not take place simply in response to the so called 'pull' factors: labour appears to have continued to shift out of agriculture even though the conditions of the non-agricultural economy (particularly in Latin America and sub-Saharan Africa) had greatly deteriorated, real wages in many of these economies had fallen sharply and urban unemployment had increased. This conclusion, however, should be viewed as tentative since labour force data of the 1980s are projections made, presumably, on the basis of past trends and expectations about future intersectoral movement of labour, expectations which may not have materialised due to the onset of the crisis.

The decline in the share of agriculture in the labour force and employment of course accords with the broad historical pattern in the process of economic development, as indicated in the well-known studies of today's advanced countries by Kuznets (1966 and 1971). Analytically, there are two significant forces at work here – the income elasticity of demand (η) and the rate of productivity growth (p) – which lead to *long-term* changes in the shares of the three economic sectors (agriculture, industry (manufacturing), and services) as *per capita* income increases. The essential stylised facts concerning 'η' and 'p' in the three sectors can be summarised as follows:

$$\eta_a < \eta_m \simeq \eta_s$$
$$p_a \simeq p_m > p_s$$

where the subscripts refer to the economic sectors. If these relationships hold, it can be shown that, over time, the share of agriculture and manufacturing in employment will eventually be greatly reduced and most of the labour force will tend to be employed in the service sector, as is increasingly the case in the advanced economies. As the bulk of economic activity initially originates in the agricultural sector, in the early stages of development, and until a fairly high level of *per capita* income is reached, the manufacturing sector will expand at the expense of agriculture, in terms of both output and employment; it is only in the very long term that labour will shift out of manufacturing into services.[18]

However, although the significance of agriculture will decline with economic growth over the long run, as the above account suggests, the important policy question for a specific country or for developing countries as a whole is whether the observed decline is, in some sense, 'optimal'. Or, to put it more simply, is 'de-ruralisation' (in the sense of a decline in the share of agriculture in output and employment) occurring at too fast a pace or much too slowly? Should economic policy be geared towards accelerating the decline in the share of agriculture or should it rather attempt to slow it down?

A number of economists argue that, in general, the actual decline in agriculture's share in recent decades in developing countries has been less than optimal, in view of the large underemployment of labour in agriculture and the very low levels of productivity in that sector. Others suggest, on the basis of the poor living conditions in many Third World cities (slums and urban squalor), that 'de-ruralisation' has been, if anything, too rapid. In view of its policy significance, the concept of the optimal degree of de-ruralisation requires precision.

Following Singh's (1977, 1987, 1989) definition of an efficient manufacturing sector in the context of 'de-industrialisation' of an advanced economy, we may conceptualise an 'efficient' size and composition of the agricultural sector, and hence the optimal degree and rate of de-ruralisation for a developing country as one which best enables it to achieve its *overall long-term growth potential* as well as meet the country's *social objectives with respect to poverty alleviation, income distribution, and employment*. To illustrate, there was a large fall in the share of agriculture in Nigeria in the oil boom decade, 1973–83. This was largely an indirect consequence of the rising exchange rate and other factors associated with the oil price rise (the 'Dutch disease' syndrome). In 1973 agricultural production accounted for 54 per cent of GDP; by 1983 this share had fallen to 34 per cent as a result of both the rise in oil revenues and the attendant decline in agriculture, as resources were sucked away from the sector. In terms of the analytical scheme outlined here, such de-ruralisation would be regarded as much too fast and inefficient since most economists would agree that this has reduced the long-term growth potential of the Nigerian economy as a whole (see, for example, Collier, 1988). Over the same period in the Republic of Korea, the share of agriculture in GDP fell from 35 to 15 per cent. This even more rapid rate of de-ruralisation may be regarded as having been efficient since it did not undermine the long-term growth potential of its economy; it was also consistent with the alleviation of poverty and creation of adequate employment opportunities outside agriculture. Thus to make this conception of an optimal pace of 'de-ruralisation' operational from a policy perspective would require, *inter alia*, a careful analysis of agriculture's various contributions, including, in particular, to the balance of payments and to employment.

Employment

The question of employment looms large for most Third World governments. Despite some slowdown in the rate of population growth in Asia and Latin America, the labour force in developing countries in the 1980s was increasing at a slightly faster rate than before in all the main regions, including Asia and Latin America; the acceleration in the rate in these two continents being due to previous demographic growth (Ghose, 1990). In the 1980s, the average labour force growth rate in the developing countries as a whole was expected to be around 2.3 per cent per annum (ILO, 1986).

To appreciate the nature of the overall employment problem the Third World countries have to contend with, consider a specific country example. In Mexico, the rate of labour force growth is currently about 3 per cent per annum. Before the economic crisis of the 1980s, the long-term trend rate of productivity growth in that country was also of the order of 3 per cent per annum (Brailovsky, 1981). On the basis of past economic relationships, therefore, the Mexican economy would need to grow at a rate of 6 per cent per annum just to provide jobs for new entrants to the labour force; economic growth would need to be faster still if the existing large backlog of unemployment and underemployment were to be appreciably reduced. In fact, between 1982 and 1990 the average growth rate of the economy was close to zero, which, regrettably, is fairly typical of many other Latin American countries during the 1980s.

In relation to agriculture, a very important question, therefore, is the capacity or the desirability of this sector to employ more labour. Here there is a significant dilemma. For the structural reasons outlined earlier, as well as because technical progress in agriculture is generally both labour-saving and land-saving, the long-run employment elasticity of agricultural output tends to be very small, if not negative. Some values of the 'measured employment elasticity' in agriculture for different groups of countries, over the period 1961–90, are given below:[19]

Developed market economies	− 1.94
Developing market economies	0.48
Latin America	0.25
Sub-Saharan Africa	0.90
South and South-east Asia	0.43

These are crude elasticities and are obtained as the ratio of the rate of growth of the 'economically active population' in agriculture to that of agricultural output. Thus the figures do not necessarily reflect solely the supply response of the labour force to increases in agricultural production. The 'economically active population' in agriculture can rise without any concomitant expansion of the agrarian economy if there are no or insufficient employment opportunities outside the sector. All the same, the measured employment elasticities for the developed market economies are negative and for the Latin American countries quite small.

As opposed to this crude global analysis of employment elasticity in agriculture, there is some detailed microeconomic evidence on 'genuine' employment elasticities – the response of agricultural employment to increases in agricultural production – which is more significant. Empirical research on the Indian Green Revolution indicates that, as the agrarian economy moves from one to two or more crops, the demand for agricultural labour rises. But once multiple cropping has been achieved, 'genuine' employment elasticity begins to decline and it may even become negative, as is the case in the advanced countries. Thus even though in a number of developing countries there may be a short- to medium-term increase in the employment capacity of the agrarian economy as the new Green Revolution-type technologies are introduced, over the longer term (say, after a decade) the employment elasticity would be expected to decline.

There has also been some recent evidence on changes in employment elasticities in the organised manufacturing sector in developing countries which make the long-term overall employment problem for these countries much more complex. Normally, as implied by our earlier discussion, in the course of economic development this elasticity is generally positive, fairly high and remains stable until a high level of *per capita* income is reached; this permits labour gradually to shift out of agriculture into manufacturing. The actual experience of developing countries has been that the employment elasticity of the organised or the formal manufacturing sector is of the order of 0.5 to 0.7 (Singh, 1984). However, recent Indian evidence indicates that the value of this elasticity has already begun to decline, even though *per capita* income in India is still very low (see, in particular, the study by Ghose, chapter 4 in this volume).

If the Indian experience of employment in the organised manufacturing sector is repeated for other countries, it will inevitably mean that the bulk of new jobs will, increasingly, have to come from the informal sector in manufacturing and from services. From the point of view of long-term employment in the 1990s and beyond in the developing countries, the significant issue therefore is not so much the older question of the relationship between agriculture and industry as that between agriculture, on the one hand, and the informal and formal sectors in manufacturing as well as services, on the other. The important issue for research is how the complexities of such relationships should be modelled.

Analytical and theoretical work

A further impulse towards a re-evaluation of the long-term role of agriculture in economic development comes from the analytical and theoretical work on these subjects during the last three decades. In the light of the actual experience of developing countries and its observed variance with previous theoretical constructs, development theorists and policy-makers became increasingly sceptical of the validity of Feldman–Mahalanobis and Lewis-type structural models of long-term development in which agriculture plays a basically passive and accommodating role to the requirements of the 'modern sector'.[20] Long before the theses concerning 'urban bias' gained popularity in development circles in the West,[21] Mao Tse-Tung provided a trenchant critique of the Preobrazhensky–Feldman–Mahalanobis kinds of analyses[22] of the role of the agrarian economy in economic development. Evaluating the first seven years of economic development in China, when the country had by and large followed the Soviet model, Mao observed in his famous 1956 speech, 'The Ten Major Relationships', that although

the production of the means of production must be given priority ... it definitely does not follow that the production of the means of subsistence, especially grain, can be neglected ... Heavy industry can also accumulate capital, but, given our present economic conditions, light industry and agriculture can accumulate more and faster.

Mao went on to argue that greater emphasis on agriculture and light industry would eventually 'lead to a greater and faster development of heavy industry and, since it ensures the livelihood of the people, it will lay a more solid foundation for the development of heavy industry' (Mao Tse-Tung, 1977, pp. 285–6).

As Singh (1979) noted, Mao's essential point was that forced-draft industrialisation, which neglects agriculture and the standard of living of the people, would be counter-productive. He still believed heavy industry to be essential for the long-term industrialisation of the country, but he thought that better results would be achieved in this sphere if agriculture were put on a secure foundation and the consumption levels of the peasantry improved. Otherwise the peasantry would feel exploited; and not only would that mean lower motivation (as had been the case in some other socialist countries),[23] but it would destroy the worker/peasant alliance which had been the cornerstone of the Chinese revolution, with serious consequences for long-run development.

Mao's analysis thus also represented an early critique of the simple 'surplus' models, whereby the main task of development policy is to extract surplus from agriculture in order to foster industry. He stressed the complexities of the political economy of this process and the fact that the size of the surplus may itself be affected by the nature, mode and politics of its extraction. The Maoist thesis was also prescient for favouring a 'balanced development' of heavy industry, light industry and agriculture, a view later conceptualised in the slogan 'agriculture as the foundation and industry as the leading sector'.

Prominent among the theoretical economists with a broadly 'structural' approach to economic development – i.e., those who regard industry's role as pre-eminent ('engine of growth') in the process but nevertheless see agriculture as a binding constraint – were Kaldor and Kalecki. Kaldor observed that industrialization ... can be expected to follow, almost automatically, upon the growth of the food surpluses of the agricultural sector. Once this is recognized, the efforts of underdeveloped countries could be concentrated – far more than they are at present – on tackling the problem of how to raise productivity on the land, as a prior condition of economic development. (Kaldor, 1960, p. 242)

Kaldor was perhaps too sanguine at the time about the 'almost automatic' translation of food surpluses into industrial development, as later experience in developing countries was to demonstrate. But he was right to emphasise the necessity of raising productivity on the land in order to sustain the industrialisation drive. Similarly, in Kalecki's (1972) model, the rate of growth of food supply did not simply adjust passively to the requirements of industrialisation but constantly threatened to fall short of it.

By the 1970s, Lewis, in significant contributions, was also suggesting that the chief constraint on future economic development in the developing countries was the rate of growth of agricultural productivity. This was for two reasons. First, reflecting on the actual experience of the less developed countries (LDCs) in the previous two decades, he observed:

Agriculture has been the weakest link in the development chain. Industry in LDCs has grown at around 7 per cent per annum, the number of children in school has multiplied by four, the domestic savings ratio has risen by three percentage points – the picture is everywhere bright until one turns to agriculture, where the dominant fact is that, in LDCs as a whole, food production has failed to keep pace with the demand for food, thereby causing or aggravating a whole series of other problems. (Lewis, 1984, p. 418)

Secondly, in the context of a deceleration in world economic growth, Lewis put forward an important analytical argument for giving primacy to raising agricultural productivity. He suggested that

the individual LDC does not have to be so dependent on exports in its development strategy. It should look more to the home market. What limits industrial production for the home market is the small agricultural surplus of that 50 per cent or more of the labor market that is engaged in growing food for home consumption. Transform this mass of low-level productivity, and the whole picture changes. (Lewis, 1978, p. 74)

He went on to provide the following policy message for developing countries:

The most important item on the agenda of development is to transform the food sector, create agricultural surpluses to feed the urban population, and thereby create the domestic basis for industry and modern services. If we can make this domestic change, we shall automatically have a new international economic order. (Lewis, 1978, p. 75)

Changing perceptions about the long-term role of agriculture in economic development are best exemplified by the recent debate over the future development strategy for India after nearly four decades of planning. It is ironic, but also entirely fitting, that this debate should take place in a country where the Feldman–Mahalanobis model held sway for so long. The late Professor Sukhamoy Chakravarty, long a leading 'agriculture-first' exponent (see Chakravarty, 1987), shared with Lewis a profound scepticism about the desirability as well as the feasibility of an export-led growth strategy in a slow-growing world economy, particularly for a large country like India. In such international economic circumstances, he suggested that long-term economic growth in India must primarily be based on the expansion of internal rather than external demand. This, he believed, was best achieved by a large-scale government programme of investment in irrigation and other agriculture-related infrastructure which would enable the Green Revolution technologies to be spread from Punjab and Haryana to other parts of the country. Such an investment strategy should lead to an acceleration in the rate of growth of agricultural productivity, a rise in farm incomes and reduced rural poverty, and hence an expansion in demand for the products of both large- and small-scale industry.[24]

Chakravarty's 'agriculture-first' development programme may be contrasted with an alternative long-term strategy favoured by the World Bank as well as by many Indian policymakers. In this view India, at its current stage of development, should follow essentially a long-term policy of 'industry-first'. Agriculture, in this alternative analysis, is no longer regarded as a constraint on Indian development and hence, it is argued, should be subject to 'benign neglect'. Liberalisation of domestic markets and imports will, it is believed, lead to 'efficient' and faster growth of industry and overall GDP, based on the demands generated by the growing middle class.

This programme, aptly termed by Lance Taylor the 'Brazilian model', was actually implemented in India during the 1980s, particularly after 1984.[25] In terms of overall economic growth it appeared to be successful, since the growth rate was higher than in the previous two decades. However, because of the high import intensity of the industrial investments undertaken to cater to middle-class demands, it also seriously affected the balance of payments and left the Indian economy subject to the danger of a Latin American-type debt trap in the 1990s.[26] Its vulnerability manifested itself in 1991 with an acute liquidity crisis which forced the Government to turn to the IMF for support in order to restore financial stability. The recently elected Congress Government has subsequently adhered even more closely to the liberal strategy adopted in the 1980s.[27]

Whether or not India will abandon this strategy and adopt instead Chakravarty's 'agriculture-first' programme will depend in part on the dimensions of the economic crisis the country faces in the 1990s, but above all on the relative political strength of the urban middle classes and upper-income groups and the rural peasantry. India's case is by no means unique. Many developing countries, particularly in Latin America and Africa, are faced with similar crucial strategic decisions as they attempt to rescue themselves from what for many of them has been the lost decade of the 1980s.

The studies in this volume

Apart from this Introduction, this book consists of two Parts. Part I of the volume includes four studies which are concerned with the effects of the world economic crisis on agrarian development in different parts of the Third World. The first by Singh and Tabatabai (chapter 2) provides a global overview of the agricultural development in the Third World in the 1980s with a focus on the following main questions: (a) how did this development differ from the experience of the 1960s and 1970s and in particular how was it affected by the world economic crisis? and (b) to what extent, if any, could the Third World's severe economic difficulties during the last decade be attributed to the previous poor performance of the agrarian economy itself (the reverse causation question)?

Inter alia, a significant conclusion of this study is that the Third World's agrarian economy was much less affected by the world economic slowdown of the early 1980s than either industry or GDP as a whole. In Africa and Latin America, the two continents which were most adversely affected by the world economic crisis in the last decade, the agricultural sector suffered relatively little setback while industrial and GDP growth collapsed. As discussed in chapter 2, the experience of the Third World's agrarian economy during the 1980s has been rather similar to that of United States agriculture in the Great Depression of the 1930s.

There are, however, some significant differences too. First, in the 1930s – as in the 1980s – there was an adverse movement in the international terms of trade against agriculture. But, unlike the situation in the developing countries in the 1980s, the United States government in the 1930s made no attempt to counteract that effect and US *internal* terms of trade remained highly unfavourable to agriculture. As observed earlier, most Third World governments, particularly in sub-Saharan Africa and Latin America, invariably tried, often under the impetus of structural adjustment programmes, to move the internal terms of trade in favour of agriculture in the 1980s, despite falling world commodity prices. This was attempted through measures such as devaluations and import liberalisation of industrial products. Second, in part as a consequence of such policies, the standard of living of rural populations in Africa and Latin America generally declined relatively less than that of the urban population. During the Great Depression, not only did rural wage rates fall far more than the industrial wages in the United States, because of the adverse movement in external as well as internal terms of trade against food and agricultural products, the standard of living of urban workers – those who did not lose their jobs, but were still in employment – most likely improved as a result.

Regional experiences are more fully analysed by the three remaining studies in Part I. That on Africa by Jamal (chapter 3) dwells on the parallels and contrasts between some of the current issues arising in connection with the role of African agriculture in structural adjustment and their historical antecedents. These relate to the relative balance between export and food crops, the importance of price incentives and the proper role of agriculture in economic recovery. Jamal is rather sceptical of the general validity of the 'urban bias' thesis, which is at the core of the model that provides the intellectual underpinnings of adjustment programmes in Africa. He nevertheless concludes that agriculture has indeed been squeezed to finance the development of non-agricultural sectors, industry in particular, although this fact neither explains the current crisis nor points to a cure for it (by putting a stop to the squeeze). The fault lay rather in the weakness in state policy which failed to plough back some of the surplus to modernise agriculture itself, a conclusion similar to that of Karshenas in chapter 7. Jamal ends his study on a somewhat pessimistic note, concluding that, while agricultural exports now contribute the only sure means of fuelling the economy, as they did at the turn of the century, the current conditions are nowhere near as favourable as they were then.

The study by Ghose on Asia (chapter 4) has the happier task of trying to explain some success stories along with some less successful ones. This leads him to adopt a comparative framework for a detailed analysis of four Asian countries: India, the Republic of Korea, the Philippines and Thailand. Ghose identifies foreign exchange as the binding constraint that explains the pace and pattern of economic growth and considers the ways in which different countries sought to overcome it. He finds that none of the four sample countries attempted to promote agricultural exports, relying instead on policies that sustained manufacturing exports or on debt accumulation. Though contrary to the prescriptions of orthodox stabilisation and adjustment programmes, this approach was very much in line with developments in the world economy which witnessed a stagnation of demand for agricultural products and a decline in their relative prices in international markets. Ghose then considers the implications of the changes in the world economy for the industrialisation strategy in the sample countries.

The last study in Part I by de Janvry and Sadoulet on Latin America (chapter 5) starts off by creating a typology of nine countries in terms of their relative success or failure in stabilising their economies and the role of agriculture in this. The authors observe that those countries in which agriculture had the capacity to grow (and hence increase agricultural exports or substitute for agricultural imports) were more successful in their stabilisation efforts. The instruments of stabilisation, however, had contradictory impacts on agriculture with real exchange depreciation generally favouring its growth while contraction of the economy, reduction of public investment expenditure and inflation tending to have the opposite effect. On balance, the authors find, the growth of agriculture has been more a function of non-price factors such as public investment and overall economic growth than of price incentives created through devaluation. Using a variety of indicators, they further conclude that the main burden of the crisis was borne primarily by those in the formal sector in urban areas rather than by the poorer farmers. Contrary to Jamal's assessment of present-day conditions in Africa, however, de Janvry and Sadoulet advance the view that the emerging realities in Latin America have opened up opportunities for a new model of rural development of which the main features are a redefined role for the State, the involvement of grass-roots organisations and the promotion of enabling conditions that emphasise the development of human capital, local institutions and employment opportunities in non-farm activities.

The two studies in Part II of the book are concerned with longer-term issues in relation to the role of agriculture in economic development. Bhaduri's study (chapter 6) provides a comprehensive critique of a number of influential models of agrarian change and economic development in the structuralist tradition – the Preobrazhensky model, the Feldman–Mahalanobis model, and the Lewis model. He points out the drastic simplifications and shortcomings of these models in relation to economic development in a country with a mixed economy which is attempting to industrialise in the face of a foreign exchange constraint. Specifically, the author draws attention to four important aspects of the relationship of agriculture to industry and to the rest of the economy which are either ignored or inadequately treated in these models: (i) the complex political economy of the generation of marketed surplus in the agricultural sector and the related issues of terms of trade and intersectoral resource flows; (ii) the adjustment of the real wage rate and the political economy of this process; (iii) the question of incentive to invest; and (iv) with respect to rural–urban migration, the enormous resource costs of urbanisation. When some of these elements are incorporated into the traditional models, their conclusions change dramatically with respect to the role of agriculture in a development strategy, the appropriate pace and content of industrialisation, and how it should best be financed.

The financing of industrialisation and of intersectoral resource flows are the subject matter of the study by Karshenas (chapter 7). He examines, both theoretically and empirically, the vexed but extremely important question of who bears the burden of industrialisation during the course of economic growth: agriculture or industry; the rural peasantry or the urban proletariat and other social groups. Karshenas shows analytically that the burden of industrialisation has often not been, and does not necessarily have to be, borne mainly by the rural sector. If urban wages fall in real terms (due to an adverse movement in the terms of trade of manufacturing, for example), most of the burden may be borne by the industrial sector itself. Agriculture provides industry with food, raw materials and markets, and industry in turn gives to agriculture consumer and producer goods as well as markets. Thus measuring empirically the 'net burden' of industrialisation, and establishing who bears it, becomes very complicated. There are, in addition, factors relating to government fiscal policy and the incidence of taxation and benefits provided by the State. Karshenas provides an appropriate accounting framework for making these empirical measurements. He applies this framework to five countries: India (during the period 1951–70); Taiwan, China (1911–60); the Islamic Republic of Iran (1963–77); Japan (1888–1937) and China (1952–80). He finds that, except in Japan and Taiwan, China, agriculture's net contribution to industrial accumulation was negative in the other three countries for much of the relevant period. Despite the inevitable limitations of such empirical estimates, which Karshenas is quick to acknowledge, theses concerning ubiquitous 'urban-bias' in the developing countries need at the very least a re-examination.

Notes

Comments by Samir Radwan, Vali Jamal, Ajit Ghose and Hans Singer on an earlier draft of this Introduction are gratefully acknowledged. The usual caveat applies. A somewhat different version of this Introduction was published in Singh and Tabatabai (1992).

1 Kuznets distinguished between the 'product', 'market' and 'factor' contributions of agriculture. Although he did not refer explicitly to the foreign exchange contribution, it was implicit in his analysis and could be subsumed under his 'market' contribution. A similar classification was also suggested by Johnston and Mellor (1961), among others.
2 The views of several leading 'structuralist' economists – Kaldor, Kalecki, Lewis and Chakravarty – are discussed later in this Introduction.

3 These papers have been selected from those presented originally at the ILO/ Swedish Agency for Research and Economic Cooperation with Developing Countries (SAREC) workshop on the 'Interrelationship between Macroeconomic Policies and Rural Development' (Geneva, 11–13 December 1989). They were subsequently revised by the authors in the light of the discussion at the workshop and the comments of the editors.

4 United Nations General Assembly Resolution 35/36, 5 December 1980, para. 20.

5 For the basic data on the subject see World Bank (1992). For an analysis of the issues involved see Sachs (1985), Singh (1986a) and Hughes and Singh (1991).

6 The source of these figures is Binswanger (1990), table 1, p. 237. The original sources are the United States Bureau of the Census (1945) and Johnson (1950).

7 As we shall see later in chapter 2, Singh and Tabatabai suggest that, in the developing countries in the 1980s too, there was a significant fall in fertiliser consumption without much evident effect on overall agricultural output.

8 In addition to sources referred to in the text, see also Hansen (1932), Kirk (1933), Schultz (1945), Hicks (1974), Kalecki (1971) and Kaldor (1976). For more recent discussion of this older literature in relation to current issues, see Binswanger (1990), Goldin and Rezende (1990), de Rezende (forthcoming) and Contré and Goldin (1991). We are grateful to K. Griffin, I. Goldin and G.C. de Rezende for bringing this literature to our attention.

9 See also Chhibber (1989).

10 For a recent review of the literature and a careful statement of this argument, see Saith (1990). For an opposite point of view, see I. Singh (1991).

11 See further Johnson and Salop (1980), Heller *et al.* (1988), Ray (1988), and the discussion by Braverman (1990) on Binswanger (1990).

12 See, for example, Ahluwalia (1985) and Saith (1990). Following Bliss (1985), Gaiha (1989) has argued that it is not inflation as such but unanticipated inflation which has an independent negative influence or rural poverty. See also Ghose (1989).

13 It is instructive in this connection to compare the IMF's policy of promoting export crop production with that of the European Community with respect to steel. At the end of the 1970s there was a large global excess capacity of steel, capacity exceeding demand perhaps by as much as 40 per cent. However, the European Commission's response to this situation was not to encourage every country to produce even more steel but rather to bring about an orderly reduction in steel capacity in the Community countries. See Singh (1986b).

14 Another related piece of evidence comes from Gilbert's investigation of the relationship between international indebtedness and commodity prices. Gilbert concluded:

Apparently, the efforts of each developing country acting independently to meet debt service obligations [have], by reducing export earnings for all exporters of these commodities, collectively made it more difficult for the developing country primary producers as a group to meet their obligations. If this analysis is correct, the costs of a particular country in meeting its debt service obligations are not confined to the domestic costs: there are additional costs imposed on other developing countries, whether or not in debt, who export the same commodities. (Gilbert, 1989, pp. 783–4)

See also Sarkar and Singer (1991) and Goldin and Winters (eds.) (1992).

15 For further elaborations of Kaldor's argument, see Currie and Vines (1988).

16 See also Anderson and Hazell (1988), Mellor (1989) and Tyers and Anderson (1987).

17 The pace of structural change decelerated in the 1980s, as evidenced by the slower decline, or in some regions even a rise, in the share of agriculture in GDP. For an analysis of this issue with respect to African countries, see Jamal and Weeks (1988, forthcoming).

18 For a full discussion of this subject, see Singh (1987) and Rowthorn and Wells (1987).

19 These elasticities are based on agricultural output data from UNCTAD Economic Time-Series Data Bank and on data on economically active population in agriculture from FAO: *World-wide Estimates and Projections of the Agricultural and Non-agricultural Population Segments, 1950–2025* (Rome: FAO, 1986).

20 For a fuller discussion of these various models and for an analysis of the differences between them, see Bhaduri's study (chapter 6 in this volume). Briefly, in the Feldman–Mahalanobis analysis, both the supply of labour and food from the agricultural sector accommodate themselves to the needs of the industrial sector; in the Lewis model, only labour does and the supply of food may not.

21 A vigorous and influential exponent of this view has been Lipton (1977).

22 See Preobrazhensky (1965). See also Sah and Stiglitz (1984, 1987).

23 For Mao's discussion of the failure of agriculture in the European socialist countries and other shortcomings of their development, see Mao Tse-Tung (1977).

24 Chakravarty's 'agriculture-first' programme seems on the face of it to be similar to Mellor and Johnston's (1984) 'unimodal development' strategy which also favours agricultural development and Green Revolution-type technological change in the agrarian economy. There are, however, important analytical differences between these two views since Chakravarty's analysis continues to be embedded in a structuralist view of the development process; moreover, as a planner, Chakravarty remained committed to the 'balanced growth' of agriculture and industry. For a critical examination of the unimodal development strategy, see Timmer (1988).

25 For a fuller analysis of the new Indian development strategy in the 1980s, see Singh and Ghosh (1988).

26 See Singh and Ghosh (1988). See also the *Report of the Indian Council of Economic Advisors on the State of the Indian Economy*: New Delhi (Planning Commission, 1990).

27 For a thorough analysis of a number of relevant issues in this context, see Storm (1992). Storm's analysis, which relies on a computable general equilibrium model of India during 1985–90, finds strong support for Chakravarty's thesis.

References

Ahluwalia, M.S., 1985. 'Rural poverty, agricultural production, and prices: A reexamination', in Mellor and Desai (eds.), (1985).

Anderson, J.R. and P.B.R. Hazell, 1988. *Variability in Grain Yields*, Baltimore: Johns Hopkins University Press.

Antonelli, G. and A. Quadrio-Curzio (eds.), 1988. *The Agro-Technological System Towards 2000*, Amsterdam: Elsevier Science Publishers BV.

Askari, H. and J.T. Cummings, 1976. *Agricultural Supply Response: A Survey of the Econometric Evidence*, New York: Praeger.

1977. 'Estimating agricultural supply response with the Nerlove model: A survey', *International Economic Review*, vol. 18, no. 2, June, pp. 257–92.

Avramovic, D., 1988. 'Conditionality: Facts, theory and policy – Contribution to the reconstruction of the international financial system', *Working Paper*, no. 37, Helsinki: World Institute for Development Economics Research.

Balassa, B., 1986. 'Economic incentives and agricultural exports in developing countries', paper presented at the Eighth Congress of the International Economic Association, New Delhi, India, December.

Banuri, T. (ed.), 1991. *No Panacea: The Limits to Liberalisation*, Oxford: Clarendon Press.

Barker, T. and V. Brailovsky (eds.), 1981. *Oil or Industry?*, London: Academic Press.

Binswanger, H., 1990. 'The policy response of agriculture', in *Proceedings of the World Bank Annual Conference on Development Economics 1989*, Washington, DC: World Bank.

Bliss, C., 1985. 'A note on the price variable', in Mellor and Desai (eds.) (1985).

Bond, M.E., 1983. 'Agricultural responses to prices in sub-Saharan African countries', *IMF Staff Papers*, vol. 30, no. 4, December, pp. 703–26.

Brailovsky, V., 1981. 'Industrialisation and oil in Mexico: A long-term perspective', in Barker and Brailovsky (eds.) (1981).

Braverman, A., 1990. 'Comment on "The policy response of agriculture", by Binswanger', *Proceedings of the World Bank Annual Conference on Development Economics 1989*, Washington, DC: World Bank.

Chakravarty, S., 1987. *Development Planning: The Indian Experience*, Oxford: Oxford University Press.

Chenery, H. and T.N. Srinivasan (eds.), 1988. *Handbook of Development Economics*, vol. I, Amsterdam: Elsevier Science Publishers BV.

Chhibber, A., 1989. 'The aggregate supply response: A survey', in Commander (ed.) (1989).

Collier, P., 1988, 'Oil shocks and food security in Nigeria', *International Labour Review*, vol. 127, no. 6, pp. 761–82.

Commander, S. (ed.), 1989. *Structural Adjustment and Agriculture: Theory and Practice in Africa and Latin America*, London: Overseas Development Institute in collaboration with James Currey and Heinemann.

28 Ajit Singh and Hamid Tabatabai

Contré, F. and I. Goldin, 1991. 'L'agriculture en période d'ajustement au Brésil', *Revue Tiers-Monde*, vol. 32, no. 126, April–June, pp. 271–302.

Cornia, G.A., 1987. 'Adjustment policies 1980–1985: Effects on child welfare', in Cornia, Jolly and Stewart (eds.) (1987).

Cornia, G.A., R. Jolly and F. Stewart (eds.), 1987. *Adjustment with a Human Face: Protecting the Vulnerable and Promoting Growth*, vol. 1, A study by UNICEF, Oxford: Clarendon Press.

Currie, D. and D. Vines, 1988. *Macroeconomic Interactions between North and South*, Cambridge: Cambridge University Press.

FAO, 1986. *World-wide Estimates and Projections of the Agricultural and Non-Agricultural Population Segments, 1950–2025*, Rome: FAO.

Gaiha, R., 1989. 'Poverty, agricultural production and prices in rural India – A reformulation', *Cambridge Journal of Economics*, vol. 13, no. 2, June, pp. 333–52.

Galbraith, J.K. and J.D. Black, 1938. 'The maintenance of agricultural production during depression: The explanations reviewed', *Journal of Political Economy*, vol. 46, no. 3, June, pp. 305–23.

Ghose, A.K., 1989. 'Rural poverty and relative prices in India', *Cambridge Journal of Economics*, vol. 13, no. 2, June, pp. 307–31.

1990. *Economic Growth and Employment Structure: A Study of Labour Outmigration from Agriculture in Developing Countries*, Geneva: ILO.

Gilbert, C.L., 1989. 'The impact of exchange rates and developing country debt on commodity prices', *Economic Journal*, vol. 99, no. 397, September, pp. 773–84.

Glyn, A., A. Hughes, A. Lipietz and A. Singh, 1990. 'The rise and fall of the Golden Age', in Marglin and Schor (eds.) (1990).

Goldin, I. and G.C. de Rezende, 1990. *Agriculture and Economic Crisis: Lessons from Brazil*, Paris: OECD.

Goldin, I. and L.A. Winters (eds.), 1992. *Open Economies: Structural Adjustment and Agriculture*, Cambridge: Cambridge University Press.

Hansen, A.H., 1932. 'The business cycle and its relation to agriculture', *Journal of Farm Economies*, vol. 14, pp. 59–68.

Harrod, R.F., 1936. *The Trade Cycle*, Oxford: Clarendon Press.

Heller, P.S. et al., 1988. *The Implications of Fund-Supported Adjustment Programs for Poverty: Experiences in Selected Countries, Occasional Paper*, no. 58, Washington, DC: IMF.

Hicks, J.R., 1974. *The Crisis in Keynesian Economics*, New York: Basic Books.

Hollist, W.L. and F.L. Tullis (eds.), 1987. *Pursuing Food Security: Strategies and Obstacles in Africa, Asia, Latin America, and the Middle East*, Boulder, Col. and London: Lynne Rienner Publishers.

Hughes, A. and A. Singh, 1991. 'The world economic slowdown and the Asian and Latin American economies: A comparative analysis of economic structure, policy and performance', in Banuri (ed.) (1991).

ILO (International Labour Office), 1976. *Employment, Growth and Basic Needs: A One-World Problem*, Geneva: ILO.

1986. *Economically Active Population: 1950–2025*, vol. V, Geneva: ILO.

Jamal, V. and J. Weeks, 1988. 'The vanishing rural–urban gap in sub-Saharan Africa', *International Labour Review*, vol. 127, no. 3, pp. 271–92.

forthcoming. *Africa Misunderstood or Whatever Happened to the Rural-Urban Gap*, London: Macmillan.

Johnson, D.G., 1950. 'The nature of the supply function for agricultural products', *American Economic Review*, vol. 40, no. 4, September, pp. 539–64.

Johnson, O. and J. Salop, 1980. 'Distributional aspects of stabilization programs in developing countries', *IMF Staff Papers*, vol. 27, no. 1, pp. 1–23.

Johnston, B.F. and J.W. Mellor, 1961. 'The role of agriculture in economic development', *American Economic Review*, vol. 51, no. 4, September, pp. 566–93.

Kaldor, N., 1960. *Essays on Economic Growth and Stability*, London: Duckworth.

1976. 'Inflation and recession in the world economy', *Economic Journal*, vol. 86, no. 344, December, pp. 703–14.

1983. 'Devaluation and adjustment in developing countries', *Finance and Development*, vol. 20, no. 2, June, pp. 35–7.

Kalecki, M., 1971. *Selected Essays on the Dynamics of the Capitalist Economy*, Cambridge: Cambridge University Press.

1972. 'Problems of financing economic development in a mixed economy', in M. Kalecki, *Selected Essays on the Economic Growth of the Socialist and the Mixed Economies*, Cambridge: Cambridge University Press.

Keynes, J.M., 1974. 'The international control of raw materials', *Journal of International Economics*, no. 4.

Kirk, J.H., 1933. *Agriculture and the Trade Cycle*, London: P.P. King & Son.

Kuznets, S., 1965. *Economic Growth and Structure: Selected Essays*, London: Heinemann.

1966. *Modern Economic Growth: Rate, Structure and Spread*, New Haven: Yale University Press.

1971. *Economic Growth of Nations: Total Output and Production Structure*, Cambridge, Mass.: Harvard University Press.

Lawrence, P. (ed.), 1986. *World Recession and the Food Crisis in Africa*, London: *Review of African Political Economy* and James Currey.

Lewis, W.A., 1978. *The Evolution of the International Economic Order*, Princeton: Princeton University Press.

1984. 'Development strategy in a limping world economy', in Meier (ed.) (1984).

Lipton, M., 1977. *Why Poor People Stay Poor: Urban Bias in World Development*, Cambridge, Mass.: Harvard University Press.

Maizels, A., 1988. 'Commodity instability and developing countries: The debate', *Working Paper*, no. 34. Helsinki: World Institute for Development Economics Research.

Mao Tse-Tung, 1977. *Selected Works of Mao Tse-Tung*, vol. V, Beijing: Foreign Languages Press.

Marglin, S. and S. Schor (eds.), 1990. *The Golden Age of Capitalism*, Oxford: Clarendon Press.

Meier, G.M. (ed.), 1984. *Leading Issues in Economic Development*, 4th edn., New

30   Ajit Singh and Hamid Tabatabai

York: Oxford University Press.

Mellor, J.W., 1987. 'Opportunities in the international economy for meeting the food requirements of the developing countries', in Hollist and Tullis (eds.) (1987).

1989. 'Food demand in developing countries and the transition of world agriculture', *European Review of Agricultural Economics*, vol. 15, no. 4, pp. 419–36.

Mellor, J.W. and G.M. Desai (eds.), 1985. *Agricultural Change and Rural Poverty: Variations on a Theme by Dharm Narain*, Baltimore and London: Johns Hopkins University Press.

Mellor, J.W. and B.F. Johnston, 1984. 'The world food equation: Interrelations among development, employment and food consumption', *Journal of Economic Literature*, vol. 22, no. 2, June, pp. 531–74.

Preobrazhensky, E., 1965. *The New Economics*, 2nd edn., Oxford: Clarendon Press.

Ray, A., 1988. 'Agricultural policies in developing countries: National and international aspects', in Antonelli and Quadrio-Curzio (eds.) (1988).

Rezende, G.C. de, forthcoming. 'External adjustment and agriculture in Brazil', in Twomey and Helwege (eds.) (forthcoming).

Rowthorn, R.E. and J.R. Wells, 1987. *Deindustrialization and Foreign Trade*, Cambridge: Cambridge University Press.

Sachs, J.D., 1985. 'External debt and macroeconomic performance in Latin America and East Asia', *Brookings Papers on Economic Activity*, 2, Washington, DC: Brookings Institution.

Sah, R.K. and J. Stiglitz, 1984. 'The economics of price scissors', *American Economic Review*, vol. 74, no. 1, March, pp. 125–38.

1987. 'Price scissors and the structure of the economy', *Quarterly Journal of Economics*, vol. 102, no. 1, February, pp. 109–34.

Saith, A., 1990. 'Development strategies and the rural poor', *Journal of Peasant Studies*, vol. 17, no. 2, January, pp. 171–244.

Sarkar, P. and H.W. Singer, 1991. 'Manufactured exports of developing countries and their terms of trade since 1965', *World Development*, vol. 19, no. 4, April, pp. 333–40.

Schultz, T.W., 1945. *Agriculture in an Unstable Economy*, New York: McGraw-Hill.

Singh, A., 1977. 'UK industry and the world economy: A case of de-industrialisation?', *Cambridge Journal of Economics*, vol. 1, no. 2, June, pp. 113–36.

1979. 'The "basic needs" approach to development *vs* the new international economic order: The significance of Third World industrialization', *World Development*, vol. 7, no. 6, June, pp. 585–606.

1984. 'The interrupted industrial revolution of the Third World: Prospects and policies for resumption', *Industry and Development* (Vienna, UNIDO), no. 12, June, pp. 43–68.

1986a. 'The world economic crisis, stabilisation and structural adjustment: An overview', *Labour and Society*, vol. 11, no. 3, September, pp. 277–93.

1986b. 'A commentary on the IMF and World Bank policy programme', in Lawrence (ed.) (1986).

1987. 'Manufacturing and de-industrialization', in J. Eatwell, M. Milgate and P. Newman (eds.), *The New Palgrave: A Dictionary of Economics*, London: Macmillan.

1989. 'Third World competition and de-industrialisation in advanced countries', *Cambridge Journal of Economics*, vol. 13, no. 1, March, pp. 103–20.

1990. 'Southern competition, labor standards and industrial development in the North and the South', in US Department of Labor: *Labor Standards and Development in the Global Economy*, pp. 239–64, Washington, DC.

Singh, A. and J. Ghosh, 1988. 'Import liberalisation and the new industrial strategy: An analysis of their impact on output and employment in the Indian economy', *Economic and Political Weekly*, Special Number, November, pp. 2313–42.

Singh, A. and H. Tabatabai, 1989. 'The agrarian economy of the Third World in the 1980s: International economic conditions, agricultural development and rural poverty', paper presented at the ILO/SAREC Workshop on the 'Interrelationship between Macroeconomic Policies and Rural Development' (Geneva, 11–13 December 1989).

1992. 'Agriculture and economic development in the 1990s: A new analytical and policy agenda', *International Labour Review*, vol. 131, nos. 4–5, pp. 405–30.

Singh, I., 1991. *The Great Ascent: The Rural Poor in South Asia*, Washington, DC: Johns Hopkins University Press for the World Bank.

Storm, S., 1992. *Macroeconomic Considerations in the Choice of an Agricultural Policy: A Study into Sectoral Interdependence with Reference to India*, Amsterdam: Thesis Publishers.

Taylor, L., 1988. *Varieties of Stabilization Experience: Towards Sensible Macroeconomics in the Third World*, Oxford: Clarendon Press.

Timmer, C.P., 1988. 'The agricultural transformation', in Chenery and Srinivasan (eds.) (1988).

Twomey, M.J. and A. Helwege (eds.), forthcoming. *Modernization and Stagnation: Latin American Agriculture in the 1980's*. Westport, Conn.: Greenwood Press.

Tyers, R. and K. Anderson, 1987. 'Liberalizing OECD agricultural policies in the Uruguay Round: Effect on trade and welfare', *Working Papers in Trade and Development*, no. 87/10, Canberra: Australian National University.

UNCTAD (United Nations Conference on Trade and Development), 1992. *Handbook of International Trade and Development Statistics 1991*, New York: United Nations.

United States Bureau of the Census, 1945. *Statistical Abstract of the United States, 1944–45*, Washington, DC.

World Bank, 1986. *World Development Report*, New York: Oxford University Press.

1988. *Adjustment Lending: An Evaluation of Ten Years of Experience*, Washington, DC: World Bank.

1990. *Adjustment Lending Policies for Sustainable Growth*, Washington, DC: World Bank.

1992. *World Development Report*, New York: Oxford University Press.

Part I

2 The world economic crisis and Third World agriculture in the 1980s

AJIT SINGH AND HAMID TABATABAI

Introduction

Adopting a global and comparative continental approach,[1] this chapter sets out to examine how the Third World's agrarian economy fared in the 1980s in the wake of the world economic crisis. The first substantive section attempts an analytical description of the observed trends in the developing countries' agriculture during the past decade compared with the record of the 1960s and 1970s. The second section is concerned with two questions: (i) How has the world economic crisis affected agricultural development in these countries? (ii) Did the performance of the agrarian economy itself lead to the economic crisis in the Third World during this decade? The third section considers briefly the implications of agricultural performance in the 1980s for rural poverty in the Third World. The main conclusions are presented in the final section.

To provide the context to the main issues discussed in this chapter, it will be recalled that, largely as a consequence of foreign borrowing, the less developed countries were in general able to cope with the consequences of the first oil shock reasonably well. Although the tempo of economic expansion in the Third World slowed between 1973 and 1979, the decline was small compared with that suffered by the developed economies. However, the impact on the poor countries of the 1979 oil price rise and the associated changes in United States monetary policy (the so-called Volcker shock), as well as that of tight economic policies in the United Kingdom and other advanced economies,[2] has been enormous and far-reaching. The trend rate of growth of GDP in the developing countries other than China between 1980 and 1988 was less than half that recorded in the 'golden age' years of 1961–73. A large number of developing countries experienced negative growth rates of GNP *per capita* during the 1980s.[3]

Singh (1990) has shown that, like GDP as a whole, the pace of industrialisation in the Third World in the 1980s suffered a major setback.

In this connection a significant issue examined in this chapter is whether the fate of agricultural development in the poor countries during this decade was similar to that of GDP and industry; and if not, why not?

Maddison (1985), Sachs (1985), Fishlow (1987) and Hughes and Singh (1988) have observed that not all parts of the Third World suffered an acute economic crisis in the 1980s. There is in fact what Singh (1986c) has called a 'great continental divide': while economic growth in many Latin American and sub-Saharan African countries more or less stopped or even regressed in the 1980s, the Asian countries were by and large able to maintain their growth momentum. The economic success of the East Asian countries in particular is regarded by the IMF and the World Bank as eloquent proof of the fact that it is not world economic conditions but rather domestic mismanagement and inappropriate policies that are largely responsible for the economic failure in Latin America and sub-Saharan Africa.[4] In an influential paper, Sachs (1985) argued that an important reason for the 'wrong' economic policies followed in Latin America was the dominance of urban and industrial interests over agrarian interests in the political economy of these countries. In relation to such theses, it clearly is of interest to analyse the actual performance of the agrarian economy in the three developing continents.

The main trends

Agricultural and food production

Table 2.1 provides summary information on agricultural and food production since 1961 for all developing countries and for certain regional groupings.[5] For analytical and comparative purposes, the period is subdivided into: (a) the pre-oil-shocks 'golden age' of 1961–73, when the world economy was growing at the unprecedented rate of 5 per cent per annum and the economies of the developing countries expanded even faster; (b) the period 1973–80, spanning the two oil shocks; and (c) the crisis period of 1980s. The following main observations may be made.

First, over the whole period 1961–90, the rate of growth of both agricultural and food production in developing market economies just kept ahead of the rate of growth of population. It is significant that this was true even in the crisis years of the 1980s. If the Asian centrally planned economies (CPEs) are included among the developing countries (last row), the overall record of the Third World turns out to be appreciably better, owing to the outstanding success of China throughout the period, but particularly in the 1980s.

Second, table 2.1 reveals important interregional differences. Not only

Table 2.1. *Trends in total and per capita agricultural and food production, 1961–90 (average annual percentage growth)*

Country group	Agricultural production				Food production			
	1961–73	1973–80	1980–90	1961–90	1961–73	1973–80	1980–90	1961–90
Total								
Developing market economies	2.6	3.0	2.8	2.7	2.7	3.2	2.9	2.9
Latin America	2.6	3.4	2.2	2.7	3.1	3.6	2.3	3.0
Sub-Saharan Africa	2.4	1.1	2.5	2.0	2.3	1.5	2.5	2.0
South and South-East Asia	2.5	3.3	3.3	3.0	2.5	3.4	3.3	3.1
Asian centrally planned economies	4.8	3.1	4.4	4.1	4.7	3.3	4.3	4.0
Developing, all	3.1	3.0	3.2	3.1	3.2	3.2	3.3	3.2
Per capita								
Developing market economies	0.1	0.6	0.5	0.3	0.2	0.8	0.5	0.5
Latin America	−0.1	1.0	0.1	0.3	0.5	1.3	0.2	0.6
Sub-Saharan Africa	−0.2	−1.8	−0.6	−0.9	−0.3	−1.5	−0.6	−0.9
South and South-East Asia	0.1	1.1	1.1	0.7	0.1	1.2	1.1	0.8
Asian centrally planned economies	2.3	1.5	3.0	2.2	2.2	1.7	2.9	2.1
Developing, all	0.6	0.9	1.2	0.9	0.7	1.1	1.2	0.9

Source: FAO data as available in the UNCTAD Economic Time-Series (ETS) Data Bank.

Table 2.2. *Trends in sectoral production performance, 1965–90* (average annual percentage growth)

Country group	GDP		Industry		Agriculture	
	1965–80	1980–90	1965–80	1980–90	1965–80	1980–90
Low-income economies (excl. China and India)	4.8	3.9	8.0	3.7	2.4	2.6
Middle-income economies	6.3	2.5	6.7	2.3	3.4	2.4
Latin America and the Caribbean	6.0	1.6	6.6	1.2	3.1	1.9
Sub-Saharan Africa	4.2	2.1	7.2	2.0	2.0	2.1
South Asia (incl. India)	3.6	5.2	4.3	6.5	2.5	3.0
East Asia and the Pacific (incl. China)	7.3	7.8	10.8	10.2	3.2	4.8

Source: World Bank (1992), table 2, pp. 220–1.

did the developing Asian CPEs perform very well during the 1980s, but the South and South-East Asian developing market economies also experienced a sustained rise in *per capita* agricultural and food production. By contrast, Latin American countries, which enjoyed strongly rising *per capita* production in the 1970s, saw virtually no growth in the 1980s. In sub-Saharan Africa *per capita* agricultural and food production fell markedly in the 1980s, by 0.6 per cent per annum – the third consecutive decade of decline. However, between 1973 and 1980 the drop had been far steeper.

Third, it is interesting to compare the trends over time in agricultural GDP with those in total GDP and industrial output. Table 2.2 shows that, for both low-income (excluding China and India) and middle-income economies, GDP and industrial output in the 1980s suffered generally greater setbacks than agriculture. In Latin America and sub-Saharan Africa the slowdown in the trend rates of growth of GDP and of industry was particularly sharp; by contrast, agricultural growth fell relatively much less in Latin America in 1980–90 than in the preceding fifteen years and did not fall at all in sub-Saharan Africa. South Asia (including India) stands out as the one region where some improvement in agricultural growth in the 1980s was accompanied by an acceleration of growth in GDP and industrial output.

Fourth, the developing countries as a group were experiencing something akin to an 'industrial revolution' during the 1960s and 1970s (a rate of growth of manufacturing value added of about 7 per cent per annum).[6] Since the rate of growth of agriculture over this period did little more than

Table 2.3. *Variability^a of total food production, 1961–90* (%)

Country group	1961–73	1973–80	1980–90
Developing market economies	1.6	1.5	1.0
Latin America	1.8	1.6	1.7
Sub-Saharan Africa	1.9	1.6	2.5
South and South-East Asia	3.0	2.4	2.1
Asian centrally planned economies	4.9	3.1	2.2
Developing, all	1.4	0.7	0.8
Developed market economies	1.2	1.3	2.7

Note:
^{a} The measure of instability used is the trend-corrected coefficient of variation $= CV\sqrt{1 - \bar{R}^2}$ where $\bar{R}^2$ is the adjusted R^2 of the semi-logarithmic regression of food production on time (see Cuddy and Della Valle, 1978).
Source: FAO data as available in the UNCTAD Economic Time-Series (ETS) Data Bank.

keep pace with population, agriculture's share in GDP halved from 32 per cent in 1960 to 15 per cent in 1980 (UNCTAD, 1992, p. 446). In the 1980s, with the collapse of industry in many parts of the Third World and a more stable performance of agriculture, the share of agriculture remained unchanged between 1980 and 1989. In sub-Saharan Africa the share rose from 25 to 28 per cent over this period (UNCTAD, 1992, p. 448).

Lastly, an important aspect of the performance of the Third World's agrarian economy relates to the variability of agricultural and particularly food production. The latter is especially important in view of its impact on the standard of living of the poor (Mellor, 1987). Table 2.3 shows, for each sub-period, the variability of total food production using a trend-corrected measure. The central point which emerges is that during the 1980s food production in the developing market economies has *not* become more unstable over time.[7] Of the developing regions, only sub-Saharan Africa exhibited a perceptible increase in instability in the 1980s compared with the record of the previous two sub-periods. In this respect, the developing countries in general performed much better than the developed market economies (see last row of table 2.3) where there was a very large *increase* in intertemporal instability in the 1980s.

Food availability and food adequacy

Table 2.4 provides information on the supply of food available for human consumption in caloric terms. The indicator measures the quantity of food

Table 2.4. *Average food supply availability, 1961–89* (calories/*per capita*/day)

Country group[a]	1961–63	1969–71	1979–81	1987–89
Developing economies	1930	2100	2330	2470
Latin America and Caribbean	2370	2510	2700	2720
Sub-Saharan Africa	2030	2080	2150	2120
Near East and North Africa	2220	2380	2840	3020
Asia	1820	2020	2250	2430

Note:
[a] These FAO groupings are somewhat different from those used in other tables.
Source: FAO: *The State of Food and Agriculture 1991* (Rome, 1992), table 3, p. 14.

that reaches the consumer but not necessarily the amount that is actually consumed (which would be less to the extent that edible food and nutrients are lost within the household). However, these data are a useful measure of *changes* in *per capita* calorie consumption – assuming that the incidence of 'waste' remains roughly constant over time.

For developing countries as a whole, table 2.4 shows an appreciable rise in *per capita* food availability – an increase of 21 per cent over the period from 1961–63 to 1979–81. Food availability continued to increase in the 1980s in the Third World as a whole. It is significant that even in regions (Latin America and sub-Saharan Africa) where GDP *per capita* fell appreciably in the 1980s, average food availability was maintained. In view of the trend decline in *per capita* food production in table 2.1 the steady level of food availability in sub-Saharan Africa was obviously due to growth in food imports.[8]

Land and labour productivity in agriculture

A large part of the increase of agricultural and food production in the developing countries during the past three decades has resulted from higher yields per hectare. However, technical progress has been not only land-saving but labour-saving as well, leading to both increased land and labour productivity. To the extent that the nature of technical progress in agriculture, and especially its adoption and spread in the rural sector, is induced by relative factor scarcities, one would expect land productivity to increase faster in Asia and labour productivity to grow more rapidly in Latin America and sub-Saharan Africa.[9]

With respect to land productivity, Mellor and Johnston (1984) report that, in the Third World as a whole, increased yields accounted for more than half the rise in production of the main food crops in the 1960s and 1970s. In Asia the contribution of the rise in land productivity was 70 per cent; it was smaller in Latin America, and actually negative during the 1960s in sub-Saharan Africa – i.e., increased production was (more than) entirely due to bringing more land into cultivation. Table 2.5 gives data on the growth rates of agricultural production (as in table 2.1), economically active population (EAP) in agriculture and the implied productivity of labour in this sector. In interpreting table 2.5 it is important to bear in mind that an increase in the economically active population in agriculture is not necessarily a response to a rise in production; it may equally well stem from reduced employment opportunities in manufacturing and in urban services, leading to what de Janvry (1987) has called the 'trapped' unemployed labour in agriculture.

Nevertheless, the figures in table 2.5 indicate that labour productivity in agriculture in the developing countries as a whole rose at well over 1 per cent per annum throughout the past three decades. In general, productivity growth was somewhat faster in Latin America than in South and South-East Asia during this period except in the 1980s when growth rates were much the same in both continents.[10] In sub-Saharan Africa productivity fell in the 1970s, as a consequence of the sharp reduction in the rate of growth of agricultural production and an acceleration in the growth of the farm labour force. With the rise in agricultural growth rates in the 1980s, labour productivity in the region has again started to increase. Thus in contrast to the Asian and the Latin American experience – where both land and labour productivity rose throughout the three decades, albeit at different rates – sub-Saharan Africa suffered a fall in land productivity in foodgrain production in the 1960s and a decline in labour productivity in the 1970s. Parenthetically, we also note that, for the Third World as a whole, over the 20 years of generally sustained economic expansion between 1960 and 1980, the rate of growth of labour productivity was much the same in agriculture as in industry (Lindbeck, 1986; UNIDO, 1984).

The world economic crisis and Third World agriculture

This section examines two analytical issues raised by the performance of Third World agriculture during the past decade. The first is: in what ways and through which channels has the sharp deceleration in industrial countries' economic growth at the end of the 1970s affected agricultural development in the South? A significant conclusion of the previous section was that in Latin America and sub-Saharan Africa, while there was a large

Table 2.5. *Trends in labour productivity in agriculture (output/EAP[a]), 1961–90 (average annual percentage growth)*

Country group	1961–73			1973–80			1980–90			1961–90		
	Agric. prod.	EAP in agric.	Lab. prod.	Agric. prod.	EAP in agric.	Lab. prod.	Agric. prod.	EAP in agric.	Lab. prod.	Agric. prod.	EAP in agric.	Lab. prod.
Developing market economies	2.6	1.2	1.4	3.0	1.3	1.7	2.8	1.4	1.4	2.7	1.3	1.4
Latin America	2.6	0.8	1.8	3.4	0.6	2.8	2.2	0.5	1.7	2.7	0.7	2.0
Sub-Saharan Africa	2.4	1.8	0.6	1.1	2.0	-0.9	2.5	1.7	0.8	2.0	1.8	0.2
South and South-East Asia	2.5	1.2	1.3	3.3	1.3	2.0	3.3	1.4	1.9	3.0	1.3	1.7
Asian centrally planned economies	4.8	1.6	3.2	3.1	1.9	1.2	4.4	1.2	3.2	4.1	1.6	2.5
Developing, all	3.1	1.4	1.7	3.0	1.6	1.4	3.2	1.3	1.9	3.1	1.5	1.6

Note:
[a] EAP = economically active population.
Sources: ILO and FAO data as available in the UNCTAD Economic Time-Series (ETS) Data Bank and FAO: *World-wide Estimates and Projections of the Agricultural and Non-agricultural Population Segments, 1950–2025* (Rome, 1986).

decline in the GDP and industrial growth rates in the 1980s, agricultural growth was relatively little affected. Therefore, the second question is: what factors can account for the differential performance of agriculture and industry in the 1980s, particularly in Latin America and sub-Saharan Africa?

The agrarian economy of a typical developing country is influenced both directly, and often more importantly indirectly, by changes in the level of world economic activity. For commodity-exporting developing countries, the *direct* effects of an international economic recession work through the obvious channels of a fall in world demand and hence in commodity prices. International commodity prices are known to be highly sensitive to short-run changes in world demand (IMF, 1986). The indirect effects operate in less obvious ways, but essentially through their impact on the developing countries' balance of payments. Balance-of-payments or foreign exchange constraints have serious adverse consequences not only for a country's agricultural development but also for its economy at large and hence for both urban and rural poverty.

Table 2.6 indicates that the world free market prices of food products dropped by 40 per cent and those of agricultural raw materials by a quarter between 1980 and 1982. Despite the economic recovery in the industrial countries since the bottom of the trough in 1982 and the longest period of upturn in United States economic activity since the Second World War, commodity prices generally remained low throughout the 1980s. By the end of the decade the nominal index of food prices was still less than two-thirds of its value in 1980, although that of agricultural raw materials had recovered its former level. The last column of table 2.6 shows that the 'real' prices of non-fuel primary commodities exported by the developing countries fell by 17 per cent between 1980 and 1982; following the very fast rate of growth of the United States economy in 1983 and 1984, real commodity prices recovered somewhat, but by the end of the decade they were nearly 40 per cent below their 1980 level (and 50 per cent below their previous peak reached in 1977).

There is also evidence of a marked increase in commodity price instability since the 1960s. Mellor (1987) reports that in the 1970s the coefficient of variation for export prices of wheat was more than eight times (and for rice twice) as high as in the 1960s.

Turning to the *indirect* effects of the changes in international economic conditions on Third World agriculture, it is necessary first to consider their impact on the balance-of-payments position of the less developed countries. In addition to the commodity price shock and the demand shock (which affected the demand for both agricultural and non-agricultural products exported by the developing countries), the new economic policies

Table 2.6. *Indices of primary commodity prices, 1980–90* (1980 = 100)

Year	Agricultural commodities (nominal price indices)		Non-oil commodity exports of developing countries[b] (real price index)
	All food	Agricultural raw materials[a]	
1980	100.0	100.0	100.0
1981	81.3	87.0	90.0
1982	60.0	75.5	82.8
1983	64.1	80.9	91.1
1984	61.7	81.2	97.5
1985	52.3	73.3	83.6
1986	56.2	74.5	70.3
1987	53.0	87.5	65.3
1988	65.7	94.7	72.4
1989	66.2	94.4	71.5
1990	61.1	100.6	60.6

Notes:
[a] Including forestry products.
[b] These include metals in addition to food, beverages and agricultural raw materials. Prices are deflated by the unit value of manufactures exported by industrial countries.
Sources: UNCTAD (1992), table 2.7, for agricultural commodities and IMF (1989), p. 155, and (1992), p. 135, for non-oil commodity exports.

of the advanced nations also led to a severe interest rate shock for the Third World at the beginning of the 1980s. Application of restrictive monetary policies through quantitative targeting of money supply aggregates, inaugurated in the United States in 1979, resulted in a sharp jump in nominal and real interest rates. If real interest rates are measured in terms of the difference between the LIBOR (London interbank offer rate) and the rate of change of the export price index for developing countries (a more appropriate deflator from the point of view of commodity exporters), the average real rate for developing countries shot up from about − 8 per cent in 1980 to nearly + 22 per cent in 1982 (World Bank, 1987, p. 19). Despite a certain decline in later years, real interest rates on the developing countries' external debt remained at a high level throughout the 1980s.

The combined effect of reduced demand, worsening terms of trade and the interest rate shocks was to place severe balance-of-payments constraints on the non-oil developing countries at the beginning of the 1980s.[11] In addition, the foreign exchange constraint for many Third World countries was further exacerbated by a sharp decline in capital flows in the wake of the Mexican debt crisis in the summer of 1982.[12] While in 1980 there was a net financial resource transfer of more than $40 billion to 98 'capital-importing' developing countries, in 1983 these transfers dried up completely. Since then, resources have been flowing in the opposite direction. By 1988 these same 98 countries were paying out $32.5 billion more in debt servicing, dividend payments and negative transfers than they received in new loans and investments, development assistance and other inflows.[13] The position is particularly serious in Africa and Latin America, the two continents which suffered most from the world economic slowdown in the 1980s.

Foreign exchange constraints and agriculture

The rural economy in developing countries may be affected in a number of different ways by a binding foreign exchange constraint. With respect to agricultural production, on the positive side, the foreign exchange constraint may lead to lower food imports, drive food prices up, and hence provide incentives for increased domestic production *over time*. However, cutbacks in non-food imports, lower domestic production of fertilisers and other agricultural inputs, together with reduced oil imports, can hamper agricultural production both immediately and also over longer periods. Indirectly, as a consequence of reduced *domestic* industrial production resulting from a shortage of foreign exchange and import compression, there may also be an additional unfavourable effect on agricultural production because the so-called incentive goods for farmers (soap, bicycles, etc.) become scarcer.[14] Moreover, Khan and Knight (1988) provide evidence that import compression not only threatens agricultural and industrial production but, paradoxically, it also reduces exports. The analytical reason for this is not far to seek. Raw cotton may, for example, be produced in the hinterland in the United Republic of Tanzania, but an acute scarcity of foreign exchange may mean that it cannot be processed (owing to the lack of spare parts for ginning mills) or conveyed to the port of Dar es Salaam for export (because of the shortage of fuel).

Apart from these 'real' effects of lower agricultural and industrial production and exports, the rural economy may be adversely affected by a variety of financial disequilibria caused by a foreign exchange crisis. The State's fiscal balance is likely to deteriorate because of a fall in import duties and sales and excise tax receipts resulting from lower imports and industrial production. A decrease in government revenues may in turn lead to less public spending on agriculture and on the rural economy. Moreover, in a decentralised economy, competing claims by various groups over a diminished rate of growth of national product is likely to lead to inflation. As noted in chapter 1, a number of studies suggest that inflation, by reducing the purchasing power of the landless poor, is an important determinant of rural poverty.[15]

Lastly, it is important to emphasise two points. The first, which follows from the above analysis, is that a foreign exchange constraint not only tends to reduce the overall growth of GDP in an economy but also has an important bearing on the distribution of income and the satisfaction of people's basic needs. Secondly, as we recall from the discussion of stabilisation issues in chapter 1, the degree to which different sectors of the economy may be affected or the overall growth rate may be reduced, or how income distribution may change, is determined not only by the severity of the foreign exchange constraint but also, *inter alia*, by the nature of the government's policy response and by the level of development and the degree of flexibility in the productive structure of the economy (Singh, 1986b).

Differential sectoral and regional performance

It has been argued so far that Third World countries found themselves facing an acute foreign exchange constraint at the beginning of the 1980s. We have also seen that, in developing economies, a foreign exchange constraint can lead to 'external strangulation' or 'import compression', which in turn can have extremely serious consequences for all aspects of the economy. However, data presented earlier suggest a differential sectoral as well as a differential regional performance in the 1980s. How are these differences to be explained?

The first essential point to note here is that, in relation to agriculture, the significant issue is one of differential sectoral rather than regional impact of the world economic recession. As noted earlier, while industrial and overall economic growth maintained their momentum in the Asian countries during the 1980s, they collapsed in Latin America and sub-Saharan Africa. But this did not happen in agriculture. As table 2.1 shows, during 1980–90 agricultural production expanded at a rate of 2.2 per cent a year in Latin America, 2.5 per cent in sub-Saharan Africa and 3.3 per cent in South and South-East Asia; the corresponding figures for food production were 2.3, 2.5 and 3.3 per cent. Only in Latin America was there a trend fall in agricultural growth rates in the 1980s relative to the intershock period. Even so, agricultural GDP in Latin America in the 1980s expanded more rapidly than GDP and industry whereas its growth was only half as high during 1965–80 (table 2.2). In sub-Saharan Africa both agricultural and food production recorded a trend increase in the rate of growth during the

Table 2.7. *Fertiliser consumption and imports (total nutrients), 1961–87*
(average annual percentage growth)

Country group	Consumption		Imports	
	1961–80	1980–87	1961–80	1980–87
Developing market economies	10.6	5.7	8.9	3.2
Latin America	10.7	4.3	10.1	3.5
Sub-Saharan Africa	10.0	1.6	8.7	2.3
South and South-East Asia	11.3	7.0	8.2	2.0
Asian centrally planned economies	13.7	4.5	9.3	8.5
Developing, all	11.5	5.2	8.9	4.4

Source: FAO data as available in the UNCTAD Economic Time-Series (ETS) Data Bank.

1980s relative to the 1960s and 1970s. The central question is therefore not so much the differential regional performance of the agrarian economy during the 1980s as why agriculture performed so much better than industry and GDP.[16]

A major analytical issue here is whether the observed resilience of the Third World's agrarian economy in the 1980s can entirely be explained in terms of the same kind of structural factors which led to the stable performance of United States agriculture during the Great Depression. As in the case of the Depression, there has also been in the 1980s a big drop in the world market prices of agricultural products relative to manufactures. Moreover, the 1980s has been marked by enormous fluctuations in commodity prices. However, there are also important differences between the 1930s and the 1980s; these lie essentially in the nature of the government response to international economic forces during these two periods.

In principle, the government policy response to a foreign exchange crisis can be such as to shield domestic agriculture from the vagaries of world market prices by compensatory changes in domestic relative prices. Furthermore, the government may choose to give the agrarian economy a priority allocation of the reduced overall level of imported inputs the country can afford.

It is not easy to obtain detailed information which bears on these issues. However, table 2.7 provides some data on the use of fertilisers, an important, and for most developing countries imported, industrial input for the agrarian economy. Figure 2.1 gives information on official external assistance to agriculture in Third World countries. Table 2.7 suggests that

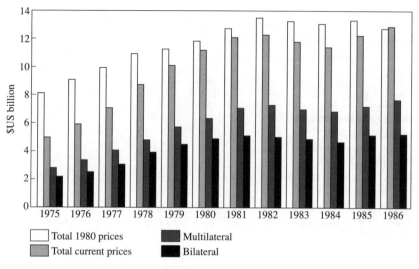

Figure 2.1 External assistance: official total commitments to agriculture, 1974–87[a].
Note:
[a] Figures refer to three-year averages centred on the year indicated. Hence the 1980 figure, for example, refers to the average for 1979–81.
Source: FAO: *The State of Food and Agriculture* (Rome, various years).

the rate of growth of fertiliser imports and consumption declined sharply in developing countries in the 1980s. The biggest drop in the growth of fertiliser consumption occurred in sub-Saharan Africa, but it could be argued that few countries would have been appreciably affected as a result since the use of chemical fertiliser is not widespread in the region. Nevertheless, it is significant that for developing countries as a whole, the data in table 2.1 suggest that the rate of growth of total food and agricultural production was more or less maintained in the 1980s notwithstanding the very marked decline in the growth of fertiliser consumption.

As for official external assistance, following the world food shortage and the rise in food prices of the early 1970s, Western aid-giving countries and international agencies such as the World Bank began to emphasise rural and agricultural development in their aid programmes. As figure 2.1 indicates, there was a substantial increase in *real* terms in official aid to agriculture during the 1970s. In the 1980s, while total aid growth ceased, agricultural assistance was maintained in real terms at about the levels it had reached at the end of the 1970s. According to the FAO, agriculture's share of official commitments to all sectors increased from 12 per cent in 1974/75 to 18–20 per cent between 1979/80 and 1983/84 (Alexandratos,

1988, p. 49). Concessional assistance has averaged about 60–70 per cent of total official assistance to agriculture and has grown particularly rapidly in Africa. The focus of official commitments to agriculture has been increasingly on low-income countries with, for example, the share of low-income food-deficit countries rising from 59 per cent in 1974 to 65 per cent in 1984.

Agricultural inputs are not the only factors to affect the health of the agrarian economy: others include the prices of agricultural products, government expenditure on irrigation, rural roads and the general rural infrastructure. After the first oil shock, a number of Third World governments began to give greater attention to agriculture, and this trend has continued since, particularly in sub-Saharan Africa.[17] Moreover, the maxi-devaluations which many Third World countries underwent as part of adjustment programmes in the 1980s will have shifted the internal terms of trade in favour of agriculture despite adverse movements in the *external* terms of trade between agriculture and industry. Whether the relatively favourable performance of agriculture in the 1980s can be ascribed to changes in the internal terms of trade (i.e., 'getting the prices right') or to the intrinsic structural factors which characterise the nature of supply conditions in agriculture (see chapter 1) is a moot question. This issue cannot in any case be settled by the small amount of evidence at the global aggregate level presented here. It is best analysed by systematic studies at the individual country level.[18]

Is agriculture responsible for the Third World's economic crisis?

We have studied so far the impact of the world economic crisis on the rural economy of the developing countries in the 1980s. Now we consider the reverse side of the question: to what extent, if any, did the past performance of agriculture in the developing countries contribute to their overall economic failure during this decade?

Much of the information already presented has a bearing on this question. Table 2.1 showed that, in the period preceding the crisis (1973–80), in the developing market economies as a whole as well as in all regional groupings except sub-Saharan Africa, both agricultural and food production were growing at a faster rate than during the 'golden' years of 1961–73. The evidence on labour productivity in agriculture in table 2.5 indicated much the same. Similarly there was no increase in the variability of agricultural production in the pre-crisis period in any of the regions, including sub-Saharan Africa (table 2.3). Thus, at the simplest level, it would appear that poor agricultural performance in the 1970s could not have caused the subsequent economic failure in the developing countries except perhaps in sub-Saharan Africa.

Table 2.8. *Net export ratio [(X − M)/(X + M)] in agricultural products,* *1961–90* (three-year arithmetic averages)

Country group	1961–63	1972–74	1979–81	1988–90
Developing market economies	0.34	0.20	0.05	0.01
Latin America	0.54	0.47	0.40	0.44
Sub-Saharan Africa	0.56	0.46	0.20	0.23
South and South-East Asia	0.20	0.05	0.05	− 0.04
Asian centrally planned economies	− 0.18	− 0.04	− 0.24	0.17
Developing, all	0.31	0.18	0.03	0.03

Source: FAO data as available in UNCTAD Economic Time-Series (ETS) Data Bank.

However, before such a conclusion is accepted, it is necessary to consider other dimensions of the Third World's agricultural performance – particularly the sector's trading position. During the process of economic development and industrialisation, agriculture usually (but not always) also provides, *inter alia*, net foreign exchange earnings which can be used for infrastructural and industrial development.[19] Table 2.8 shows that the trade performance ratio – the ratio of trade balance to total trade – of the agricultural sector of the developing countries had been declining throughout the 1960s and 1970s. There are, however, important structural reasons for expecting a long-run decline in the value of the ratio for countries at an intermediate stage of development (Mellor, 1987). As economic development proceeds, growth of population and high income elasticity of demand for food lead to consumption outstripping food production, particularly for countries that achieve rapid economic growth. As a result reliance on imports grows, a tendency that is consistent with Mellor's observation that 'rates of growth in food imports in the developing world seem to vary positively with the rate of *per capita* income increase' (Mellor, 1987, p. 57).

However, table 2.8 also shows that in the 1980s there was an apparent halt in this trend for the developing countries as a whole with a mixed picture at the level of country groups. The value of the trade performance ratio significantly declined in South and South-East Asia but it increased in other developing regions during the decade. This could reflect either genuinely improved trading performance in the latter regions or simply the special circumstances of the 1980s, i.e., a reduction in agricultural imports caused by the foreign exchange constraint.

Table 2.9 provides a more accurate measure of the annual rate of change in the trade performance ratio, calculated by regression analysis for the

Table 2.9. *Average annual percentage growth rates of ratio of agricultural exports to agricultural imports* $(X/M)^a$, *1961–90*

Country group	1961–73	1973–80	1980–90	1961–90
Developing market economies	−1.9[b]	−3.0	0.1	−2.8
Latin America	−1.1	−1.4	1.5	−1.0
Sub-Saharan Africa	−1.6	−6.8	2.6	−3.7
South and South-East Asia	−3.2	1.5	−1.6	−1.4
Asian centrally planned economies	4.7	−7.3	10.5	1.9
Developing, all	−1.5	−3.2	0.9	−2.5

Notes:
[a] Because the ratio $[(X - M)/(X + M)]$ is often negative, it is not possible to fit logarithmic time trend regression equations to this variable. Instead the equation fitted was: $\log (X/M) = a + bt + e$.
[b] A negative value indicates that the trend rate of growth of imports was greater than that of exports.
Source: FAO data as available in the UNCTAD Economic Time-Series (ETS) Data Bank.

various periods. It shows that, for the developing market economies as a whole, the rate of decline in the trade performance ratio increased somewhat during 1973–80 as compared with the 'golden' years. For Latin America this increase was marginal but in the case of sub-Saharan Africa it was, as one would expect, very substantial. By contrast, in South and South-East Asia the trade performance ratio greatly improved to show positive growth in the period 1973–80.[20]

The trade performance indicators reported in tables 2.8 and 2.9 are value measures which indicate the combined influence of changes in volumes as well as prices. An examination of the FAO data on the *volume* of agricultural exports[21] shows that for the developing market economies as a whole there was a small trend increase in the growth rate of such exports between the two periods 1961–73 and 1973–80, from 2 to 2.5 per cent per annum. However, the Latin American and the Far Eastern countries recorded a very appreciable trend increase in the volume of agricultural exports during the period preceding the crisis.

The overall picture which emerges from the production, productivity and trading evidence for the agricultural sector reviewed above is that, for the developing countries as a whole and for Latin America and the South and South-East Asian countries, agricultural performance in the preceding period could not be regarded as the sole or contributory cause of the economic crisis of the 1980s. However, this evidence also indicates that in sub-Saharan Africa poor agricultural performance in the intershock period is likely to have contributed to the economic failure of the countries in the region both in the 1970s and in the 1980s. It is nevertheless important to bear in mind two essential points with respect to this conclusion. First, the agricultural failure itself may have been due to external factors – war (in the continental sub-Saharan Africa, at least a quarter of the countries were affected by armed conflict), drought and changes in world economic conditions leading to a foreign exchange constraint in the sense outlined earlier – rather than to domestic mismanagement. Secondly, even if poor past agricultural performance did contribute to the economic crisis in the sub-Saharan African countries in the 1980s, this contribution might be quite small relative to that of the sea change in world economic conditions which came about in the period after the second oil shock.[22]

Implications for rural poverty

We turn now to some implications of the observed trends in the Third World's agrarian economy in the 1980s for the rural poor. While far from being the sole factor at work, agricultural growth has a decisive influence on the evolution of rural poverty, particularly at the level of major groupings of countries.[23] The differential patterns of agricultural growth performance observed earlier are thus likely to have affected poverty differently, both intertemporally and interregionally.

The most recent trend estimates of the incidence of absolute poverty and the number of poor people are presented in table 2.10. These estimates suggest that while the number of those living in absolute poverty in developing countries (excluding China) rose by about one-fifth between 1970 and 1985, the incidence of poverty dropped from 52 per cent to 44 per cent. The improvement was greater in the rural than in the urban sector. Nevertheless, because of the higher incidence of rural poverty and the higher share of the rural sector in total population, the bulk of the poor (nearly three-quarters of the total) still live in rural areas. Only in Latin America is the share of the population in the rural sector comparatively low (around a quarter).

The decline in the incidence of poverty is unlikely to have been uniform throughout the period since 1970. Much of it probably occurred during the 1970s before the economic crisis set in. It is only in Asia that the sustained growth of agricultural and non-agricultural sectors into the 1980s is likely to have permitted a continued reduction in poverty levels in both urban and rural areas. Elsewhere, poverty intensified although, given the differential performance of major sectors, this was more true of the urban than rural areas.

Table 2.10. *Trends in absolute poverty*[a] *in developing countries, 1970 and 1985*

Country group	Incidence of poverty (%)		No. of poor (millions)	
	1970	1985	1970	1985
All developing countries				
Total	52	44	944	1 156
Rural	59	49	767	850
Urban	35	32	177	306
Africa				
Total	46	49	166	273
Rural	50	58	140	226
Urban	32	29	26	47
Asia[b]				
Total	56	43	662	737
Rural	61	47	552	567
Urban	42	34	110	170
Latin America				
Total	40	36	116	146
Rural	62	45	75	57
Urban	25	32	41	89

Notes:
[a] The absolute poverty line is that income level below which a nutritionally adequate diet and essential non-food items are not affordable.
[b] Excluding China.
Source: United Nations, Department of International Economic and Social Affairs, as reported in United Nations: *1989 Report on the World Social Situation* (1989), table 24, p. 39.

As we saw earlier, agricultural growth in Latin America declined in the 1980s relative to the 1970s, with the growth of labour productivity falling from 2.8 per cent per annum in 1973–80 to 1.7 per cent in 1980–90 (table 2.5). The latter figure, while positive, appears to have been barely high enough to overcome the disequalising tendencies of severely dualistic agrarian structures, and rural poverty did not decline in the 1980s. In fact, ILO/PREALC estimates suggest that its incidence rose from 54.3 per cent in 1980 to 58.6 per cent in 1985 (García *et al.*, 1989, p. 471) although another set of estimates by ECLAC puts this incidence at 60 per cent in both 1980 and 1986 (ECLAC, 1990, p. 60). Both these sources agree, however, that poverty incidence rose sharply in urban areas: from 20.7 to 28.9 per cent between 1980 and 1985 (ILO/PREALC) and from 30 to 36 per cent between 1980 and 1986 (ECLAC). This contrast between poverty trends in rural and urban areas of Latin America is consistent with the more severe effect of recession on non-agricultural sectors in this region.

Africa is the only region in which rural poverty incidence is estimated to have risen between 1970 and 1985 (table 2.10). This is not surprising in view of its agricultural performance over this period but, as we saw earlier, this performance was actually somewhat less poor in the 1980s than in the 1970s. Agricultural labour productivity in sub-Saharan Africa fell at an annual rate of 0.9 per cent during 1973–80 but grew at the rate of 0.8 per cent a year during 1980–90 (table 2.5). This growth, however, was probably too small to have prevented a rise in rural poverty in the 1980s.

Conclusion

Three main conclusions emerge from the above discussion. First, even in sub-Saharan Africa and Latin America, where the overall economy and industry were hard hit by the international economic recession in the 1980s, for a variety of reasons the agricultural sector fared a great deal better than other sectors. Second, as a consequence, rural poverty during the 1980s increased much less than urban poverty in these two regions. In Asia, a region which by and large was not much affected by the world economic crisis, both rural and urban poverty diminished appreciably during the 1980s.

Third, on the reverse causation issue, i.e., whether the past agricultural performance in Latin America and sub-Saharan Africa was itself responsible for the crisis of these economies in the 1980s, it is concluded here that the answer for Latin America is a clear 'no'. On a range of indicators, the Latin American agrarian economy in the period preceding the crisis was doing better than before; moreover, its performance in the 1970s was at least as good as, if not superior to, that of the Asian agrarian economies. Thus a Sachs-type explanation for the much better overall economic record of the Asian than of the Latin American countries, on account of the greater domination of agrarian interests in the political economy of the former, does not sit easily with the actual performance of agriculture in the two continents during the pre-crisis period.[24] In sub-Saharan Africa, on the other hand, the unfavourable record of the agrarian economy in the 1970s did contribute to the subsequent economic downturn. Nevertheless, it was noted that agriculture's poor performance in the earlier period may itself have been due to exogenous factors and not just to domestic mismanagement. It was also suggested that even if agriculture was in part responsible for the acute foreign exchange difficulties faced by the sub-Saharan African countries since the beginning of this decade, its contribution to the crisis is likely to have been small as against that of external factors, i.e., the enormous change in world market conditions, drought and war.

Appendix: comparative analysis of agricultural and food performance

Data on the production of and trade in agricultural products in many developing countries are often unreliable, may display significant year-to-year variations, and are liable to be constantly revised. Analysts also use different periods and definitions (what is 'food'?) and employ different methodologies to summarise the data and their trends. As a result the literature is replete with seemingly inconsistent findings which may be used selectively to 'substantiate' a favourite argument or to 'refute' an equally plausible counter-argument. Many of the controversies that crop up with disconcerting regularity in the literature (on adjustment in Africa, for instance) could easily be clarified, if not settled, with a greater awareness of the nature of the data available and of the way in which they have been handled. The adage that statistics can be made to tell any story is particularly true of agricultural statistics in developing countries.

   In an effort to reduce inconsistencies that inevitably arise from differences in sources, definitions, periodisation and methods of calculation of summary statistics, this chapter has strived to follow, inasmuch as possible, the same 'rules' for gathering and handling data related to food and agriculture. These are:
(a) using the latest available FAO source for any given piece of data;
(b) using the three periods 1961–73, 1973–80 and 1980–latest year; if this proved impossible, 1960–70, 1970–80 and 1980–latest year;
(c) using FAO's comprehensive definition of 'food'; two alternative definitions may have also been used: cereals; cereals combined with 'roots and tubers' and pulses (weighting scheme: *one* for cereals, *one-third* for roots and tubers and *one* for pulses, these weights reflecting approximately the calorie content of these different crop groups); and
(d) computing average annual growth rates by fitting a semi-logarithmic trend equation to the annual time-series data based on the least-squares method.
   These ground rules help reduce inconsistent results, but two questions remain: (i) how do our results compare with those of other researchers? and (ii) how robust are they? This Appendix examines these questions in

relation to the food production performance of the three developing regions: Latin America, sub-Saharan Africa and Asia (excluding Asian CPEs).

Comparison with other results

For this purpose we focus on a comparison with results reported in Mellor and Johnston (1984) and Mellor (1989). Their results and our own are assembled in table 2A.1 for the 1960s and the 1970s (items I, II and III) along with some pertinent facts which may account for their differences.

In the case of Asia all three studies are more or less in agreement, in particular on the fact that there was a certain acceleration in the growth of food production in this region from the 1960s to the 1970s. The differences in the periodisation, the method of calculation of the growth rate and the exact definition of 'food' apparently do not make all that much of a difference, or at least their effects tend to cancel each other out. But there are rather important discrepancies in the case of the other two regions. Latin America's food production performance deteriorated sharply in the 1970s relative to the 1960s according to the first two sources (I showing a change of -2.6 percentage points and II showing a change of -1.0 percentage point) but our results (III) in fact show a slight improvement ($+0.5$). In the case of sub-Saharan Africa Mellor and Johnston (I) show a deterioration (-1.1), which we (III) also find although to a lesser extent (-0.8), but Mellor (II) reports no deterioration and even a slight improvement ($+0.3$).

Such differences may be due to differences in periodisation, in the method of calculation of growth rate, in the definition of food, or in the data used which, coming from different sources, may be different. In order to identify the sources of discrepancies more precisely, consider the results for Latin America and sub-Saharan Africa, the two regions for which discrepancies are patent. The method of estimation of the growth rates is the same in I and III but the periods are somewhat different. In order to control for this confounding factor the relevant growth rates for 1961–70 and 1971–80 (periods of I) are also given in parentheses under item III. A further step, involving a change in the definition of 'food' from *all* food (FAO definition) to staple food crops (cereals + (1/3) roots and tubers + pulses, see (c) above), produces the results reported under item IV in table 2A.1.

The analysis of growth rates for Latin America suggests that the difference in intertemporal growth rates, which is $+0.5$ according to our results (III), is reduced to -0.1 when our periods are modified to conform to those used by Mellor and Johnston (I), and further to -2.2 when our comprehensive definition of food (following FAO) gives way to a definition involving staple food crops only. The remaining discrepancy (between

Table 2A.1. *Comparative average annual growth rates of food production by developing region, 1960s and 1970s* (%)

Source and specificities	Latin America	Sub-Saharan Africa	Asia[a]
I. Mellor and Johnston (1984), table 2			
Period: 1961–70	4.3	2.3	2.7
1971–80	1.7	1.2	3.3
Difference	−2.6	−1.1	+0.6
Method: Semi-logarithmic			
'Food': Major food crops			
II. Mellor (1989), table 1			
Period: 1961–3 to 1971–3	3.7	1.5	2.4
1971–3 to 1981–3	2.7	1.8	3.3
Difference	−1.0	+0.3	+0.9
Method: Average based on end points			
'Food': Major food crops			
III. This chapter, table 2.1[b]			
Period: 1961–73 (1961–70)	3.1 (3.6)	2.3 (2.6)	2.5 (2.6)
1973–80 (1971–80)	3.6 (3.5)	1.5 (1.5)	3.4 (3.4)
Difference	+0.5 (−0.1)	−0.8 (−1.1)	+0.9 (+0.8)
Method: Semi-logarithmic			
'Food': All food (FAO definition)			
IV. Our data base			
Period: 1961–73 (1961–70)	3.5 (4.1)	2.0 (2.3)	—
1973–80 (1971–80)	1.6 (1.9)	1.3 (1.7)	—
Difference	−1.9 (−2.2)	−0.7 (−0.6)	—
Method: Semi-logarithmic			
'Food': Staple food crops			

Notes:
[a] Excluding centrally planned economies.
[b] Growth rates put in parentheses do not come from table 2.1 but are calculated to permit comparison with those in Mellor and Johnston (1984) shown in item I (see text, p. 56).

−2.2 in IV and −2.6 in I) is minor and is explainable in terms of slight differences in the choice of major crops and/or in original data.

While in the case of Latin America the definition of 'food' is of considerably more importance than the difference in time periods in accounting for the seemingly incompatible results in I and III, in the case of sub-Saharan Africa both these factors seem to be of little consequence in terms of the size of their effect. The contrast between these regions reflects the fact that, while in Latin America non-staple food output is relatively large and grew faster than staples (non-staple foods are often exported), in sub-Saharan Africa the importance of staples in total food output is considerably greater.

The real difference requiring explanation in the case of sub-Saharan Africa concerns the results in I and II which show a significant discrepancy in the intertemporal growth differences. The definition of 'food' does not enter into the explanation since it is the same in both. Instead, it is the combination of a particular choice of periods and the method of calculation of growth rates (which uses only the data pertaining to the *end points* of the selected periods) in II that accounts for the difference between I and II.

The main point to underline, therefore, is that, given the nature of data used in such exercises, apparent discrepancies will inevitably arise and it is important to be aware of the potential sensitivity of the results to the exact choice of period, definition of the variable, methods of analysis, etc.

Robustness of the results

Given the preceding discussion regarding the potential importance of various factors in influencing intertemporal differences in growth rates it would be legitimate to wonder if the apparent differences among growth rates for 1961–73, 1973–80 and 1980–90 are actually statistically significant. Two alternative methods are available to test these differences: the Chow test and the dummy variable technique. Both methods yield the same overall results but the latter is more appealing from a statistical point of view (it explicitly identifies the source of the difference in sub-period regressions, whether intercept or slope) and is computationally more convenient (only a single regression is required). The results reported (table 2A.2) here are based on the dummy variable technique.

These results indicate that in Latin America a statistically significant change (deterioration) in growth performance occurred in the 1980s relative to 1973–80 but the difference between the first sub-period and the middle sub-period (taken as reference) is not statistically significant. In sub-Saharan Africa the differences in growth rates of food production in the first and third sub-periods are both significantly different from the base (middle) sub-period. In Asia, however, the difference between the first and the reference sub-periods is significant (at 5 per cent level) while that between the reference and final sub-periods is not.

Table 2A.2. Significance tests of intertemporal differences in food production growth rates

Country group	Intercept	D1	D1 × Time	Time	D3	D3 × Time	$\bar{R}^2$	N	DW
Latin America	10.6** (252.3)	0.071 (1.64)	−0.004 (−1.27)	0.036** (14.26)	0.258** (4.12)	−0.013** (−4.24)	0.996	30	1.43
Sub-Saharan Africa	10.3** (196.5)	−0.119* (−2.22)	0.010** (2.83)	0.015** (4.62)	−0.240** (−3.09)	0.011** (2.92)	0.987	30	1.62
Asia	11.2** (199.3)	0.121* (2.09)	−0.010* (−2.61)	0.035** (10.45)	0.082 (0.99)	−0.004 (−0.90)	0.994	30	1.54

Notes:
** Significant at 1 per cent level.
* Significant at 5 per cent level.
D1 = 1 if observation in first sub-period (1961–72)
    = 0 otherwise.
D3 = 1 if observation in third sub-period (1981–90)
    = 0 otherwise.
D1 = D3 = 0 if observation in middle period (1973–80).

Notes

A somewhat different version of this study was published earlier (Singh and
Tabatabai, 1990). The authors acknowledge their gratitude to Ajit Ghose, Vali
Jamal, Samir Radwan, Victor Tokman and, particularly, Keith Griffin. Thanks are
also due to Carlos García who prepared the data files from the UNCTAD ETS Data
Base.

1 Notable examples of recent studies taking a global view of the agrarian economy
  of the South include Alexandratos (1988), Griffin (1987), Hollist and Tullis
  (eds.) (1987), Mellor (1987, 1988, 1989), Mellor and Johnston (1984) and
  Paulino (1986).
2 For a fuller discussion of the reasons for the changes in the economic policies of
  the leading industrial countries, see Glyn *et al.* (1990). For various interpretations of the economic record of the developing countries during the 1980s, see
  the World Bank's *World Development Reports*, UNCTAD's *Trade and Development Reports*, and the IMF's *World Economic Outlooks* among others.
3 See World Bank (1992).
4 See for example de Larosière (1986).
5 For information and comments on the sources of data, definitions and methods,
  and for a comparison of our figures with those of other researchers, see
  Appendix, pp. 55–9. This Appendix also reports the results of testing the
  statistical significance of intertemporal differences in growth rates.
6 On the 'industrial revolution' of the Third World countries during 1960–80, see
  Singh (1984, 1989).
7 See Mellor (1987) for somewhat different results.
8 Between 1969–71 and 1979–81, food imports by sub-Saharan African countries
  increased from 160 to 290 calories *per capita* per day; between 1979–81 and
  1983–85 they rose further to 300 calories *per capita* per day (Alexandratos, 1988,
  table 2.7, p. 39). The index of the volume of food imports rose by 26 per cent
  between 1979–81 and 1988–90 (FAO, 1991, p. 34).
9 Hayami and Ruttan (1985) and Timmer (1988) provide a comprehensive
  discussion of the relationship between land and labour productivity in agriculture in different parts of the world and at different stages of development.
10 It should perhaps be noted that labour force trends in the 1980s, on which the
  productivity trends are based, are projections made in the mid-1980s and hence
  do not reflect any changes in trends in rural-to-urban migration due to
  slowdown in the urban economies in many developing countries.
11 For evidence and a comprehensive analysis of the impact of the world economic
  crisis on the balance-of-payments position of developing countries see Singh
  (1986b, 1990). See also Cline (1984), Dornbusch (1985) and Cornia, Jolly and
  Stewart (eds.) (1987).
12 Fishlow (1987) and Hughes and Singh (1991) pay particular attention to the
  adverse impact on developing countries, particularly in Latin America, of an
  exogenous change in the flow of foreign capital.
13 These estimates refer to the net flow of foreign financial resources available for
  imports of goods and services (i.e., after payment of income on foreign capital

outstanding). The flows include both private and public capital flows as well as direct investment and official grants. See United Nations (1989).

14 For a detailed discussion of the impact of the foreign exchange crisis and import compression on industrial development in developing countries, see Khan and Knight (1988) and Singh (1990).

15 See for example Ahluwalia (1985), Gaiha (1989) and Saith (1990).

16 There is a large literature on the differential overall economic performance of Asian and Latin American countries: see Maddison (1985), Sachs (1985), Fishlow (1987) and Hughes and Singh (1988). On the differential performance of sub-Saharan African economies, see Singh (1986a, 1986d, 1988) and references contained in those papers.

17 See for example Ghai (1987) and Green (1985).

18 See for example Jamal (1986).

19 For an analysis of the relationship between agriculture and industry in the course of economic development, see Johnston and Mellor (1961), Mellor and Johnston (1984), Singh (1979, 1987) and Timmer (1988).

20 This probably reflects a trend reduction in food imports by countries like India for 'genuine' reasons – i.e., a trend increase in food production.

21 See Singh and Tabatabai (1989), table 18, p. 27.

22 See further Singh (1988).

23 The world economic recession may adversely affect rural poverty in the developing countries through three distinct channels: (a) reduced agricultural growth; (b) inflation; (c) reduced public spending on rural health, education, infrastructure, etc. See the Introduction to this volume.

24 On the issues raised by Sachs in this context, see the excellent contribution by Fortin (1990).

References

Ahluwalia, M.S., 1985. 'Rural poverty, agricultural production, and prices: A reexamination', in Mellor and Desai (eds.) (1985).

Alexandratos, N. (ed.), 1988. *World Agriculture: Toward 2000*, London: Belhaven Press.

Banuri, T. (ed.), 1991. *No Panacea: The limits to Liberalisation*, Oxford: Clarendon Press.

Chenery, H. and T.N. Srinivasan (eds.), 1988. *Handbook of Development Economics*, vol. I, Amsterdam: Elsevier Science Publishers BV.

Cline, W.R., 1984. *International Debt: Systematic Risk and Policy Response*, Washington, DC: Institute for International Economics.

Cornia, G. A., R. Jolly and F. Stewart (eds.), 1987. *Adjustment with a Human Face: Protecting the Vulnerable and Promoting Growth*, vol. I, A study by UNICEF, Oxford: Clarendon Press.

Cuddy, J.D.A. and P.A. Della Valle, 1978. 'Measuring the instability of time series data', *Oxford Bulletin of Economics and Statistics*, vol. 40, no. 1, February, pp. 79–85.

de Janvry, A., 1987. 'Latin American agriculture from import substitution industrialization to debt crisis', in Hollist and Tullis (eds.) (1987).

de Larosière, J., 1986. 'The debt situation', *Labour and Society*, vol. 11, no. 3, September, pp. 305–12.

Dornbusch, R., 1985. 'Policy and performance links between LDC debtors and industrial nations', *Brookings Papers on Economic Activity*, 2, Washington, DC: Brookings Institution.

ECLAC (Economic Commission for Latin America and the Caribbean), 1990. *Magnitud de la pobreza en America Latina en los años ochenta*, LC/L. 533, 31 May.

FAO, 1991. *Trade Yearbook 1990*, Rome: FAO.

Fishlow, A., 1987. 'Some reflections on comparative Latin American economic performance and policy', *Working Paper*, no. 8754, Berkeley: University of California.

Fortin, C., 1990. 'The rise and decline of industrialisation in Latin America', paper presented at the ICCDA Conference in Paris, April.

Gaiha, R., 1989. 'Poverty, agricultural production and prices in rural India – A reformulation', *Cambridge Journal of Economics*, vol. 13, no. 2, June, pp. 333–52.

García, A., R. Infante and V.E. Tokman, 1989. 'Paying off the social debt in Latin America', *International Labour Review*, vol. 128, no. 4, pp. 467–83.

Ghai, D., 1987. 'Successes and failures in growth in sub-Saharan Africa: 1960–82'. World Employment Programme, *Research Working Paper*, WEP 10–6/WP83, Geneva: ILO.

Glyn, A., A. Hughes, A. Lipietz and A. Singh, 1990. 'The rise and fall of the Golden Age', in Marglin and Schor (eds.) (1990).

Green, R.H., 1985. 'From deepening economic malaise towards renewed development: An overview', *Journal of Development Planning*, no. 15, pp. 9–43.

Griffin, K., 1987. *World Hunger and the World Economy*, London: Macmillan.

Hayami, Y. and V.W. Ruttan, 1985. *Agricultural Development: An International Perspective*, Baltimore and London: Johns Hopkins University Press.

Hollist, W. L. and F.L. Tullis (eds.), 1987. *Pursuing Food Security: Strategies and Obstacles in Africa, Asia, Latin America, and the Middle East*, Boulder, Col. and London: Lynne Rienner Publishers.

Hughes, A. and A. Singh, 1991. 'The world economic slowdown and the Asian and Latin American economies: A comparative analysis of economic structure, policy and performance', in Banuri (ed.) (1991).

IMF, 1986. *World Economic Outlook*, May, Washington, DC: IMF.

    1989. *World Economic Outlook*, April, Washington, DC: IMF.

    1992. *World Economic Outlook*, May, Washington, DC: IMF.

Jamal, V., 1986. 'Economics of devaluation: The case of Tanzania', *Labour and Society*, vol. 11, no. 3, September, pp. 379–93.

Johnston, B.F. and J.W. Mellor, 1961. 'The role of agriculture in economic development', *American Economic Review*, vol. 51, no. 4, September, pp. 566–93.

Khan, M.S. and M.D. Knight, 1988. 'Import compression and export performance in developing countries', *Review of Economics and Statistics*, vol. 70, no. 2, May, pp. 315–21.

Lawrence, P. (ed.), 1986. *World Recession and the Food Crisis in Africa*, London: Review of African Political Economy and James Currey.

Lindbeck, A., 1986. *The Role of the Public Sector in Economic Development*, Stockholm School of Economics, *Discussion paper*.

Maddison, A., 1985. *Two Crises: Latin America and Asia 1929–38 and 1973–83*, Paris: OECD.

Marglin, S. and S. Schor (eds.), 1990. *The Golden Age of Capitalism*, Oxford: Clarendon Press.

Mellor, J.W., 1987. 'Opportunities in the international economy for meeting the food requirements of the developing countries', in Hollist and Tullis (eds.) (1987).

  1988. 'Global food balances and food security', *World Development*, vol. 16, no. 9, September, pp. 997–1011.

  1989. 'Food demand in developing countries and the transition of world agriculture', *European Review of Agricultural Economics*, vol. 15, no. 4, pp. 419–36.

Mellor, J.W. and G.M. Desai (eds.), 1985. *Agricultural Change and Rural Poverty: Variations on a Theme by Dharm Narain*, Baltimore and London: Johns Hopkins University Press.

Mellor, J.W. and B.F. Johnston, 1984. 'The world food equation: Interrelations among development, employment and food consumption', *Journal of Economic Literature*, vol. 22, no. 2, June, pp. 531–74.

Paulino, L.A., 1986. *Food in the Third World: Past Trends and Projections to 2000*, *Research Report*, no. 52, Washington, DC: International Food Policy Research Institute.

Sachs, J.D., 1985. 'External debt and macroeconomic performance in Latin America and East Asia', *Brookings Papers on Economic Activity*, 2, Washington, DC: Brookings Institution.

Saith, A., 1990. 'Development strategies and the rural poor', *Journal of Peasant Studies*, vol. 17, no. 2, January, pp. 171–244.

Singh, A., 1979. 'The "basic needs" approach to development *vs* the new international economic order: The significance of Third World industrialization', *World Development*, vol. 7, no. 6, June, pp. 585–606.

  1984. 'The interrupted industrial revolution of the Third World: Prospects and policies for resumption', *Industry and Development* (Vienna, UNIDO), no. 12, June, pp. 43–68.

  1986a. 'Tanzania and the IMF: The analytics of alternative adjustment programmes', *Development and Change*, vol. 17, no. 3, July, pp. 425–54.

  1986b. 'The world economic crisis, stabilisation and structural adjustment: An overview', *Labour and Society*, vol. 11, no. 3, September, pp. 277–93.

  1986c. 'The great continental divide: Asian and Latin American countries in the world economic crisis', *Labour and Society*, vol. 11, no. 3, September, pp. 415–27.

1986d. 'A commentary on the IMF and World Bank policy programme', in Lawrence (ed.) (1986).

1987. 'Manufacturing and de-industrialization', in J. Eatwell, M. Milgate and P. Newman (eds.), *The New Palgrave: A Dictionary of Economics*, London: Macmillan.

1988. 'Exogenous shocks and de-industrialisation in sub-Saharan Africa: Prospects and policies for re-industrialisation', in Research and Information Systems of Non-Aligned and Developing Economies, *African Economic Crisis*, New Delhi.

1989. 'Third World competition and de-industrialisation in advanced countries', *Cambridge Journal of Economics*, vol. 13, no. 1, March, pp. 103–20.

1990. 'The state of industry in the Third World in the 1980s: Analytical and policy issues', *Working Paper*, no. 137, Notre Dame, Indiana: Kellogg Institute, University of Notre Dame.

Singh, A. and H. Tabatabai, 1989. 'The agrarian economy of the Third World in the 1980s: International economic conditions, agricultural development and rural poverty', paper presented at the ILO/SAREC Workshop on the 'Interrelationship between Macroeconomic Policies and Rural Development' (Geneva, 11–13 December 1989).

1990. 'Facing the crisis: Third World agriculture in the 1980s', *International Labour Review*, vol. 129, no. 4, pp. 479–500.

Timmer, C.P., 1988. 'The agricultural transformation', in Chenery and Srinivasan (eds.) (1988).

UNCTAD (United Nations Conference on Trade and Development), 1992. *Handbook of International Trade and Development Statistics 1991*, New York: United Nations.

UNIDO, 1984. *Industry in a Changing World*, New York: UNIDO.

United Nations, 1989. *World Economic Survey*, New York: United Nations.

World Bank, 1987. *World Development Report*, Washington, DC: World Bank.

1992. *World Development Report*, Washington, DC: World Bank.

3 Surplus extraction and the African agrarian crisis in a historical perspective

VALI JAMAL

Introduction

While perhaps it has never been stated quite so starkly, agreement could be mustered for the proposition that most structural adjustment programmes in sub-Saharan African (SSA) countries (and there are at least 30 such programmes in operation in SSA countries currently) start from the premise of urban bias, i.e., the operation of policies that systematically enrich the urban sector at the expense of the rural sector, with the rural-urban terms of trade as the transfer mechanism. The World Bank's 1981 report on Africa, known after its chief author as the 'Berg Report' (World Bank, 1981), from which most World Bank analyses of the agrarian crisis and adjustment programmes have issued, and Bates' influential book of the same year may be cited in partial evidence.[1] The policies singled out in support of the urban-bias hypothesis are those relating to wages for the urban employees and pricing policies for the farmers. Adjustment programmes strive to 'correct' the bias in these policies by freezing wages and raising agricultural prices. Jamal and Weeks (1987, 1988, forthcoming) have questioned the almost automatic acceptance of urban bias in terms of favouritism towards the wage-earning class, and their results will be summarised later. On the agricultural side, studies of pricing policies have been more common and systematic. However, a synthesis has so far been lacking, especially in the context of the debate on adjustment programmes. It is the objective of this chapter to fill this lacuna by looking at the question of agricultural surplus extraction in Africa from a long-term historical perspective. We look back to the initial introduction of export crops into the sub-Saharan countries to adduce the role of agriculture at different stages of African economic development, the nature of competition between export crops and food crops, and, most importantly for development, the modes of surplus extraction from the agricultural sector. This examination should enable us to put in context recurrent arguments about the relative balance between export crops and food crops, the importance of price incentives as a cause and cure of the African crisis and the proper role of agriculture in African development.

The introduction of export crops in Africa is described in the first section. For the current debate the points of interest are the role of price incentives in export expansion, the marshalling of resources for exports and the distribution of export incomes among farmers, processors and government. I shall in particular look at the argument that the current food crisis in Africa can be attributed to the concentration on exports. The next section analyses the modes of surplus extraction from agriculture. In Africa these have taken the form of withdrawals from export incomes, rather than the more common Asian method of terms of trade 'twists' on food crops. The following section quantifies the impact of exports on living standards by looking at producer real prices. The final section examines the linkages between agricultural surplus extraction, wages and the African crisis.

Exports and 'vent for surplus'

The establishment of agricultural exports is the one unequivocal success story out of Africa this century. To take just two examples, in Nigeria export volume doubled in the first twelve years of this century and again in the next twelve, followed by a further 25 per cent increase between 1924 and 1929 (Helleiner, 1966, p. 7 and table II-A-2). In Uganda cotton exports increased from a mere 56 bales (400 lb each) in 1905 to 418,000 bales in 1938. By then almost half of the cultivated land in the country was devoted to cotton (Jamal, 1976b, table II.1). From the 1930s the land-locked East African country experienced a second export boom, this time for African-grown coffee. By the early 1960s some 2 million acres of land had been brought under cotton and coffee, representing around 40 per cent of total acreage cultivated in Uganda at that time. Similar stories can be told of most other African countries.[2]

How the initial expansion of exports occurred in basically subsistence-oriented economies has much to tell us about current efforts to revive the export sector in African countries after nearly two decades of decline. Three questions in particular are relevant: (i) What was the role of price incentives; (ii) how were resources created for the export industry; and (iii) what were the implications of export expansion for food production?

The newly introduced export crops – cotton, coffee, cocoa, groundnuts, palm products – although generally unknown to Africans[3] were nevertheless readily accepted by them because they could be easily integrated into the traditional rotations (McPhee, 1926; Johnston, 1964, 1980). Cotton could be grown alongside sorghum and millet, coffee and cocoa with plantains and root crops, groundnuts with pulses, while palm trees grew wild in the forest. The same farm tools sufficed for the cultivation of export crops as of food crops – the machete for clearing the bush, the hoe for digging, weeding and uprooting, and specialised knives for harvesting.

The major changes required for exporting were rather in the non-agricultural sectors, involving the importation of foreign technologies and, in many cases, foreign personnel. That put the stamp on income distribution not only within the export industry but throughout the economy. Three non-farm sectors were involved – transport, processing and trade. Establishment of the first two was imperative for a successful export drive since African commodities were not only bulky but also weight-losing. In the early days of exporting, and when head-porterage was still the norm, cotton, coffee and cocoa were exported in their raw form. Obviously these were temporary expedients. Gradually the railway and processing plants penetrated the hinterland and exports took off rapidly. The trading network too had to be imported from abroad – Europe, India, the Levant – and provided the vital link for African farmers between growing what to them were commodities of unknown utility and buying what soon became coveted consumer goods – cloth, shoes, utensils, candles, matches and cigarettes.

The role of coercion in export expansion should nevertheless not be underestimated, à propos the emphasis in current adjustment programmes on incentives. In the traditional economy the chiefs had enlisted their subjects to raid neighbouring tribes and build houses and roads. With the establishment of international trade they had them cultivating export crops, sometimes on their own estates. This overt coercion was sanctioned by the colonial powers whose main concern was to make their dependencies financially self-sufficient. Covert coercion existed in the form of the poll tax. The required cash could be earned by selling food to the foreign population in towns, taking up wage employment as servants or farm hands, or growing export crops. Wherever the last choice was available it was the one preferred.

Given this institutional framework for export expansion, what were the resource costs? In particular, were resources withdrawn from existing economic activities? As Jones (1968) has noted, there are basically four sources of labour for new production: (i) idle labour, (ii) labour employed on products and services of low value, (iii) labour employed inefficiently, and (iv) labour unemployed because of illness. In the African case the most important sources of labour initially were idle labour and labour released as a result of the substitution of local goods and tools by imported ones.[4]

At the turn of the century the African economies were basically subsistence-oriented;[5] the major occupation of the population was food production, everywhere the responsibility of women. Although men helped out peripherally by clearing the bush and harvesting, their main duties were the provision of shelter and clothing, and hunting. Some specialised in skilled work, notably iron-making and pottery. In the more organised societies they joined the chiefs' army, or worked on their (chiefs') compounds building houses, fences and roads. These activities did not exhaust the available labour time and the remaining time constituted a ready source of labour for the cultivation of exports.

The surplus labour was augmented by the inflow of imports. However, there was no wholesale displacement or extinction of traditional crafts, as most were geared to the specialised needs of the population. Thus, while bark-cloth in Uganda gave way to *amerikani*[6] (grey unbleached cloth) and *basta* (bleached cloth), the art of bark-cloth making survived for ceremonial wear. In West Africa cotton cloth which had been made from the eighth century onwards also withstood the competition from mass-produced textiles from Lancashire[7] (Hopkins, 1973, p. 121). Similarly, though many locally-made iron tools and utensils were superseded by imports, others survived such as specialised knives used in harvesting millet, and pots and pans used for collecting water and storing grains.

The indirect impact of imports in releasing labour – by increasing labour productivity – was probably greater than the direct displacement impact. The imported tools speeded up the tasks, releasing time for other activities. Hoes, axes, fishing hooks and nets, spears and knives, and hammers and nails were universally adopted. The railway, lorries and processing plants which followed in quick succession displaced porters, again increasing the labour supply for agriculture. In the service sector too there was a substitution effect of sorts as medicine men, diviners and traditional judges gave way to doctors, missionaries and lawyers. Most importantly, the standing armies of the chiefs were disbanded in favour of modern police forces.

The process of export expansion just described is the classical 'vent-for-surplus' model enunciated by Myint (1958) and earlier postulated by Adam Smith.[8] The model applies to land-abundant economies[9] and embodies the notion that the sparse population can provide for its needs well within its production frontier. External demand spurs the surplus land and labour into useful production. The implied underemployment means that farmers can take up exports without sacrificing existing activities, in particular food production. In fact, as we have seen, in most cases export crops were grafted on to traditional rotations without causing any disruption and represented a net addition to national output. There is obviously a limit to such growth based on idle resources and in later years exports can only expand in line with growth of the labour force or the introduction of new technology. The vent for surplus eventually disappears.

The above model of export expansion applies most appropriately to peasant-based African economies, which comprise the majority of the sub-Saharan countries. However, a second model of African development that came to the fore with colonialism is sometimes advanced to refute several points deriving from the peasant model.

At the start of Africa's colonisation, the expectation was that the colonies would be developed on the basis of European-operated plantations. This was the tried model of development until then, with notable successes in the West Indies, Indonesia, Malaysia and elsewhere. Around the turn of the century plantations were established in most West African countries – Ivory Coast, Dahomey, Togo, the Cameroons, the Gold Coast, Nigeria (Hopkins, 1973, p. 211). It was asserted that plantations would produce a better and more regular supply of raw materials for processing factories. There was also a fear that 'the greater efficiency achieved by plantation development in other parts of the world would make it impossible for indigenous producers in West Africa to compete in international markets' (Hopkins, 1973, p. 211). None the less, apart from those in Ivory Coast (and Liberia in the 1920s), plantations made little headway in West Africa and in the meantime peasant-based exports – palm products, groundnuts, cocoa – took off with the establishment of the three marketing networks described earlier.

In East Africa attempts to establish plantations were made in Uganda (coffee) and Tanganyika (sisal, tea and coffee), but side by side with peasant-based exports. The Ugandan coffee plantations failed miserably with the price slump in the second decade of the century and, after a period of dormancy, coffee too passed into the hands of African smallholders in the 1930s (Ehrlich, 1965; Jamal, 1976b). In Tanganyika plantations coexisted with peasant agriculture well into the present era but without ever dominating the agricultural economy.

It was in Kenya and the southern African countries that plantations reached their apogee in Africa. The plantations (estates) specialised in coffee, tea and sisal for the export market and maize and livestock for the domestic market. These plantations differed from the Asian model in being operated by permanent settlers rather than contracted expatriates. As Brett (1973, p. 174) has shown in his study of Kenya, the settlers made many more demands on the Government for long-term social and political security than would itinerant planters. African smallholders had to be prevented from growing the same crops as European planters, tariff protection had to be given on wheat and livestock products, railway rates had to be fixed to favour European products and, above all, a reliable, plentiful and cheap supply of labour had to be ensured. Africans did not come forward to take up wage employment on the estates because of the safety net provided by subsistence agriculture.[10] Thus, as in the peasant model, taxes were imposed which in the context of closed entry into export farming could be paid only through wage labour. For safe measure special rules directed labour to plantations. After the mid-1920s Kenya's African population increased considerably. The ensuing pressure on the land (only 20 per cent of Kenya's land is fertile and of this more than one-half had been appropriated by the Europeans) 'naturally' pushed the growing labour force into wage employment, gradually obviating the need for coercion. While up to 1912/13 African production had accounted for 70 per cent of Kenyan exports, from 1925 even the absolute value of African exports declined (Wrigley, 1965, p. 243).

Here then is the model of export expansion at the expense of the peasantry – and, some contend, at the expense of food production, one exponent of this viewpoint being the influential writer on the African crisis, Michael Lofchie (1987). According to him export production in Africa resulted from plantation agriculture;[11] this caused a dualism within the agricultural sector between an export enclave producing for the external market and the hinterland producing food for the domestic market (Lofchie, 1987, p. 104, citing Leys, 1973); to survive, plantations needed a supply of cheap migratory labour, but since peasants were the only source of supply, their 'living standards ... had to be deliberately lowered to the point that wage labor became the only alternative to starvation or utter destitution' (Lofchie, 1987, p. 106, citing Stavenhagen, 1975); policies such as the poll tax, labour laws and outright coercion were instituted to compel 'formerly self-sufficient peasants to become agricultural workers' (Lofchie, 1987, p. 106); in the long run the most effective method of impoverishment was the introduction of price controls on food crops which 'lowered peasant family incomes to the point at which survival depended upon some income' (Lofchie, 1987, p. 106).

Lofchie considers this the principal model of African export expansion and derives from it the chief explanation of the 'food crisis that began within a decade of the end of formal colonial rule' (Lofchie, 1987, p. 106). He rejects the vent-for-surplus model, with support from other authorities;[12] that model failed to recognise 'just how ubiquitous ... enclave development was and, therefore, how deeply its development depended upon the suppression of domestically oriented agricultural production' (Lofchie, 1987, p. 108).

Lofchie's ultimate conclusion from this line of reasoning – that exports do not provide the salvation for Africa's current problems – is one to which I subscribe, although only partly. However, his path to this conclusion may be questioned. Central to his argument is the contention that there was no vent for surplus and that this manifested itself in the food crisis within a decade of independence. What would have to be shown is that export crops led to a food crisis *within a decade of their introduction*, if not straightaway. In reality, food imports in any significant quantity are very much a phenomenon of the late 1970s and 1980s and, far from signifying a losing battle of domestic production with exports, occurred *concurrently* with a *decline* in export crops.[13] The African crisis is not just a food crisis, and perhaps not even primarily a food crisis, but very much an export-related crisis.[14] Lofchie's assertion that the plantation model was the predominant model of development in Africa would also be contested, as would his implicit notion of dualistic development between an 'export crop sector' and a 'food crop sector', the former being relatively advanced in its capital intensity and technology (Lofchie, 1987, p. 104). In most African countries one looks in vain for distinct export crop and food crop 'sectors'. Indeed, it is an argument of this chapter that no such dichotomy exists and that the symbiotic relationships between the two types of crops grown side by side has much to teach us about the nature of the African crisis.

Surplus extraction

The role of coercion in the establishment of export crops fostered a belief that African farmers took up cash work only because of coercion and that by the same token burdensome taxes would not discourage them unduly. The upshot was that neither in the colonial period nor subsequently did African farmers receive a fair return for their efforts. Poll taxes, marketing board surpluses and exchange-rate manipulation were the means used to squeeze farmers.

Poll tax

In the early years, given the small acreages that most farmers cultivated, the poll tax represented a heavy burden. For example, in Uganda, the poll tax of Sh 6.66 in 1914 could have been met from the proceeds of one-fifth of an acre of cotton – but farmers in most districts grew no more than that amount of cotton. Thus the bulk of their cash income went to pay the poll tax. Various native government taxes that traditionally had been met through personal service and tribute claimed as much as the poll tax in many districts. In Buganda in the late 1930s, with the poll tax fixed at Sh 15, commutation of labour obligation (*luwalo*) was assessed at Sh 10, while in the cotton-growing districts of Eastern Province, farmers had additionally to contribute a produce tribute (*busulu*) of Sh 3–6. The importance of these native taxes may be gauged from the fact that in 1939 they raised £311,000 compared with £580,000 for the poll tax. In some parts of Uganda, Africans owning more than five acres of land paid a land tax of Sh 20 per farm, while those owning less than five acres could be taxed at Sh 2 at the discretion of the native government. Every Ganda landowner was likewise liable to a tax of 10 per cent of the rent he received.

The worst aspect of the tax regime was its discriminatory nature, which in most African countries acquired racial overtones because of the division of labour between farmers, processors and traders. In Uganda non-African incomes remained untaxed for over twenty years after the start of the protectorate and non-African crops for even longer (see Jamal, 1976a, 1978). When in 1919 the poll tax was finally imposed on Asians and Europeans the rate was fixed at only twice the African rate. Not until 1945 was an income tax proper introduced. Throughout the colonial period no export tax was charged on plantation rubber, even though non-plantation rubber, tapped by Africans, was taxed. In the 1940s when coffee finally became subject to the export tax and marketing board control, only the African industry was affected; estate coffee, still mostly in the hands of non-Africans, remained untaxed and uncontrolled.

The consequences of government tax policies in Uganda are demonstrated in table 3.1. Taking 1937 as an illustration, farmers paid £761,000 in direct taxes (poll tax and local government tax) and £133,000 in cotton (export) tax. Thus they contributed £894,000 in taxes out of their potential income of £3.15 million – a tax rate of 28 per cent. In 1947, owing to withdrawals made by the Lint Marketing Board, the rate of taxation reached almost 50 per cent. Non-Africans, by contrast, paid a minute proportion of their income in tax. In 1937, their poll tax raised £29,877 when, as estimated elsewhere (Jamal, 1976a), ginners' income alone amounted to £533,000. Thus, even on the assumption that all non-African poll tax came from cotton ginners and cotton ginning income was their only income, the rate of taxation works out at 5.4 per cent.

Marketing board taxation

Taxation by marketing boards represented the most extreme form of taxation in Africa. The boards were a British colonial invention, created in the early 1940s to meet war-time exigencies, though the idea, as Bauer (1954, 1975) has suggested, came from powerful traders and processors bent on eliminating competition in the export trade.[15] With export prices rising, the marketing boards were reluctant to pass on the benefits to farmers, justifying this initially on the grounds that increasing producer prices would fuel inflation in the face of war-induced shortages. Later, the rationale was advanced that marketing boards were there to stabilise producer prices and that financial surpluses would be liquidated in due course to compensate for falling prices. In the event, only a small fraction of

Table 3.1. *Uganda: farm taxes, incomes and tax incidence, 1927, 1937 and 1947* (£000 and %)

	1927	1937	1947
Farm taxes			
(i) Export tax[a]	51	133	2653
(ii) Poll tax[b]	453	495	550
(iii) Native government tax	—	266	341
(iv) Total farm taxes (all above)	504	894	3544
Farm incomes			
(v) Farm cash income	2851	3015	4634
(vi) Farm potential income[c] ((v)+(i))	2902	3148	7287
Tax rate (%)			
(vii) Farm taxes (iv) to farm potential income (vi)	17.4	28.4	48.6

Notes:
[a] In 1927 and 1937 only cotton export tax. In 1947 £90,000 worth of coffee export tax and £1.66 million worth of marketing board surplus.
[b] Net of poll tax paid by wage earners.
[c] Identified as the income farmers could have received in the absence of export taxes and marketing surplus, i.e., farm potential income = payment to growers plus export duty and marketing board surplus.
Source: Jamal (1976b), table VI.2.

the huge surpluses accumulated by the marketing boards was used to top up producer prices. Most was spent on development projects, so that the surpluses resembled an export tax. And by the time the farmers saw any benefit of the price stabilisation fund, consumer goods prices had increased considerably; the money the boards paid out in the late 1950s and early 1960s was worth only two-thirds of its value in the period it was collected.

As Bauer (1954, table 22) showed, in the Gold Coast the cocoa marketing board taxed away 35 per cent of sales proceeds between 1939/40 and 1950/51, on top of the 9 per cent export duty. During the same period the Nigerian cocoa board deducted 37 per cent on top of the 7 per cent export duty (Bauer, 1954, table 22). The 1950/51 season saw a peaking of withdrawals (marketing board and export duty), with 49 per cent deducted from Gold Coast cocoa, 53 per cent from Nigerian cocoa, 57 per cent from Nigerian groundnuts, 36 per cent from Nigerian palm kernels and 33 per cent from Nigerian palm oil (Bauer, 1954, table 22). Helleiner (1966) continued the story for Nigerian products up to 1962 – see table 3.2.

Table 3.2. *Nigeria: export tax and marketing board surplus, 1947–62*
(£ million, except as indicated)

	Export duties (1)	Marketing board surplus (2)	Total with-drawals[a] (3) = (1) + (2)	Potential producer income[b] (4)	Withdrawals: potential income (%) (5) = (3)/(4)
Cocoa 1947/48–1961/62	64.5	46.6	115.7	363.0	31.9
Groundnuts 1947/48–1960/61	32.2	25.7	61.9	248.4	24.9
Palm kernels 1947–1961	27.0	37.0	68.3	243.0	28.1
Palm oil 1947–1961	17.0	10.8	32.4	154.0	21.0
Cotton 1949/50–1960/61	8.5	5.3	14.5	65.8	22.1
Total	149.2	125.4	292.8	1 074.2	27.2

Notes:
[a] Including minor withdrawals by way of produce purchase tax.
[b] I.e., the income producers could have received had there been no
withdrawals = producer income (not shown but derivable) plus withdrawals.
Source: Helleiner (1966), table 38.

Between 1947 and 1962 32 per cent of cocoa proceeds, 25 per cent of groundnuts, 28 per cent of palm kernels, 21 per cent of palm oil and 22 per cent of cotton proceeds were taxed away. In each case, the marketing board surplus amounted to at least one-third total of withdrawals, the average being 43 per cent and the highest figure 54 per cent (for palm kernels).

In Uganda high export prices lasted from around 1945 to 1952. In the first four years of this period, £7.3 million was deducted from cotton proceeds and £1 million from coffee (Jamal, 1976b). Between 1949 and 1952 deductions reached their peak, with withholdings of £27.4 million from cotton and £11.9 million from coffee incomes. The surplus collected from cotton amounted to 33 per cent of cotton growers' potential income and that from coffee 45 per cent. At the same time, the Government deducted around 20 per cent of export incomes through the export tax, so that in this period more money was extracted from cotton and coffee growers than was paid out to them. In the next decade a small part of the surplus collected was

Table 3.3. *Sierra Leone: effective rates of taxation,[a] 1968/69–1981/82*

	Palm kernels	Coffee	Cocoa
1968/69–1972/73	− 1.5	44.4	38.2
1973/74–1976/77	26.6	54.4	53.9
1977/78–1981/82	29.6	43.3	35.8

Note:
[a] Figures show marketing board surplus and export tax as a proportion of producer potential income, defined as previously.
Source: Jamal (1986), table 4, p. 344.

repaid to the farmers (in the period 1953–62, £9.5 million to coffee producers and in 1958–62, £7.1 million to cotton producers) to cushion sharply falling export prices. The remaining funds were used for development projects or recurrent government expenditures.

In Sierra Leone marketing board 'action' lasted well into the 1980s. Writing in 1986 I had singled out this small West African country as having the most persistent and onerous agricultural taxation (Jamal, 1986, p. 340). Effective tax rates of 40 per cent and more were common for coffee and cocoa for the period 1968/69 to 1981/82, and for palm kernels reached that level at least three times during these 13 years (Jamal, 1986, table 4). Average figures by sub-periods are given in table 3.3.

I also estimated the incidence of taxation for 1979/80 (when for all three crops the effective rate of taxation was around 40–45 per cent). The estimates took account of farmers' subsistence income, but on the tax side included only the export tax and marketing board surplus, i.e., poll tax and indirect taxes were omitted. Taxes totalled Le 31 million, equal to 9.9 per cent of total agricultural income or 19.2 per cent of agricultural cash income. By comparison, non-farmers who on average had an income over five times that of farmers paid taxes at just 5.6 per cent (Jamal, 1986, table 6).

Exchange-rate taxation

Since the mid-1970s the overt forms of agricultural taxation have been dismantled, with abolition of export duties and the virtual disappearance of the poll tax amid the general collapse of the physical and administrative infrastructure. Their place has been taken by what might be termed 'exchange-rate taxation', the essence of which is the operation of different sets of prices on the external and internal markets through exchange-rate manipulation. On the external front the country receives foreign exchange and purchases cloth, utensils and other goods at international prices; on the internal front farmers receive local currency and purchase similar necessities at local prices. The Government, which can decide the exchange rate, usually overvalues the local currency so that the conventional ratios of border prices to producer prices fail to reflect the actual tax burden. We shall illustrate with examples from Uganda and Ghana.

Table 3.4 shows the pertinent data for coffee and cotton in Uganda. Some columns need explanation. Column (2) converts the producer price in column (1) for the unprocessed product (say seed cotton, i.e., lint plus cotton seed) to give a price for the processed product (lint). This is to facilitate a comparison with the export price which will always be for lint.[16] Column (8) converts the price in column (7) to 'parity price' – i.e., the price the farmer could have received for the crop after allowing for essential processing and marketing charges. This price can then be compared with the price in column (2), as in column (9) – except that exchange rate distortions can make intertemporal comparisons misleading. For example, the figures in column (9) for cotton imply that the farmer was receiving a 'subsidy'. That would be quite wrong; by 1980 the Ugandan shilling was hopelessly overvalued, with the price in the parallel market being around Sh 50 per dollar. If this price is used in the calculation then the shilling-equivalent price in New York was not Sh 12.52 but Sh 89.50, meaning that the farmer received only 24 per cent of the potential parity price. The Government squeezed farmers by letting domestic inflation diverge from imported inflation while defending the exchange rate.

The situation in Ghana was similar. For this West African country we have a series for international terms of trade all the way back to 1900. The series ends in 1960 but we have extended it to 1987 using for the 1960s the real price of cocoa and for 1970–87 Ghana's terms of trade as estimated by UNCTAD (1989, table 7.2). The result is shown as Series A in figure 3.1. Superimposed on Series A is a series of the real producer price of cocoa from 1950 to 1985 (Series B). The figures show that farmers' terms of trade fell by a catastrophic 95 per cent in the course of just three decades from the 1950s at a time when the country's terms improved by 22 per cent. Put even more vividly, while between 1965 and 1977–79 (average) the country's terms of trade doubled, farmers' terms declined by 60 per cent; the Ghanaian cocoa farmer never saw the benefit of the late 1970s' beverages boom. By contrast, the conventional tax ratios show an 'improvement': in 1953 30 per cent of farm income was taxed away whereas by 1980 the rate halved. In reality, farm 'taxation' tripled.[17]

Table 3.4. *Uganda: comparison of producer and export prices of coffee and cotton, 1972 and 1980*

	Producer price for unprocessed product Sh/kg (1)	Equivalent price for processed product Sh/kg (2)	Uganda CPI (1972=100) (3)	Real producer price (1972 prices) Sh/kg (4) =100×(1)/(3)	New York price US$/kg (5)	Exchange rate Sh/US$ (6)	New York price Sh/kg (7) =(5)×(6)	Equivalent potential price to grower Sh/kg (8) =0.85×(7)	Ratio of grower price to potential price (9) =(2)/(8)	Import unit value index (1972=100) (10)	New York real price (11)= 100×(5)/(10)
Coffee											
1972	1.19	2.38	100	1.19	0.99	7.00	6.96	5.92	0.40	100	0.99
1980	7.00	14.00	3 348	0.21	3.24	7.00	22.66	19.26	0.73	294	1.10
Cotton											
1972	1.25	3.75	100	1.25	0.75	7.00	5.28	4.49	0.84	100	0.75
1980	6.00	18.00	3 348	0.18	1.79	7.00	12.52	10.64	1.69	294	0.61

Sources and notes: (1) Jamal (1985); (2) derived from (1) using a ratio for processed to unprocessed of 0.5 for coffee and 0.33 for cotton; (3) Consumer price index, Jamal (1985); (5) IMF (1988), p. 180: New York price for Uganda coffee and 'US 10 market' price for cotton; (6) IMF (1988), tables on Uganda; (8) assumes processing and marketing costs at 15 per cent of New York price; (10) UNCTAD (1989), table 7.2 for Uganda.

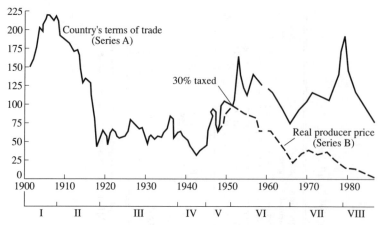

Figure 3.1 Gold Coast (Ghana): net barter terms of trade, 1900–60 and 1960–87 and real producer price of cocoa, 1950–87 (1953 = 100).
Sources: Country's terms of trade (Series A), 1900–60 from Hymer (1971) quoted in Hopkins (1973); for the 1960s, real price of cocoa; 1970–87 from UNCTAD (1989), table 7.2. Discontinuity at 1960 signifies a switch between data sources. Producer's real price of cocoa (Series B) from Bequele (1980) and Tabatabai (1988, alternative B).

Exports and living standards

Figure 3.1 also illustrates a point about the gains from trade to African countries and farmers. For countries, eight sub-periods can be discerned (marked on the horizontal axis). During the first decade of the century – also the first decade of the export industry – prices rose. This not only facilitated the establishment of the industry but also helped consolidate colonial rule by reducing the burden on home taxpayers. During the next decade prices fell more or less continuously, while for the two following decades they fluctuated around a rising trend. Between the late 1930s and the late 1970s prices went through four major cycles starting with a fall in the pre-war period and culminating in the price boom of the late 1970s. The story since then is of an almost continuous fall in prices, quite sharp if we take the unusual late 1970s' peak as a reference, but still considerable when averaged out. As Hopkins (1973, p. 183) has shown, exporting crops bought for West Africa four times as many imports in 1960 as 50 years previously. Since during this period the population doubled, import purchasing power doubled in *per capita* terms. After 1960 catastrophe hit Ghana. Terms of trade declined by 34 per cent up to 1987, while output declined by 38 per cent. Thus the purchasing power of cocoa exports fell by

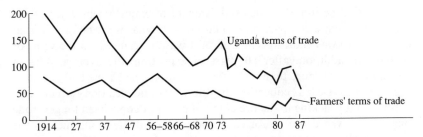

Figure 3.2 Uganda: barter terms of trade of cotton textiles for cotton lint,
1914–87 (yards of cloth for 100 lb lint).
Sources: Jamal (1976b), up to 1973; then IMF (1988) and Jamal (1988a).

over 60 per cent. This means that in 1987 the country's ability to purchase
imports was no higher in *per capita* terms than in 1910. And in 1987 quite a
large proportion of imports will have been essential inputs for the remaining functioning industries; Ghana could almost certainly import many
fewer consumer goods than 80 years previously.

Up to the late 1940s Ghanaian farmers' terms of trade followed the same
pattern as the country's (so that Series A and B coincide between 1900 and
1950); after that their terms began to diverge sharply – for the worse. By the
late 1980s cocoa farmers' earnings from (official) exports were lower even
than in 1920 and certainly only a fraction of their level in 1953 when the
great slide in producer prices began.

Figure 3.2 gives similar information to figure 3.1 for Uganda, with terms
of trade ratios represented by the barter terms of trade of cotton textiles for
cotton lint. Uganda's terms fluctuated much more than Ghana's, although
data intervals may be partly responsible. The trend decline after 1973
observed for Ghana comes through clearly, as does the relative profitability
of growing cotton in the earlier years. However, there is a trend decline for
the whole period 1914–87, in both external and internal markets. Around
1914 Uganda could import 200 yards of cotton textiles for 100 lb of lint,
whereas by the mid-1980s this had fallen to 63 yards; the farmers' terms of
trade halved. The gap between the two terms of trade shows the extent of
farm taxation, albeit approximately.[18] Given that the same amount of
cotton went into the making of, say, a shirt, one realises how much 'value
added' was retained in the advanced countries. 'Surplus extraction' is a
favourite catch-phrase of free market economists to encapsulate state
exploitation of the peasantry. The extent of surplus extraction through free-
market international exchanges is less often acknowledged and is therefore
well worth emphasising.

The pessimistic view of exporting must be qualified. The above comparison is with a period after the establishment of export crops whereas the more appropriate comparison should be with what went before. In that case the gain was enormous and all of it was net gain, given the vent for surplus. In addition, after 60 years of exporting, the average African consumed much more than just consumer goods; he or she had access to social services such as education, health, water and electricity which were almost totally lacking in the pre-colonial period. People lived longer, rode bicycles or even drove motor cars, and enjoyed distractions such as the cinema and sports matches. Of course, there was always 'urban bias' and farmers benefited much less from social services and public amenities than townspeople.

Surplus extraction and development

As we stated at the beginning, 'urban bias' is very much at the heart of the model by which African economies are understood and the notion of a pampered wage earning class very much a part of this model.[19] In addition, there is a belief that African industrialisation has been inefficient.[20] Recent ILO research (see in particular Jamal and Weeks, 1987, 1988, forthcoming; also Jamal, 1989) has questioned many aspects of this stylisation of African economies, especially the assertion that agricultural taxation went to benefit the urban wage earners. The linkage is missing as African exports are not wage goods, and even the wage goods – food crops – have been mostly traded on free markets, so that if price twists have occurred, the blame should be put not on government manipulation but on the markets.

ILO research has also shown that the 'labour aristocracy' was in fact very much an East African phenomenon, ephemeral and quite likely illusory. West Africa, where the notion of the rural–urban gap was born, saw few minimum wage increases after independence. Indeed, such countries as Sierra Leone and Liberia have never had effective minimum wages (Jamal and Weeks, 1988, forthcoming; also Rimmer, 1970). Only the East African countries of Kenya, Uganda, the United Republic of Tanzania and Zambia provide examples of sharp minimum wage increases after independence; in no case, it now appears, could the resulting minimum wage be considered 'aristocratic'. For example, Tanzania (then Tanganyika) was singled out in two ILO documents (ILO, 1964; Smith, 1969) as the African country where wages increased fastest between 1956 and 1964 (Smith, 1969, table 1). Because of the alleged rural–urban gap such large increases were said to need 'special scrutiny' (Smith, 1969, p. 32). In fact, out of the average non-agricultural wage of Sh 224 per month in 1964, Sh 120 – or 54 per cent – would have been needed just to purchase the most basic foods for the family; adding non-food needs would exhaust the rest (Jamal, 1989).[21] The *minimum* wage would certainly not have supported an average family in town. That only happened ten years later, in 1974, when the minimum wage was at a record level in real terms. In Uganda the minimum wage reached its highest level in 1964 after three successive hikes within a decade, yet 46 per cent of the wage was necessary to purchase 9,000 staple calories – the barest sufficiency for four people. Adding non-staple foods, not to mention fuel and non-food items, would easily exhaust the minimum wage. The 'aristocrats' lived on a tight budget.

What is true is that the situation of wage earners did improve considerably after the mid-1950s and the change was deliberately engineered to 'stabilise' the labour force, a policy enunciated in the 1955 *Report of the Committee on African Wages* in Kenya. The migratory pattern of wage employment engendered by low wages was deplored because of its negative implications for productivity in both the urban and rural sectors.[22] The report recommended an immediate change in the fixing of the minimum wage – 'from one which takes account only of the needs of a single man to one based on the needs of a family unit'. The family-based wage became the norm from the late 1950s and remained so through the first decade of independence. It resulted in considerable sedentarisation of the labour force.

In the last fifteen years this carefully nurtured urban–rural dichotomy has broken down with a catastrophic decline in wages (Jamal and Weeks, 1988, forthcoming). Once again, urban wage earners have to make forays into the countryside to collect food and to grow their own food in the urban areas in order to survive. We have here the paradoxical situation that just when surplus extraction from agriculture increased (through exchange rate taxation), the class that was alleged to be gaining from the squeeze itself got squeezed. In the extreme cases of Uganda, Ghana and the United Republic of Tanzania, the minimum wage fell by almost *three-quarters* between the early 1970s and 1986. Even the more normally functioning African economies suffered wage declines – Kenya, Côte d'Ivoire and Burkina Faso by around 40 per cent, Malawi and Senegal by just under 50 per cent, Zambia by 35 per cent, and so on.

While it is questionable whether surplus extraction directly helped wage earners, whose position has in any event by now weakened, other aspects of urban bias are undeniable. There was agricultural taxation, and government expenditure was slanted in favour of the urban areas. There was also costly industrialisation, partly financed through export surpluses. Altogether, if we look at African economic structures we cannot but conclude that agriculture was squeezed in favour of industry.[23]

But the historical perspective also makes us answer 'no' to two recurring questions about the current predicament of African countries: did surplus extraction cause the African crisis, and would removing it be a cure? The argument has two parts: one points to evidence such as that in figures 3.1 and 3.2 to show that the African crisis is a by-product of trends in commodity markets. With African economies dependent on exports to the extent of 25–30 per cent of their GDP, falls in external prices were bound to cause major declines in incomes.

The other part of the argument accepts that there was surplus extraction and that this was necessary as one of the roles of agriculture à la Johnston and Mellor (1961),[24] but points to its inefficient uses. Agriculture in Africa became the provider of foreign exchange because of chance historical circumstances – the availability of surplus resources to take up export production. But the productivity increases which are essential to successful surplus extraction never occurred. In the meantime agriculture had to feed an ever-increasing urban population, another of its roles in the transformation of the economy, but again without any commensurate increases in productivity. In terms of the perceptive synthesis offered by Timmer (1988, figure 8.1, p. 282) African agriculture was squeezed before it could 'get moving' and it never attained the conditions necessary for successful fulfilment of the Johnston–Mellor functions.

Would the retention of surplus within the agricultural sector have helped the process of accumulation and technological change? That is of course a difficult question to answer but, given the lack of spontaneous innovation on the continent, one rather doubts it. The catalytic role had to be played by the State and nowhere did it do so. The State siphoned off huge surpluses from the farmers – and 'lost' them through expensive industrialisation. In the final analysis the weakness in state policy was not extraction of surplus per se but rather that so little of it was used to modernise the agricultural sector.

Looking ahead one cannot but be overawed by the task facing Africa – the revival of not only the agricultural sector but also the urban sector. The impetus, despite poor export markets and the ultimate desirability of reducing export dependency, must come from the export sector. In this we differ from Lofchie. While diversification away from traditional exports must be the ultimate objective, that objective can be achieved initially only from export expansion: the internal market is simply too small to provide an alternative. We are back to the start of the century when too exports constituted the only sure means of fuelling the economy; unfortunately, as table 3.5 shows, current conditions are not half as propitious.

The only benign factor present now is that there is once more vent for surplus. In most African countries exports have fallen drastically in the last decade and hence 'excess capacity' has appeared in the agricultural sector.[25] Otherwise there are no positive factors in favour of agriculture's

Table 3.5. *Conditions for expanding exports, c. 1900 and 1990*

	Then (c. 1900)	Now (c. 1990)
Vent for surplus	Yes: new activity	Yes: excess capacity because of export decline
Food imports	None	Yes: around 15 per cent of total calories consumed
Marketing network	None, but soon built up	Mostly destroyed
Urban sector	Import-dependent but able to supply inputs and consumer goods	Import-dependent, but import strangulation and urban collapse
Population pressure	No	Yes
Soil fertility	Stable	Declining because of population pressure and reduction of fallow
Price prospects	Good	Poor
Division of export proceeds	Farmers, traders, Government	Government, farmers
Farmer morale	?	Low
Accumulated technology	No	Yes/no

revival. The marketing network – roads, sheds, scales – has disappeared and the prospects for rebuilding it are dim, given the demands on resources; the urban sector too has collapsed and cannot now be relied upon to supply the inputs and services necessary for agriculture. Population pressure has increased so that a much larger population has to be fed and accommodated on the farms,[26] while soil fertility has been declining. Export prices have fallen for the whole of the last decade and longer-term prospects remain bleak in the face of continuing substitution by synthetics. Meanwhile, the division of export proceeds is even more weighted against the farmers than it was at the height of marketing board taxation. In consequence, farmer morale is low; farmers have too long been denied a just price, in recent years often being paid 'chits' that are never redeemed. Their crops rot because of lack of processing capacity and they have again to head-load their produce as even their bicycles have broken down. There is more accumulated technology in the world for increasing agricultural productivity but very little has percolated down to Africa. In consequence, technology remains at an arrested stage.

Dare one suggest that there is at least one unlisted benign condition present now that was not present at the beginning of the century: that governments have learned the lesson about the limits to squeezing the agricultural sector? Recent increases in agricultural prices suggest that they may have done, but there are obvious limits to that itself, given the weak external markets and the widespread squeeze on the urban wage earners that has already happened. More and more the task remains how to increase productivity levels in agriculture. Its achievement will not only trigger all-round growth, but also facilitate agriculture's contributions to the economy, something that agriculture must eventually do as the dominant sector in African countries.

Notes

1 Further references on both sides of the argument may be found in Jamal (1988b, n. 13).

2 The degree of export expansion before 1914 was everywhere remarkable, particularly in West Africa. Thus, as W. Arthur Lewis (1970, p. 15) has shown, in West Africa export volume increased by 484 per cent between 1883 and 1913, in Central Africa by 398 per cent and in East Africa by 272 per cent. In India by comparison the growth was 135 per cent.

3 Some of these crops were not entirely new to the region. Cotton was grown in small quantities in Nigeria and Uganda long before its formal introduction by the British around the turn of the century (to fill the gap left by a fall in supplies from the United States). Groundnuts were introduced from the Americas around 1800 and used in local diets, as was palm oil. See further Hogendorn (1975).

4 Improved availability of health services did not initially contribute much to labour supply. Warfare and epidemics which accompanied the establishment of the new regimes actually reduced the population. Medical facilities were mostly concentrated in towns, and the rural population suffered the ravages of disease well into the recent period.

5 This does not mean that African countries remained untouched by trade until the start of the colonial era. As Hopkins (1973) has shown in his brilliant study, the West African countries had long-standing contacts with the outside world through the Sahara and the Atlantic long before the arrival of the colonial powers. In consequence they had many forms of local currency. McPhee (1926) also traces the export crop 'revolution' in West Africa to the start of the nineteenth century rather than the twentieth. Even landlocked Uganda was penetrated by traders by the 1870s, although recorded agricultural exports – excluding ivory – date from around the turn of the century. Contacts of the East African coast countries with the outside world go back to AD 100 – see Oliver and Gervase (1963, ch. IV); also Jones (1980) for an account of pre-colonial trade patterns.

6 In the eighteenth century, grey cloth was imported into Zanzibar from the

United States of America; hence its common name throughout East Africa, a name that survived subsequent changes in its source.

7 By the middle of the nineteenth century Kano in northern Nigeria 'had become in influence, if not in organisation, the Manchester of West Africa' (Hopkins, 1973, p. 48).

8 The vent-for-surplus model has by now been applied by at least a score of economists to the African situation. For a useful summary and sources see Eicher and Baker (1982); also Caves (1965).

9 As Myint (1958, p. 325) shows, this explains why despite similar climatic conditions Burma developed into a major exporter of rice whereas south India became a net importer. That the initial conditions for the introduction of exports differed between Africa and Asia (though not Latin America) is often missed by Asia-oriented observers whose implicit model assumes land scarcity. Hence Asian economists almost always conceive export expansion as occurring at the expense of food crops.

10 Practically everywhere in Africa the Africans were reluctant to take up wage employment and had to be coerced into it. See Newbury (1975) for a useful summary.

11 'To profitably produce Africa's key export crops – coffee, tea, cotton, sisal, oil palms and cocoa – fairly large farms or plantations were established' (Lofchie, 1987, p. 105).

12 Lofchie cites Freund and Shenton (1977) and Ingham (1981). Neither of these sources disputes that there was surplus capacity in African countries at the time of the introduction of exports, which of course is the central idea behind vent for surplus; rather both of them bring out neglected dimensions of the vent-for-surplus model. Freund and Shenton point to the disruptive effects of the slave trade and the disruption of existing patterns of trade, while Ingham shows the active part played by African farmers in the incorporation of export crops. She does show that by 1911 labour devoted to cocoa in Ghana amounted to only a small fraction of total agricultural labour, which runs counter to the vent-for-surplus model. However, cocoa production continued to expand thereafter, reaching by the early 1970s a volume ten times its level in 1911. Where the labour for this came from has to be explained.

13 Meier (1975, p. 447) in examining the process of cocoa expansion in the Gold Coast concurs about the impact on food production. He derives his inspiration from Johnston (1964).

14 See Jamal (1988b). Perhaps a majority of the studies on African crisis have concentrated on the food crisis. Mellor and Johnston (1984) in their important article on food hardly mention export crops in the discussion of Africa.

15 For the case of Uganda see Ehrlich (1958, 1965) and Jamal (1976b). Repeated efforts were made by powerful middlemen to secure legislation restricting competition, almost always on the grounds that competition would be harmful to the growers (competition would reduce the number of competitors and hence eventually create a monopsony!) as well as the country (the quality of exports would fall, to the detriment of Uganda's reputation in international markets).

16 Failure to do this is quite common and renders many analyses of parity prices

worthless. For example, the figures quoted in Bates (1981, Appendix B) for Nigerian cotton (e.g., 10–15 per cent of f.o.b. price returned to farmers) do not allow for converting producer prices (for seed cotton) to the export (lint) stage nor, one imagines, for processing and marketing margins. However, one set of figures Bates uses is from Jamal (1976b) where the correct conversion was made.

17 In 1953 farmers obtained 60 units of imports whereas the country obtained 100. Allowing for processing and retailing costs, this implies a tax rate of around 30 per cent. Between 1953 and 1980 the real price received by farmers fell by 90 per cent whereas the country's real price received improved by 22 per cent. Allowing for marketing costs this is equivalent to a rate of taxation of around 90 per cent.

18 A more precise calculation would require the country's terms of trade to be modified to reflect prices of exports and imports at producer point and not in Mombasa or New York as in figure 3.1, and allowance to be made for processing and marketing costs for both cotton lint and cotton cloth. When this is done for 1937 we find that, compared to the country's terms of trade at Mombasa of 208 yards of cloth for 100 lb of lint, the value at the farm-gate (without taxes, i.e., farm potential terms of trade) was 101. Because of the export tax, the c.i.f. duty on cloth and direct income taxes, farmers actually received only 57 yards of cloth for 100 lb of lint – a rate of taxation of 44 per cent. This is a restricted calculation. It attributes all of the direct tax to cotton income and assumes that all the cotton disposable income is spent on dutiable goods.

19 It is worth pointing out that the notion that African wage earners were privileged compared with other sections of the African population appeared as early as 1958 and emanated from no less an authority than W. Arthur Lewis, then economic adviser to the Ghanaian Government. He asked why the 'aristocracy' of Ghana should be favoured through a proposed minimum wage when there were other more deserving groups, such as farmers (quoted in Rimmer, 1970, p. 33).

20 Many studies have looked at the high cost of industrialisation in Africa, among them Jamal (1976c) for Uganda. Bhaduri's argument about surplus extraction and industrialisation fits exactly the African model (Bhaduri, chapter 6 in this volume). Saith (1990) also considers the question of surplus extraction and industrialisation.

21 Further, as Iliffe (1987) has pointed out, an urban wage earner could at any time expect to have to put up his kith and kin from the rural areas. 'Family wage' has a wide meaning in Africa.

22 The migratory pattern of wage employment was also exploitative, as it supplied labour for mines, plantations, factories, shops and urban homes at a cheap rate. See Newbury (1975) and Elkan (1961). However Elliot Berg, writing for an International Institute for Labour Studies conference in 1966, argued strongly against the family wage, viewing the migratory system 'as the most efficient way to meet money needs in the village' (Berg, 1966, p. 147). He also argued that the labour stabilisation policy was costly, requiring large social overhead investments in housing and other facilities.

23 The squeeze is continuing even though urban wages have collapsed and African

countries are actually 'de-industrialising'. Unfortunately, surplus extraction now takes the form of blatant extortion.

24 The roles of agriculture in development specified by Johnston and Mellor (1961) were to: (1) increase the supply of food for domestic consumption; (2) release labour for industrial employment; (3) enlarge the size of the market for industrial output; (4) increase the supply of domestic savings; and (5) earn foreign exchange.

25 It may be objected that 'idle labour' has already been shed to the urban sector through migration, but there is no evidence of migration *increasing* in the last decade or changing its character from mainly youth to farmers. Food imports do not signify a lack of surplus capacity either. As pointed out elsewhere (Jamal, 1988a), changing urban diets means that food imports cannot automatically be equated to an inability to feed the population.

26 It should be noted that sub-Saharan Africa's population growth rate was 3.1 per cent per annum for the period 1980–87, 'the highest seen anywhere, at any time in history' as the World Bank's latest report on Africa points out (World Bank, 1989, pp. 25, 39).

References

Baldwin, R.E. *et al.* (eds.), 1965. *Trade, Growth and the Balance of Payments: Essays in Honor of Gottfried Haberler*, Chicago: Rand McNally.

Bates, R.H., 1981. *Markets and States in Tropical Africa*, Berkeley, California: University of California Press.

Bates, R.H. and M.F. Lofchie (eds.), 1980. *Agricultural Development in Africa: Issues of Public Policy*, New York: Praeger.

Bauer, P.T., 1954. *West African Trade: A Study of Competition, Oligopoly and Monopoly in a Changing Economy*, Cambridge: Cambridge University Press.

1975. 'British colonial Africa: Economic retrospect and aftermath', in Duignan and Gann (eds.) (1975).

Bequele, A., 1980. 'Poverty, inequality and stagnation: The Ghanaian experience', World Employment Programme, *Research Working Paper*, WEP 10–6/WP33, Geneva: ILO.

Berg, E.J., 1966. 'Major issues of wage policy in Africa', in Ross (ed.) (1966).

Brett, E.A., 1973. *Colonialism and Underdevelopment in East Africa: The Politics of Economic Change, 1919–1939*, London: Heinemann.

Caves, R.E., 1965. '"Vent for surplus" models of trade and growth', in Baldwin *et al.* (eds.) (1965).

Chenery, H. and T.N. Srinivasan (eds.), 1988. *Handbook of Development Economics*, vol. I, Amsterdam: Elsevier Science Publishers BV.

Duignan, P. and L.G. Gann (eds.), 1975. *Colonialism in Africa, 1870–1960*, vol. IV of P. Duignan and L.G. Gann (eds.),*The Economics of Colonialism*, Cambridge: Cambridge University Press.

Ehrlich, C., 1958. 'The marketing of cotton in Uganda, 1900–1950'. Ph.D. dissertation, University of London.

1965. 'The Uganda economy, 1903–1945', in Harlow and Chilver (eds.) (1965).
Eicher, C.K. and D.C. Baker, 1982. *Research on Agricultural Development in Sub-Saharan Africa: A Critical Survey, MCU International Development Paper,* no. 1. East Lansing: Michigan State University, Department of Agricultural Economics.
Elkan, W., 1961. *Migrants and Proletarians: Urban Labour in the Economic Development of Uganda,* London: Oxford University Press.
Elkan, W. and R. van Zwanenberg, 1975. 'How people came to live in towns', in Duignan and Gann (eds.) (1975).
Freund, W.M. and R.W. Shenton, 1977. '"Vent for surplus" theory and the economic history of West Africa', *Savanna,* vol. 6, no. 2, December, pp. 191–95.
Harlow, V. and E.M. Chilver (eds.), 1965. *History of East Africa,* vol. II, Oxford: Clarendon Press.
Helleiner, G.K., 1966. *Peasant Agriculture, Government, and Economic Growth in Nigeria,* Homewood, Ill.: Richard B. Irwin.
Herskovits, M.J. and M. Harwitz (eds.), 1964. *Economic Transition in Africa,* Evanston, Ill.: Northwestern University Press.
Hogendorn, J.S., 1975. 'Economic initiative and African cash farming: Pre-colonial origins and early colonial developments', in Duignan and Gann (eds.) (1975).
Hollist, W.L. and F.L. Tullis (eds.), 1987. *Pursuing Food Security: Strategies and Obstacles in Africa, Asia, Latin America, and the Middle East,* Boulder, Col. and London: Lynne Rienner Publishers.
Hopkins, A.G., 1973. *An Economic History of West Africa,* London: Longman.
Hymer, S.H., 1971. 'The political economy of the Gold Coast and Ghana', in Ranis (ed.) (1971).
Iliffe, J., 1987. *African Poor: A History,* Cambridge: Cambridge University Press.
ILO (International Labour Office), 1964. 'Methods and principles of wage regulation', Report for the Second African Regional Conference, Geneva: ILO.
ILO/JASPA, 1986. *The Challenge of Employment and Basic Needs in Africa,* Nairobi: Oxford University Press.
IMF, 1988. *International Financial Statistics Yearbook,* Washington, DC: IMF.
Ingham, B., 1981. *Tropical Exports and Economic Development: New Perspectives on Producer Response in Three Low-Income Countries,* New York: St Martin's Press.
Jamal, V., 1976a. 'Asians in Uganda, 1880–1972: Inequality and expulsion', *Economic History Review,* vol. 29, no. 4.
  1976b. 'The role of cotton and coffee in Uganda's economic development', Ph.D. dissertation, Stanford University.
  1976c. 'Effective protection in Uganda', *Eastern Africa Economic Review,* vol. 8, no. 2, December.
  1978. 'Taxation and inequality in Uganda, 1900–1964', *Journal of Economic History,* vol. 38, no. 2, pp. 418–38.
  1985. 'Structural adjustment and food security in Uganda', World Employment Programme, *Research Working Paper,* WEP 10–6/WP73, Geneva: ILO.
  1986. 'Taxing the peasants in Sierra Leone', in ILO/JASPA (1986).

1988a. 'Coping under crisis in Uganda', *International Labour Review*, vol. 127, no. 6, pp. 679–701.

1988b. 'Getting the crisis right: Missing perspectives on Africa', *International Labour Review*, vol. 127, no. 6, pp. 655–78.

1989. 'The demise of the labor aristocracy in Africa: Structural adjustment in Tanzania', in Weeks (ed.) (1989).

Jamal, V. and J. Weeks, 1987. 'Rural–urban income trends in sub-Saharan Africa', World Employment Programme, *Research Working Paper*, WEP 2–43/WP18, Geneva: ILO.

1988. 'The vanishing rural–urban gap in sub-Saharan Africa', *International Labour Review*, vol. 127, no. 3, pp. 271–92.

Forthcoming. *Africa Misunderstood or Whatever Happened to the Rural–Urban Gap*, London: Macmillan.

Johnston, B.F., 1964. 'Changes in agricultural productivity', in Herskovits and Harwitz (eds.) (1964).

1980. 'Agricultural production potential and small-farmer strategies in Sub-Saharan Africa', in Bates and Lofchie (eds.) (1980).

Johnston, B.F. and J.W. Mellor, 1961. 'The role of agriculture in economic development', *American Economic Review*, vol. 51, no. 4, September, pp. 566–93.

Jones, W.O., 1968. 'Labour and leisure in traditional African societies', *Items*, vol. 22, no. 1, March, London: Social Science Research Council.

1980. 'Agricultural trade within tropical Africa: Historical background', in Bates and Lofchie (eds.) (1980).

Lewis, W.A., 1970. 'The export stimulus', in W.A. Lewis (ed.): *Tropical Development, 1880–1913*, Evanston, Ill.: Northwestern University Press.

Leys, R., 1973. *Dualism and Rural Development in East Africa*, Copenhagen: Institute for Development Research.

Lipton, M., 1977. *Why Poor People Stay Poor: Urban Bias in World Development*, Cambridge, Mass.: Harvard University Press.

Lofchie, M.F., 1987. 'The external determinants of Africa's agrarian crisis', in Hollist and Tullis (eds.) (1987).

McPhee, A., 1926. *The Economic Revolution in British West Africa*, London: Routledge.

Meier, G.M., 1975. 'External trade and international development', in Duignan and Gann (eds.) (1975).

Mellor, J.W. and B.F. Johnston, 1984. 'The world food equation: Interrelations among development, employment and food consumption', *Journal of Economic Literature*, vol. 22, no. 2, June, pp. 531–74.

Myint, H., 1958. 'The "classical theory" of international trade and the under-developed countries', *Economic Journal*, vol. 68, no. 270, June, pp. 317–37.

Newbury, J., 1975. 'Historical aspects of manpower and migration in Africa South of the Sahara', in Duignan and Gann (eds.) (1975).

Oliver, R. and M. Gervase, 1963. *History of East Africa*, vol. I, Oxford: Clarendon Press.

Ranis, G. (ed.), 1971. *Government and Economic Development*, New Haven: Yale University Press.

Rimmer, D., 1970. 'Wage policies in West Africa', Birmingham: University of Birmingham, Faculty of Commerce and Social Science, *Occasional Paper*, no. 12.

Ross, A.M. (ed.), 1966. *Industrial Relations and Economic Development*, London: Macmillan.

Saith, A., 1990. 'Development strategies and the rural poor', in *Journal of Peasant Studies*, vol. 17, no. 2, January, pp. 171–244.

Smith, A.D. (ed.), 1969. *Wage Policy Issues in Economic Development*, London: Macmillan.

Stavenhagen, R., 1975. *Social Classes in Agrarian Societies*, New York: Anchor Press/Doubleday.

Tabatabai, H., 1988. 'Agricultural decline and access to food in Ghana', *International Labour Review*, vol. 127, no. 6, pp. 703–34.

Timmer, C.P., 1988. 'The agricultural transformation', in Chenery and Srinivasan (eds.) (1988).

UNCTAD (United Nations Conference on Trade and Development), 1989. *Handbook of International Trade and Development Statistics 1988*, New York: United Nations.

Weeks, J. (ed.), 1989. *Debt Disaster? Governments, Banks and Multilaterals Face the Crisis*, Cambridge, Mass.: Ballinger.

World Bank, 1981. *Accelerated Development in Sub-Saharan Africa: An Agenda for Action*, Washington, DC: World Bank.

1989. *Sub-Saharan Africa: From Crisis to Sustainable Growth: A Long-Term Perspective Study*, Washington, DC: World Bank.

Wrigley, C.C., 1965. 'Kenya: the patterns of economic life, 1902–1945', in Harlow and Chilver (eds.) (1965).

4 Global changes, agriculture and economic growth in the 1980s: a study of four Asian countries

AJIT K. GHOSE

Introduction

The global economic changes in the 1980s – the depression of world trade and the persistent debt problem – which had disastrous consequences for the developing economies of Africa and Latin America, had surprisingly little impact on the growth performance of the Asian developing economies. Of course, there was the case of the Philippines whose economic difficulties in the 1980s were comparable to those of the highly indebted Latin American countries. But this was the unique exception to the rule. The growth performance of the Asian developing economies in the 1980s was in general as good as, and in some cases even better than, that in the 1970s (table 4.1).

The fact has been widely noted; several – not entirely satisfactory – explanations have also been advanced.[1] First, it has been observed that growth rates in several Asian countries had been high in the 1970s so that, despite significant deceleration in the 1980s, they still remained respectable. But cases of significant deceleration were in fact very few. It can also be pointed out that several Latin American economies, which stagnated in the 1980s, had also experienced rapid growth in the 1970s. Second, it has been argued that quite a few Asian economies were (and still are) relatively insulated from the world economy so that they were not much affected by the global economic changes of the 1980s. But the fact that a country has a low export–GDP ratio does not imply that exports are not of vital importance for sustaining growth. Third, there is a view that the Asian countries adjusted efficiently to global changes.[2] 'Efficient adjustment', unfortunately, is a vague term, but if it means the type of adjustment promoted by the Bretton Woods institutions, then the view cannot be substantiated. Fourth, it has been observed that very few Asian countries faced a debt crisis in the 1980s. This is correct, but leaves unclear how the absence of a debt crisis may have helped sustain or augment economic growth.

Table 4.1. *Annual growth rates^a of real GDP,
1970–79 and 1979–88* (%)

	1970–79	1979–88
Bangladesh	3.2	3.5
India	3.5	5.1
Indonesia^b	7.3	4.2
Korea, Republic of	9.2	8.4
Malaysia	6.6	5.2
Nepal	2.1	4.2
Pakistan	4.6	6.3
Philippines	4.6	0.7*
Sri Lanka	3.6	4.4
Thailand	6.8	5.6

Notes:
a Unless noted otherwise, all growth rates in this study
have been estimated by fitting a trend equation to
annual data.
b Refers to real GNP.
* Statistically not significant at 10 per cent.
Source: World Bank data files.

Moreover, the experience of the Asian developing economies differed
from that of the African and Latin American economies in other important
respects too. In the normal course of development, agriculture's share in
GDP, exports and employment are all expected to decline.[3] Such declines
were indeed universal in the developing world in the 1960s and the 1970s,
and they were regarded as signs of healthy development.[4] In the 1980s, the
global demand for agricultural products stagnated and their relative
international prices fell quite sharply. Logically, these changes should have
led to a sharpening of the long-term tendencies.

In reality, the long-term tendencies persisted only in the Asian economies. In a large number of African and Latin American countries,
agriculture's share in GDP and exports increased in the 1980s.[5] It appears
that growth reduced agriculture's role in the Asian economies while lack of
growth enhanced it in African and Latin American economies. Such
developments, it will be argued here, are not particularly surprising and
should in fact be expected. They are worth discussing only because in the
literature the developments in African and Latin American countries tend
to be viewed not as setbacks but as necessary adjustments. The standard
stabilisation and structural adjustment policies, which have been adopted

by many African and Latin American countries, are designed to increase agriculture's share in GDP and exports.[6] The underlying argument is that interventionist policies of the past caused a premature decline in the role of agriculture in most developing economies and that, therefore, there is a need to redress the balance.[7] This argument, however, is entirely *a priori* and ignores certain key realities.[8] Interventionist policies, after all, were as common in Asia as in Africa and Latin America, and if the signals from the global markets are to be heeded, agriculture's role in the economy should be reduced and not enhanced.

The long-term tendency which seems to have remained unchanged everywhere in the 1980s is the declining role of agriculture as a provider of employment. This fact, in the context of Asia, may in the first instance be taken to indicate a continuation of the normal process of development. But in the context of Africa and Latin America, it does not square well with theoretical expectations. If, in a large number of countries, agriculture's share in employment declined while its share in GDP and exports rose, it would seem to follow that agriculture's role in employment generation has become detached from its role in the growth process. The issue is important since it has implications for the employment consequences of economic growth. If movements in agriculture's share in employment are independent of the growth process, then it is not clear that the trends in Asia in the 1980s necessarily reflected the effects of growth.

Obviously, the developing countries' experiences in the 1980s have brought into focus quite a number of important issues. This chapter attempts to derive insights into some of these issues from a comparison of the experiences of four Asian countries (India, the Republic of Korea, the Philippines and Thailand). The countries chosen for study are quite heterogeneous in terms of economic structures, growth strategies and performance in the 1980s. The objective is not to provide a representative account of the developments in the region in the 1980s (such an account is difficult to provide in any case, given the heterogeneity of Asian countries) but rather to seek a framework for analysing the experiences of individual countries in the region.[9]

The basic hypotheses explored in the chapter are as follows. The binding constraint on the growth of manufacturing and, therefore, on the overall growth of the economy in developing countries is the foreign exchange constraint.[10] Since such countries are also typically dependent on agricultural exports, the severity of the foreign exchange constraint depends, to a significant extent, on the conditions of trade in agricultural products. Obviously, difficulties with agricultural exports adversely affect agricultural growth by discouraging the production of exportables. But, *ceteris paribus*, they also have the effect of tightening the foreign exchange constraint and, therefore, adversely affect the growth of manufacturing. This can in principle be pre-empted through increased external borrowing. But if there are factors (e.g., a debt crisis) which block a country's access to external credit, the only option is a cut in imports and the adverse impact on the growth of manufacturing can be very sharp. In such situations, a general economic stagnation may ensue and agriculture's share in GDP and exports may rise. Paradoxical though it may seem, these tendencies actually indicate a weakening of the role of agriculture in the economy, as they are necessarily associated with stagnation. In general, explanations for both the pace and pattern of economic growth in the 1980s should be sought in the movements of variables which affected the foreign exchange constraint.

In most developing countries, agriculture's capacity to absorb labour has almost reached its limit because the possibility of extending the land frontier is nearly exhausted. This means that while agricultural growth is relevant for improving employment conditions within agriculture itself, its effect on the migration of labour out of agriculture is increasingly marginal. For improvements in overall employment conditions to occur, therefore, the non-agricultural sector must grow at a high rate and such growth must be employment-intensive. The role of agriculture in promoting non-agricultural growth is more important than its role in direct employment promotion. Decline in the latter, at the present juncture, is a universal tendency which does not depend on the particularities of the growth process.

The chapter is organised as follows. The second section analyses the growth performance of the economies under study and its relation to the behaviour of agricultural exports. It is found that agricultural exports indeed suffered serious setbacks and that this adversely affected agricultural growth except in the case of the Republic of Korea (hereafter Korea) which was not dependent on agricultural exports. No systematic effect on the manufacturing sector can be discerned, however; the reasons are brought out in the third section which discusses the trends in import capacity and external debt. It is shown that the countries which were in a position to expand manufacturing exports or to benefit from increased transfer incomes from abroad or to resort to external borrowing were able to sustain the growth of manufacturing. The fourth section discusses some aspects of macroeconomic policy in the 1980s. It makes the point that none of the countries really attempted to sustain or boost agricultural exports. Except in the Philippines, policies were geared to sustaining manufacturing growth; in other words, they were not in line with the standard stabilisation and structural adjustment package. The discussion also makes explicit the choices made by countries faced with a trade-off between economic growth and growth of debt burdens. The fifth section analyses the employment

Table 4.2. *Indicators of agriculture's role in the economy, 1978–80* (%)

	Agricultural share in			Share of agricultural exports in agricultural GDP[a]	Share of exports in GDP
	GDP	Exports	Employment[a]		
India	37.9	28.5	69.9	4.0	5.4
Korea, Republic of	19.1	3.8	37.6	2.1	26.1
Philippines	26.1	37.7	52.1	21.1	15.3
Thailand	27.6	54.8	71.1	37.8	18.7

Note:
[a] Refers to 1979.
Sources: World Bank data files and Ghose (1990), Appendix table IX.

effects of growth. There are two findings here. First, the trend in agriculture's share in employment shows no systematic relation to overall growth performance. Second, the growth of manufacturing in the 1980s generated little employment so that employment conditions tended to worsen even in high-growth economies. The sixth section presents a few concluding observations.

As a preliminary, it is useful to note a few structural features of the economies under scrutiny (table 4.2). At the beginning of the 1980s, the Korean economy could almost be characterised as industrialised; agriculture's share in GDP and employment was low and agricultural exports were of little significance to the economy. In the other three economies, agriculture clearly was an important sector. The only qualifying remark which needs to be made is that, for India, agricultural exports accounted for a large proportion of export earnings but only for a very small proportion of agricultural output. That is, difficulties with agricultural exports could be expected to have a large effect on export earnings but only a very small effect on agricultural growth. The degree of openness varied widely across the economies: the Korean economy was very open while the Indian economy was quasi-closed, with the Philippines and Thailand falling somewhere in between.

Economic growth and agriculture in the 1980s

The growth performance of the four countries in the last two decades is summarised in table 4.3. For purposes of comparison, the two periods are defined as 1970–79 and 1979–88, the justification being that the second 'oil

Table 4.3. *Growth of GDP,ᵃ exports and imports,ᵇ 1970–88* (average annual percentage rate)

	Annual rate of growth		
	GDP	Exports/GDP	Merchandise imports
India			
1970–79	3.5	2.8	3.1
1979–88	5.1	−1.7	5.0
Korea, Republic of			
1970–79	9.2	13.6	11.7
1979–88	8.4	5.0	8.5
Philippines			
1970–79	5.9	−0.8	3.1
1979–88	0.7*	0.4*	−1.6*
Thailand			
1970–79	6.8	2.9	4.3
1979–88	5.6	5.2	6.1

Notes:
ᵃ GDP is at factor cost and measured in national currency and in 1980 prices.
ᵇ Exports and imports are measured in constant 1980 dollar prices.
* Statistically not significant at 10 per cent.
Source: World Bank data files.

shock' which triggered the global changes in the 1980s occurred in 1979. The striking feature is the economic stagnation of the Philippines in the 1980s. This contrasts not only with its own performance in the earlier period but also with that of the other three countries. In the 1980s, the rate of growth accelerated in India and decelerated in Korea and Thailand but was above 5 per cent in all three cases.

It is quite clear that the growth performance in the 1980s did not relate to the degree of openness in any systematic manner. Thailand and the Philippines had equally open economies (see table 4.2), yet their growth performances were radically different. Korea's economy was very open while India's was quasi-closed, but both achieved rapid growth. Moreover, the degree of openness increased in the case of Thailand and declined in the case of India; yet the rate of growth decelerated in Thailand and accelerated in India (see table 4.3).

The rate of growth of imports, on the other hand, clearly had a systematic influence on economic growth. The positive relation between the two variables is apparent from comparison across countries and over the two periods in each country. Only in Thailand did growth decelerate in the 1980s in spite of an acceleration in the growth of imports. But this odd result arises from the fact that Thailand's imports grew phenomenally (by more than 40 per cent) in 1988. The annual rate of growth of imports during 1979–87 was 3.6 per cent, below the rate in 1970–79.

These facts already suggest that economic growth in the countries concerned was foreign exchange-constrained. The point can be developed a little further. The imports of developing countries consist largely of intermediate and capital goods destined for use in the manufacturing sector – i.e., manufacturing production is import-intensive. Agricultural production, on the other hand, typically involves little use of imported inputs. For these reasons, the foreign exchange constraint is more relevant for manufacturing growth than for agricultural growth.

Another point to note is that, typically, the agricultural exports of developing countries are domestically non-competitive (i.e., domestic demand is insignificant) while manufacturing exports are domestically competitive in the sense that declining exports could conceivably be neutralised by growing domestic demand. Thus the performance of agricultural exports directly affects agricultural growth. But the performance of manufacturing exports has no direct bearing on manufacturing growth. Both manufacturing and agricultural exports affect manufacturing growth indirectly, through their effects on the foreign exchange constraint.

It is well-known that depression of demand for and prices of agricultural commodities was a major feature of the changes in the global economy in the 1980s.[11] For individual countries, this translated into a deceleration or decline in the growth of both real agricultural exports and earnings from them. This adversely affected agricultural growth on the one hand and import capacity on the other.

These points are brought out by the data in table 4.4. Before commenting on these data, two caveats need to be added. First, it should be recalled that agricultural exports are of little significance to Korea's economy. Thus little can be read into the data for Korea, which are presented here for the sake of completeness; the behaviour of its agricultural exports could have only a marginal impact on agricultural production (whose behaviour must therefore be explained by factors internal to the economy) and import capacity. Second, 1979 was a particularly bad crop-year in India. This imparts a downward bias in the rate of agricultural growth for 1970–79 and an upward bias for 1979–88. A less biased picture emerges if the two periods are taken as 1970–78 and 1980–88.

The deceleration in the growth of real agricultural exports (column (D)) and of export earnings (column (E)) is quite evident from the data. In the

Table 4.4. *Growth process in agriculture, 1970–88*

	Annual rate of growth (%)					
	(A)	(B)	(C)	(D)	(E)	(F)
India						
1970–79	1.9 (2.6)^a	2.3 (2.8)^a	−1.6	4.0	14.1	−2.7
1979–88	2.8 (2.2)^b	3.1 (2.7)^b	−2.3	−0.1*	0.0*	−6.1
Korea, Republic of						
1970–79	4.0	4.0	−5.2	12.9	22.5	−10.2
1979–88	3.0	0.8*	−5.4	3.1	4.2	−9.6
Philippines						
1970–79	4.8	5.2	−1.1	4.9	14.7	−1.5
1979–88	2.0	2.5	1.3	−3.4	−6.0	−7.7
Thailand						
1970–79	4.5	2.1	−2.3	9.1	20.6	−2.1
1979–88	3.6	3.4	−2.0	5.8	3.1	−6.3

Notes:
(A) Agricultural GDP, measured in national currency and in 1980 prices;
(B) foodgrains output: includes cereals and pulses, measured in million metric
tons; (C) agriculture's share in GDP (constant 1980 prices); (D) value of
agricultural exports in constant 1980 dollar prices; (E) value of agricultural
exports in current dollars; (F) agriculture's share in export earnings in current
dollars.
^{a} Figure in parentheses refers to 1970–78.
^{b} Figure in parentheses refers to 1980–88.
* Statistically not significant at 10 per cent.
Sources: World Bank data files; FAO data files.

1980s, both variables showed zero growth in India and large declines in the
Philippines. The consequences for agricultural production were straightforward; the growth of non-foodgrains output decelerated sharply in both
countries. Thailand experienced a less dramatic deceleration in the growth
of agricultural exports. This was largely because it was able to expand
exports of rice, in which it controlled a large share of the global market,
though at the expense of depressing prices; exports of most items other than
rice declined in volume terms.[12] These changes are clearly reflected in the
pace and pattern of output growth in agriculture.

A general consequence of these developments was that agriculture's
share in export earnings (column (F)) declined at a faster rate in the 1980s.
The same tendency, however, is not universally observed for agriculture's

share in GDP (column (C)); this is explained by two particular features of agricultural production. First, as already argued, agricultural growth is not usually foreign exchange-constrained while overall growth is. A foreign exchange crisis, therefore, is apt to increase agriculture's share in GDP. Second, foodgrains, which are not usually exported, account for the bulk of agricultural output. The growth of foodgrains output is influenced (in most cases) not by the performance of agricultural exports but by the overall growth performance of the economy and the growth of population.[13]

The clearest illustration of these points is provided by the Philippines. In the 1980s, real agricultural exports (column (D)) declined at an annual rate of 3.4 per cent and real imports also declined, indicating an increasingly severe foreign exchange constraint. Yet agricultural growth, at 2 per cent per annum, was respectable largely because the growth of food production kept pace with that of the population. The overall growth of the economy, however, was negligible and, as a consequence, agriculture's share in GDP rose.

The foreign exchange constraint, as argued above, affects GDP growth primarily through its effect on manufacturing growth. This is clearly demonstrated by the data in table 4.5. Both cross-sectionally and intertemporally, the growth of manufacturing output was clearly linked to the growth of imports. However, there was no clear relation between the growth of manufacturing output and the performance of manufacturing exports. In the 1980s, the growth of manufacturing exports decelerated in the case of India and accelerated in the case of Thailand, yet the growth of manufacturing output accelerated in India and decelerated in Thailand. In the Philippines, the growth of manufacturing exports was fairly respectable in the 1980s but the growth of output was virtually zero.

The essential point is that the rate of manufacturing growth had little to do with the degree of export-orientation of this growth and much to do with the growth of imports. For a satisfactory explanation of the differential growth performance of the countries in the 1980s, it is necessary to look into the determinants of import growth.

The growth of import capacity

The setback to agricultural exports, by itself, need not have affected the growth of imports of the countries concerned. The growth of imports depended on several other factors: the performance of manufacturing exports, net income from factor and non-factor services, net transfers from abroad on private and public accounts, movements in external terms of trade and the availability of external credit. Indeed, these factors were of almost exclusive importance for Korea.

100   Ajit Ghose

Table 4.5. *Growth process in manufacturing, 1970–88*

	Annual rate of growth (%)		
	Manufacturing output	Value of manufacturing exports in constant 1980 dollar prices	Export–output ratio in manufacturing
India			
1970–79	4.7	9.2	4.5
1979–88	7.4	2.8	−4.6
Korea, Republic of			
1970–79	16.7	24.4	7.7
1979–88	11.2	14.3	3.1
Philippines			
1970–79	6.9	25.5	18.6
1979–88	0.1*	4.9	4.8
Thailand			
1970–79	10.4	16.6	6.2
1979–88	6.2	17.5	11.3

Note:
* Statistically not significant at 10 per cent.
Source: World Bank data files.

The data presented in table 4.6 bring out a number of interesting, and occasionally surprising, facts. First, manufacturing exports (column (A)) also suffered setbacks in the 1980s in the sense that the growth of earnings decelerated quite sharply in all cases. The deceleration, however, was less sharp than for agricultural exports.

Second, despite the setbacks to both agricultural and manufacturing exports, the 'import capacity of exports' (column (D)) (earnings from merchandise exports deflated by the price index for merchandise imports) actually grew at a faster rate in the 1980s in all the economies except Korea. The reason is that import prices were rising rapidly in the 1970s but remained virtually constant in the 1980s. The external terms of trade (column (C)), which had shown rapid deterioration in the 1970s, deteriorated further only for Thailand in the 1980s; they improved significantly for India.

Third, the pattern of growth of the overall capacity for merchandise imports (column (F)) diverged markedly from that of the 'import capacity

Table 4.6. *Growth of export earnings and import capacity, 1970–88*

	Annual rate of growth (%)					
	(A)	(B)	(C)	(D)	(E)	(F)
India						
1970–79	18.6	16.8	−4.8	1.8	3.1	6.0
1979–88	7.5	6.1	1.5	5.1	5.0	0.6*
Korea, Republic of						
1970–79	33.9	32.7	−3.9	18.2	11.7	15.9
1979–88	14.3	13.8	0.3*	13.5	8.5	14.2
Philippines						
1970–79	35.3	16.2	−5.4	−0.6	3.1	−0.8
1979–88	8.0	1.7*	0.2*	1.4*	−1.6*	3.1
Thailand						
1970–79	30.4	22.7	−2.8	7.2	4.3	2.6
1979–88	17.5	9.4	−2.3*	8.6	6.1	9.1

Notes:
(A) Value of manufacturing exports in current dollars; (B) total export earnings in current dollars; (C) external terms of trade; (D) import capacity of exports; (E) value of imports in constant 1980 dollars; (F) overall import capacity. The import capacity of exports is defined as the earnings from merchandise exports deflated by the import price index. The overall import capacity is defined as the sum of the earnings from merchandise exports, net factor and non-factor incomes and net transfers from abroad on both private and public accounts, deflated by the import price index.
* Statistically not significant at 10 per cent.
Source: World Bank data files.

of exports'. The main reason was that the behaviour of net current transfers from abroad (both on private and public accounts) was far from uniform across the countries. Thus the growth of overall capacity for merchandise imports decelerated very sharply in the case of India, decelerated slightly in the case of Korea and accelerated in the cases of the Philippines and Thailand. The behaviour of net current transfers from abroad, therefore, was such as to wipe out the benefits for India of more favourable terms of trade but elsewhere to counteract the effects of the deceleration in growth of export earnings.

The discrepancies between the growth of overall import capacity and that of actual merchandise imports indicate the trends in current account

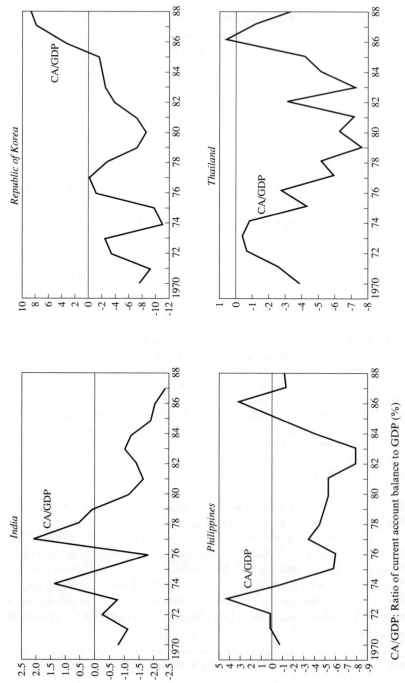

CA/GDP: Ratio of current account balance to GDP (%)

Figure 4.1 The current account balance.

Table 4.7. *Debt–GNP and debt service ratios, 1980–88 (%)*

	India		Republic of Korea		Philippines		Thailand	
	(A)	(B)	(A)	(B)	(A)	(B)	(A)	(B)
1980	9.2	11.9	19.7	48.7	26.5	49.5	18.7	25.9
1981	10.4	12.6	21.7	49.3	33.5	54.3	20.2	31.5
1982	13.9	14.9	22.4	52.3	42.4	62.5	20.5	34.8
1983	16.7	16.0	21.2	50.8	36.3	71.5	23.9	35.3
1984	18.2	17.6	21.3	48.4	33.3	77.2	25.6	36.8
1985	22.4	19.2	27.3	52.5	32.5	83.5	31.9	47.8
1986	31.6	21.1	26.7	45.5	34.4	94.1	30.1	45.5
1987	29.0	21.7	32.3	31.0	38.5	87.8	21.0	44.0
1988	21.4	28.9	21.1	14.8	74.8	31.5	37.2	18.8

Notes:
(A) Debt–GNP ratio; (B) debt service ratio. Debt–GNP ratio is the ratio of the total stock of debt to GNP expressed as a percentage. Debt service payments include repayments of principal, interest payments on long-term debt and IMF credit, and interest payments on short-term debt. Debt service ratio is the ratio of debt service payments to the value of exports of goods and services expressed in percentages.
Source: World Bank: *World Debt Tables, 1989–90 and 1990–91* (Washington, DC: December 1989 and December 1990).

balances which can also be directly observed from figure 4.1. It is clear that India could sustain a high rate of growth in the 1980s only at the cost of increasing its external debt. Korea and Thailand, on the other hand, chose to improve the current account balance (i.e., to reduce the burden of external debt) and hence restrained the rate of economic growth below the feasible limit.

The Philippines too improved its current account balance rather rapidly in the 1980s, but only through import compression which of course led to stagnation of the manufacturing sector. This can hardly be seen as the result of deliberate policy. The Philippines' overall import capacity was declining in the 1970s and a high rate of growth was sustained by high current account deficits. As a consequence, it was the only country confronted with a debt problem at the beginning of the 1980s (as we shall see shortly) which made improvement in the current account balance an overwhelming priority: its merchandise imports actually declined in the 1980s even though overall import capacity was growing.

The data in table 4.7 confirm the above findings. The Philippines, alone among the countries, suffered a 'debt shock' in the early 1980s and remained a heavily indebted country throughout the 1980s. India steadily increased its debt burden. Korea and Thailand at first allowed their debt burdens to rise and then reduced them substantially.

The major conclusions to emerge are as follows. Even though exports, both agricultural and manufacturing, suffered setbacks in the 1980s, the favourable movements in external terms of trade more than compensated. The 'import capacity of exports' grew at a faster rate in the 1980s than in the 1970s. Unfortunately, net transfers from abroad declined in the case of India and the Philippines was confronted with a debt problem. India sustained a high rate of growth of imports (and, therefore, a high rate of economic growth) by increasing its external debt. This option was not available to the Philippines; its economic stagnation was thus unavoidable. Korea and Thailand faced no real adjustment problems. They could in fact have increased their rates of economic growth in the 1980s if they had chosen to do so. However, they chose, prudently, to restrain growth so as to be able to reduce debt burdens.

Macroeconomic policies

It has been indicated above that, except in the Philippines, meaningful policy options were available: India could have restrained economic growth (in which case it would not be facing a debt problem today) and Korea and Thailand could have achieved higher growth (in which case they would have a somewhat higher debt burden today). This section explores the point further. It also demonstrates that none of the countries seriously attempted to boost agricultural exports or agriculture's role in the economy; macro-economic policies remained oriented to promoting industrialisation-led growth.

There are four key macroeconomic variables controlled by the government: the budget deficit, bank credit, the rate of interest and the exchange rate. Of these, the really important variables are the budget deficit and the exchange rate. The budget deficit usually has a determining influence on the expansion of bank credit and the rate of interest. If government borrowing is at a high level, a high rate of interest would be undesirable and restraint on the expansion of bank credit would have a crowding-out effect on private investment.

In theory, the level of the budget deficit, through its effect on the expansion of money incomes in the economy, affects simultaneously the rate of inflation, the rate of economic growth and the current account deficit.[14] The growth of expenditure on food, associated with a rise in the budget deficit, leads to a rise in food prices which, through the effect on money wages, in turn leads to a rise in the prices of manufactures which tend to be cost-determined. In general, however, food prices in these circumstances rise faster than the prices of manufactures so that the terms of trade shift in favour of agriculture. But the growth of money incomes also leads to a rise in the real demand for manufactures and thus stimulates manufacturing production and investment. This has the effect of increasing imports of intermediate and capital goods so that the current account balance tends to worsen.

Exchange-rate devaluation also affects the rate of inflation, the rate of economic growth and the current account balance simultaneously.[15] It increases the domestic prices of export crops (directly) and manufactures (by raising the domestic prices of imported intermediate and capital goods). Thus the rate of inflation increases and relative food prices decline (except where much of the food is internationally traded). The increase in the prices of manufactures reduces real demand for them in the domestic market and thereby discourages growth and investment in the manufacturing sector. This in turn has the effect of reducing the demand for imports and hence the current account balance improves.

Thus while growth of the budget deficit and devaluation are both inflationary, they have contradictory effects on aggregate domestic demand, relative food prices and the current account balance. If a substantial growth of the budget deficit is combined with a substantial devaluation, the main outcome is inflation. The policy combination which deflates the economy while encouraging agricultural exports is a reduction of the budget deficit together with a substantial devaluation; these are the policies which form the core of the standard stabilisation and structural adjustment packages. No combination of these policies, however, can effectively encourage export of manufactures. Reduction of the budget deficit is helpful only when domestic consumption and exports are mutually exclusive, i.e., when the manufacturing sector is producing at full capacity and the products are price-competitive in international markets; reduction in domestic demand may then release goods for export. These conditions are typically not met in developing countries. Devaluation increases the unit costs of production (and hence prices) of manufactures in domestic currency, by increasing the domestic currency prices of imported interme-diate goods; thus it need not increase price-competitiveness in international markets. Promotion of manufacturing exports calls for particular measures (e.g., export subsidies, tariff benefits) to reduce costs of production in manufacturing.

These observations help interpret the apparent policy shifts which occurred in the 1980s (figure 4.2 and tables 4.8 and 4.9). In India and the Philippines, the budget deficit was generally higher in the 1980s than in the

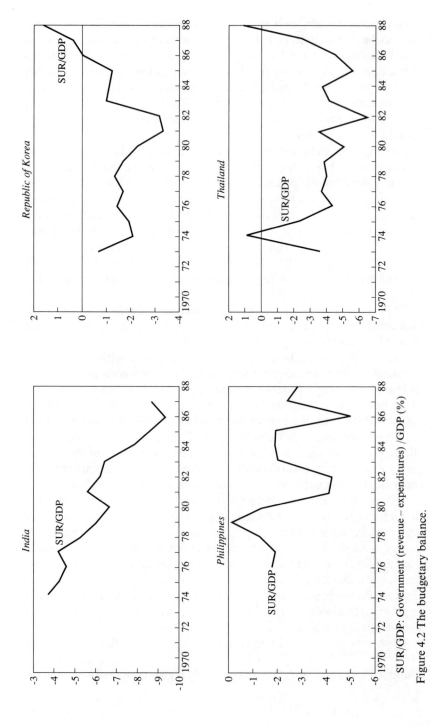

SUR/GDP: Government (revenue – expenditures) /GDP (%)

Figure 4.2 The budgetary balance.

Table 4.8. *Selected macroeconomic policy variables, 1970–88*

	Rate of change (%)		
	Domestic bank credit	Real interest rate	Nominal exchange rate
India			
1970–79	15.7	−1.2	1.5
1979–88	17.4	−6.0	7.0
Korea, Republic of			
1970–79	28.6	−18.5	4.9
1979–88	18.4	−18.3	6.4
Philippines			
1970–79	21.7	−18.1	2.3
1979–88	6.7	−10.1	14.8
Thailand			
1970–79	21.3	9.0	−2.7
1979–88	15.2	−10.4	3.0

Sources: IMF: *International Financial Statistics* (1989); World Bank data files.

Table 4.9. *Inflation, 1970–88*

	Annual rate of change of deflator (%) for		
	GDP	Agricultural GDP	Manufacturing GDP
India			
1970–79	7.8	6.1	8.6
1979–88	8.2	8.6	7.2
Korea, Republic of			
1970–79	18.3	20.3	14.8
1979–88	6.5	5.7	5.2
Philippines			
1970–79	12.3	12.6	12.2
1979–88	14.4	13.1	15.1
Thailand			
1970–79	8.8	10.7	7.7
1979–88	3.7	1.2*	4.9

Note:
* Statistically not significant at 10 per cent.
Source: World Bank data files.

1970s; it was, moreover, steadily increasing in India. In Korea and Thailand, by contrast, the budget deficit was lower and was on a declining trend in the 1980s; indeed, both countries ran a budget surplus towards the end of the period. Domestic bank credit expanded at a faster rate in the 1980s only in India. The surprise is that in the Philippines, where the budget deficit was high in the 1980s, the expansion of bank credit was restrained quite sharply. This combination of policies could have had a crowding-out effect on private investment, though the effect was probably superfluous since the foreign exchange constraint would have reduced private investment from the supply side in any case. The real rate of interest declined in all the countries so that this variable is of no significance in explaining differences in economic performance. Exchange-rate devaluation clearly was a generally adopted policy in the 1980s, but substantial devaluation occurred only in the Philippines.

When the policy changes are viewed together, the conclusions seem to be as follows. In India, policy was clearly more expansionary in the 1980s than in the 1970s. The dominant feature of macroeconomic management in the latter period was the growing budget deficit. This stimulated growth of the manufacturing sector but tended to create food imbalances. The former encouraged demand for imports at a time when import capacity was not growing and the latter led to inflationary pressure and rising relative prices of foodgrains.

In Korea and Thailand, policy was significantly less expansionary in the 1980s than in the 1970s. In these countries, too, the dominant effects resulted from the trend in the government budget deficit; the exchange-rate devaluations were quite mild. The budget deficit declined in the latter period and the rate of growth of bank credit correspondingly slowed. Consequently, the growth of manufacturing output, the current account deficit and the rate of inflation were all lower.

The Philippines, of course, had to deal with much sharper external shocks than any of the other three countries. But its macroeconomic policies in the 1980s also lacked a clear focus. Large budget deficits were combined with a substantial devaluation. The only result, predictably, was inflation with unchanging relative prices. It must be said that, given the nature of the foreign exchange constraint, it is difficult to see how the country could have avoided economic stagnation. But small budget deficits and a mild devaluation would have spared the economy inflationary pressures.

It is clear that in none of the countries was a reduction in budget deficits combined with a substantial devaluation – policies which are usually prescribed as stabilisation measures and which are designed to boost agricultural exports and agriculture's role in the economy. Agricultural exports, of course, could also be encouraged through other policies. In Thailand, for example, a sharp reduction of taxes on rice exports helped sustain export production in a situation where international prices were declining.[16] But the fact remains that encouraging agricultural exports was not a central objective of macroeconomic policies in any of the countries.

It is also to be noted that, except in the Philippines, macroeconomic policies were concerned with growth rather than with short-run stabilisation and adjustment. Korea and Thailand did not face serious stabilisation and adjustment problems; they restrained economic growth in the 1980s so as to keep their debt burdens within manageable limits. India did face a problem of adjustment, but its initial debt burdens were low so that it had easy access to external credit. To be sure, the policies were imprudent – not because external borrowing was increased in order to sustain growth but because manufacturing growth was based on domestic market expansion rather than on export expansion. Nevertheless, it remains true that the policies were concerned with growth.

The employment consequences of growth

The basic mechanism through which economic growth is expected to improve employment conditions in developing economies is the movement of labour from self-employment (or irregular wage-employment) in agriculture to regular wage-employment in modern non-agricultural sectors. This movement is supposed to generate two parallel processes. On the one hand, agriculture's role in the economy as a provider of employment declines; on the other hand, employment conditions in agriculture itself improve essentially because of a decline in underemployment.

The actual experience of developing countries has shown these ideas to be rather simplistic.[17] Two points in particular are worth emphasising. First, much of the movement of labour is from agriculture to what might be called traditional non-agricultural sectors (the rural non-farm sector and the urban informal sector) in which the employment conditions are not very different from those in agriculture. The declining share of agriculture in the labour force, therefore, neither presupposes economic growth nor implies improvements in employment conditions. Growing land scarcity is the major determinant of labour outmigration from agriculture, although employment conditions in modern non-agricultural sectors influence the process at the margin. Second, the movement of labour out of agriculture does not even necessarily imply improvements in employment conditions in agriculture; an equally important condition is healthy agricultural growth.

For an assessment of the employment consequences of growth, attention needs to be focused both on the change in under-employment in agriculture

Table 4.10. *Employment conditions in agriculture, 1970–88*

	Share of agriculture in labour force: change in percentage points between end years	Annual rate of growth (%)		
		Output per worker in agriculture	Labour force in agriculture	Arable land per worker
India				
1970–79	−1.8	1.2	1.4	−1.1
1979–88	−2.8	0.7	1.5	−1.4[a]
Korea, Republic of				
1970–79	−11.6	4.4	−0.4	0.0
1979–88	−10.6	3.6	−1.2	0.8[a]
Philippines				
1970–79	−2.7	2.9	1.9	−1.0
1979–88	−4.4	0.5	1.5	−1.1[a]
Thailand				
1970–79	−8.0	2.9	1.6	1.6
1979–88	−5.6	2.1	1.5	0.0[a]

Note:
[a] Refers to 1979–85.
Sources: ILO data files; table 4.4 in the text; and Ghose (1990).

and on the growth of employment in modern non-agricultural sectors. Unfortunately, given the nature of the data available, neither variable is directly observable. Research has shown, however, that output per worker in agriculture and employment in manufacturing can serve as reasonable proxies.[18] The analysis accordingly proceeds on the basis of data on these variables assembled in tables 4.10 and 4.11. These data suggest the following conclusions.[19]

First, a straightforward linkage between the pace of economic growth and that of labour outmigration from agriculture is clearly missing if all the four countries are considered together. In the 1980s, the pace of economic growth accelerated in India and decelerated in Thailand and these trends seem to correspond to the pace of labour outmigration; but the appearance is false since the pace of labour outmigration was higher in Thailand in both periods. In the Philippines, moreover, the rate of economic growth fell from about 6 per cent in the 1970s to virtually zero in the 1980s and yet the pace of

Table 4.11. *Growth of employment in manufacturing, 1970–86*

	Annual rate of growth (%)		Output elasticity of employment	
	ILO	UNIDO	ILO	UNIDO
India				
1970–79	1.6	3.8	0.34	0.81
1979–86	0.9	0.0	0.13	0.00
Korea, Republic of				
1970–79	12.1	11.9	0.72	0.71
1979–86	4.5	3.2	0.55	0.39
Philippines				
1970–75	5.4	—	0.78	—
1976–82	—	5.1	—	1.04
1983–86	−3.4	—	0.72	—
Thailand				
1970–79	—	7.7	—	0.74
1979–86	—	−2.4	—	−0.39

Source: ILO data files; World Bank data files.

labour outmigration accelerated in the latter period. The patterns become intelligible only when increased land scarcity is brought into the picture.

Second, in spite of different patterns of labour outmigration from agriculture, the trends in agricultural underemployment were broadly similar across the countries. The data on labour productivity in agriculture suggest that agricultural underemployment declined in all the countries in both periods, but that the rate of decline was slower in the 1980s, particularly so in India and the Philippines. The linkage with agricultural growth is quite evident.

Third, the most intriguing aspect of the growth process in the 1980s concerned the relation between output growth and employment growth in the manufacturing sector. Estimates of the rate of growth of employment and of output elasticity of employment in the manufacturing sector can be based on two sets of data available from two sources – the ILO and the UNIDO. There are some discrepancies between these data sets, for two reasons. First, except for Korea, the ILO data refer to manufacturing establishments with ten or more workers while the UNIDO data refer to those with five or more workers; in the case of Korea, both sets of data refer to establishments with five or more workers. Second, the ILO estimates include employees and working proprietors in India and the Philippines and only employees in Korea. The UNIDO estimates, on the other hand, include employees, working proprietors, active business partners and unpaid family workers in all the countries. On the whole, the UNIDO estimates roughly approximate total employment in manufacturing while the ILO estimates roughly approximate employment in organised manufacturing.

As far as the growth of total employment in manufacturing is concerned, the differences between the two periods are quite striking. In the 1970s, the rate of growth was high in all the countries except India; even in India, it exceeded the rate of growth of the non-agricultural labour force. The elasticity estimates suggest, moreover, that the growth of manufacturing was employment-intensive and that the slow growth of employment in India was to a large extent due to the slow growth of output. In the 1980s, however, manufacturing employment declined in Thailand (and very probably also in the Philippines) and stagnated in India; only in Korea did it continue to grow at a decent rate though even here the rate of growth decelerated quite sharply. The elasticity estimates clearly suggest that the growth of manufacturing was far less employment-intensive in the latter period. The changes were truly dramatic in the cases of India and Thailand.

Unfortunately, adequate data on employment in organised manufacturing were available only for India and Korea. These show that what was true of the manufacturing sector as a whole was also true of the organised subsector: output growth was much less employment-intensive in the 1980s than in the 1970s. There is little reason to doubt that the same conclusion is valid for Thailand as well. The conclusion follows immediately if it is assumed that the relative weights of the organised and unorganised subsectors in employment and output remained unchanged between the periods. The assumption may not be valid, of course. But it is hard to imagine that, in the absence of declines in employment intensities in both subsectors, a mere change of weights could have caused an absolute decline in employment in the manufacturing sector as a whole.

It seems clear that in the 1970s employment in organised manufacturing grew at a faster rate than the non-agricultural labour force everywhere except in India, but the reverse was true in the 1980s everywhere except in Korea. This observation has straightforward implications for the growth in informal sector employment in the two periods, because the trends in employment in the organised non-agricultural sector are strongly and positively related to those in organised manufacturing.[20] It can thus be concluded that in the 1970s informal sector employment was declining in relative terms everywhere except in India, while in the 1980s it expanded in both absolute and relative terms everywhere except in Korea.

This being the case, it is a curious fact that in the 1980s employment conditions deteriorated in India and Thailand, which enjoyed rapid economic growth, in much the same way as in the Philippines, which suffered economic stagnation: the pace of decline in agricultural underemployment slowed, employment in the organised non-agricultural sector at best stagnated and informal sector employment increased very rapidly. The available evidence on the incidence of poverty supports this conclusion. In Thailand, the incidence of rural poverty increased between 1980/81 and 1985/86 and declined between 1985/86 and 1988/89, but the incidence was still higher in 1988/89 than in 1980/81; the incidence of urban poverty changed little during the period.[21] In the case of India, the incidence of poverty in both rural and urban areas showed only a slight decline between 1983 and 1987/88.[22]

Concluding observations

Perhaps the most important point highlighted by the analysis in this chapter concerns the significance of the foreign exchange constraint for all the economies considered, irrespective of the degree of openness. Growth performance in the 1980s depended critically on the growth of merchandise imports. The growth of import capacity did not suffer a decline in all cases; it fell sharply in India and the Philippines but improved substantially in Korea and Thailand. Somewhat contrary to expectations, however, the growth of import capacity was not linked to export performance in any straightforward manner. The 'import capacity of exports' in fact grew at a faster rate in the 1980s than in the 1970s in all the cases. India's import capacity nevertheless suffered principally because of a decline in net transfers from abroad. The Philippines suffered because of the debt problem – in part a consequence of policies pursued in the 1970s. India, with a low debt burden at the beginning of the 1980s, had easy access to external credit and could sustain a high growth of imports through increased external borrowing. The Philippines, being heavily indebted, was obliged to compress imports.

Given the nature of the constraints on the growth of imports, meaningful choices relating to macroeconomic policies were available only to India, Korea and Thailand. Four aspects of the policies actually chosen and their consequences are highlighted by the analysis. First, there was a clear trade-off between economic growth and the growth of the debt burden. India opted for a high rate of economic growth at the cost of building up a debt problem for the 1990s. Korea and Thailand, by contrast, chose progressively to reduce their debt burdens and so restrained economic growth.

Second, the stagnation in world demand for agricultural products and the decline in their relative prices in international markets underlined the need to adjust agriculture's role in these economies. The adjustments which occurred were in line with developments in the world economy; agriculture's share in GDP and exports declined at a faster rate in the 1980s. In none of the countries were serious efforts made to protect agriculture's role; rather the focus of macroeconomic policies was on the growth of manufacturing. In this sense, the policies were quite different from those emphasised in orthodox stabilisation and structural adjustment programmes.

Third, the changes in the world economy had created a need to reorient the industrialisation strategy itself. Since agriculture's role as an earner of foreign exchange was declining in importance, the role of the manufacturing sector had correspondingly to grow. Thus if the growth process was to be sustained in the long run, an export-oriented growth strategy had to be adopted for the manufacturing sector. In reality, such a strategy was pursued only in Korea and Thailand. The growth of manufacturing in India in the 1980s was very much of the import-substitutive variety, in fact more so than it had been in the 1970s. This clearly was inappropriate and involved an intertemporal trade-off in terms of growth.

Finally, industrialisation-led growth in the 1980s performed rather poorly in terms of improving employment conditions. There were two general reasons for this. First, because of the exhaustion of land frontiers, agriculture's capacity for labour absorption had nearly reached its limit in most cases. Agricultural growth, moreover, had slowed. Second, the output elasticity of employment in the manufacturing sector was very low, much lower than it had been in the 1970s. These features were less pronounced in Korea than in India and Thailand. Employment conditions did improve in Korea in the 1980s, though less rapidly than in the 1970s. But in both India and Thailand, employment conditions almost certainly deteriorated.

There remain two intriguing questions which, unfortunately, could not be answered in this chapter. First, what explains the very low output elasticity of employment in the manufacturing sector in the 1980s? Clearly, the sector had undergone significant structural changes and the macroeconomic policies pursued in the 1980s had a role in inducing these. But the issues remain to be investigated. Second, why did India and Thailand have very similar experiences with respect to employment in manufacturing? In the 1980s, the growth of manufacturing in India was import-substitutive while that in Thailand was export-oriented. Thailand's manufacturing sector, therefore, should have performed much better than India's in terms of employment creation.[23] This was not the case. Perhaps, in today's context, exports are no more labour-intensive than import substitutes. But, again, the issues remain to be investigated.

Notes

1 See, for example, Lee (1987), Fischer (1987), Hughes and Singh (1991), Edgren
   and Muqtada (1990) and Singh and Tabatabai, chapter 2 in this volume. A good
   account of the economic difficulties of the Latin American countries is available
   in Bianchi (1987).
2 This view is promoted particularly by the World Bank in its country reports.
3 The generalisations are due to Clark (1957) and Kuznets (1965, 1971).
4 See, for example, Chenery and Syrquin (1975) and Ghose (1990).
5 For evidence, see Ghose (1990). See also the Introduction to this volume, and de
   Janvry and Sadoulet, chapter 5 in this volume.
6 The stated objective of these policies is to shift resources from the production of
   non-tradeables to that of tradeables. In the context of developing countries, this
   usually means encouraging the production of export crops. For further clarifica-
   tion, see the section on 'Macroeconomic policies' below.
7 The argument can be found in Mellor (1986), Johnson (1987), Timmer (1988),
   World Bank (1986) and de Janvry and Sadoulet, chapter 5 this volume.
8 To this author's knowledge, there has been no attempt to define optimal rates of
   decline in agriculture's share in GDP and exports. The only theoretical basis for
   the argument is the proposition that free markets always produce optimal
   allocation of resources and all interventions, therefore, must lead to suboptimal
   results. Such a proposition is empirically non-verifiable and hence unhelpful.
9 There is probably a greater degree of heterogeneity among countries in Asia
   than in other regions. The Asian region includes the Hong Kong area and
   Singapore with virtually no agricultural sector at one extreme and, at the other,
   countries such as Bangladesh and Nepal whose economies are overwhelmingly
   dominated by agriculture.
10 The constraint was recognised long ago in a celebrated paper by Chenery and
   Bruno (1962). More recent expositions are available in Bacha (1984) and Taylor
   (1983).
11 For some evidence, see Singh and Tabatabai, chapter 2 in this volume.
12 During 1980–87, rice exports in volume terms increased at an annual rate of
   about 7 per cent while the export price declined at an annual rate of about 4.5 per
   cent. Exports of rubber also increased although, again, the export price declined.
   Exports of tapioca and sugar declined substantially in both volume and value
   terms. See World Bank (1989), vol. II, table 3.2.
13 Underlying the statement is a well-known formula: rate of growth of demand for
   foodgrains = rate of growth of population + (rate of growth of *per capita*
   income × income elasticity of demand for foodgrains).
14 The theoretical conjectures which follow are derived from what might be called a
   structuralist model. For a discussion of such models, see Taylor (1983). An
   alternative monetarist model predicts inflation and the current account deficit as
   consequences of the budget deficit but not the effects on relative food prices and
   manufacturing output. See, for example, Khan, Montiel and Haque (1990).
15 Once again, the theoretical conjectures follow from a structuralist model. On a
   monetarist perspective, a devaluation increases exports, reduces imports and
   leaves the rate of economic growth unaffected.

116   Ajit Ghose

16 See Siamwalla and Sethboonsarng (1989).
17 See Ghose (1990).
18 Cf. Ghose (1990), chs. 3 and 4.
19 It should be noted that data on the labour force in agriculture tend to be less reliable than those on the total labour force. Since population censuses or labour force surveys are carried out only periodically, the data for the 1980s are estimates based on projections; projection of the total labour force is easier than that of the agricultural labour force. Consequently, it is difficult to be fully confident of the empirical results relating to intersectoral migration or productivity movements in agriculture. Not much can be done about the problem and the results have to be accepted as valid pending confirmation or contradiction by fresh rounds of censuses or labour force surveys.
20 Cf. Ghose (1990), ch. 3.
21 See Hutaserani (1990) and Jitsuchon (1990).
22 See Minhas, Jain and Tendulkar (1991).
23 It has been argued that export-oriented industries are significantly more labour-intensive than import-substituting industries. See Krueger (1983, 1988).

References

Bacha, E.L., 1984. 'Growth with limited supplies of foreign exchange: A reappraisal of the two-gap model', in Syrquin, Taylor and Westphal (eds.) (1984).
Banuri, T. (ed.), 1991. *No Panacea: The Limits to Liberalisation*, Oxford: Clarendon Press.
Bianchi, A., 1987. 'Adjustment in Latin America, 1981–86', in Corbo, Goldstein and Khan (eds.) (1987).
Chenery, H. and M. Bruno, 1962. 'Development alternatives in an open economy: The case of Israel', *Economic Journal*, vol. 72, no. 1, pp. 79–103.
Chenery, H. and T.N. Srinivasan (eds.), 1988. *Handbook of Development Economics*, vol. I, Amsterdam: Elsevier Science Publishers BV.
Chenery, H. and M. Syrquin, 1975. *Patterns of Development, 1950–1970*, London: Oxford University Press.
Clark, C., 1957. *The Conditions of Economic Progress*, 3rd edn., London: Macmillan.
Corbo, V., M. Goldstein and M. Khan (eds.), 1987. *Growth-Oriented Adjustment Programs*, Washington, DC: IMF and World Bank.
Edgren, G. and M. Muqtada, 1990. 'Strategies for growth and employment in Asia: Learning from within', in ILO/ARTEP (1990).
Fischer, S., 1987. 'Economic growth and economic policy', in Corbo, Goldstein and Khan (eds.) (1987).
Ghose, A.K., 1990. *Economic Growth and Employment Structure: A Study of Labour Outmigration from Agriculture in Developing Countries*, Geneva: ILO.
Hughes, A. and A. Singh, 1991. 'The world economic slowdown and the Asian and Latin American economies: A comparative analysis of economic structure, policy and performance', in Banuri (ed.) (1991).
Hutaserani, S., 1990. 'The trends of income inequality and poverty and a profile of

the urban poor in Thailand', *Thailand Development Research Institute Quarterly Review*, vol. 5, no. 4.

ILO (International Labour Office), 1987. *World Recession and Global Interdependence: Effects on Employment, Poverty and Policy Formation in Developing Countries*, Geneva: ILO.

ILO/ARTEP, 1990. *Employment Challenges for the 90s*, New Delhi: ILO/ARTEP.

Jitsuchon, S., 1990. *Alleviation of Rural Poverty in Thailand*, New Delhi: ILO/ARTEP.

Johnson, D.G., 1987. 'Agricultural structural policies', in Corbo, Goldstein and Khan (eds.) (1987).

Khan, M.S., P. Montiel and N.U. Haque, 1990. 'Adjustment with growth: Relating the analytical approaches of the IMF and the World Bank', *Journal of Development Economics*, vol. 32, no. 1, pp. 155–79.

Krueger, A.O. (ed.), 1983. *Trade and Employment in Developing Countries*, Chicago: Chicago University Press.

1988. 'The relationships between trade, employment and development', in Ranis and Schultz (eds.) (1988).

Kuznets, S., 1965. *Economic Growth and Structure: Selected Essays*, London: Heinemann.

1971. *Economic Growth of Nations: Total Output and Production Structure*, Cambridge, Mass.: Harvard University Press.

Lee, E., 1987. 'World recession and developing economies in Asia', in ILO (1987).

Lewis, J.P. and V. Kallab (eds.), 1986. *Development Strategies Reconsidered*, New Brunswick, New Jersey, Oxford: Transaction Books for the Overseas Development Council.

Mellor, J.W., 1986. 'Agriculture on the road to industrialization', in Lewis and Kallab (eds.) (1986).

Minhas, B.S., L.R. Jain and S.D. Tendulkar, 1991. 'Declining incidence of poverty in the 1980s: Evidence versus artefacts', *Economic and Political Weekly*, vol. 26, nos. 27 and 28, July 6–13, pp. 1673–82.

Ranis, G. and T.P. Schultz (eds.), 1988. *The State of Development Economics: Progress and Perspectives*, Oxford: Basil Blackwell.

Siamwalla, A. and S. Sethboonsarng, 1989. *Trade, Exchange Rate, and Agricultural Pricing Policies in Thailand*, Washington, DC: World Bank.

Syrquin, M., L. Taylor and L. Westphal (eds.), 1984. *Economic Structure and Performance: Essays in Honour of Hollis B. Chenery*, London: Academic Press.

Taylor, L, 1983. *Structuralist Macroeconomics*, New York: Basic Books.

Timmer, C.P., 1988. 'The agricultural transformation', in Chenery and Srinivasan (eds.) (1988).

World Bank, 1986. *World Development Report*, New York: Oxford University Press.

1989. *Thailand: Country Economic Memorandum, Building on the Recent Success – A Policy Framework*, Washington, DC: World Bank, 2 vols.

5 Adjustment policies, agriculture and rural development in Latin America

ALAIN DE JANVRY AND ELISABETH
SADOULET

Role of agriculture in economic recovery

Agriculture in Latin America has played an important cushioning role in preventing further deterioration of gross domestic product (GDP) during the crisis decade of the 1980s. We show in this chapter that aggregate agricultural output has responded positively to the real exchange-rate depreciations that have occurred as a result of foreign exchange shortages and industrial trade liberalisation. But output has been negatively affected by economic slowdown, reduced public expenditures, and the uncertainties caused by inflation. While the performance of countries in stabilising their economies remains highly unequal a decade after the beginning of the debt crisis, we observe that those countries whose agricultural sectors offer good opportunities to increase exports and to substitute for imports have been the most successful. Improving the growth of agriculture will be one of the key features of a strategy of economic recovery for the 1990s. Because the elasticity of supply response of agriculture is highly dependent on non-price factors, its performance hinges on more effective and/or higher levels of public investment in the sector as opposed to the sharp contraction experienced in the 1980s as part of fiscal austerity policies.

During the 1980s, the incidence of absolute poverty has increased, reversing the declining trend of the previous decades. While the process has been highly uneven across countries, it is in the urban areas that poverty has increased the most. This has been due to rising food prices, sharply falling real wages, and the loss of employment coming with the liquidation of large sectors of non-competitive import-substitution industries and shrinkage of the public sector. Agriculture and the rural poor have, by contrast, fared better, with some sectors of the rural poor benefiting from real exchange-rate depreciation as producers (or employees of producers) of a marketed surplus of tradeables. As a result, by 1989, for the first time in the history of Latin America, the mass of absolute poverty has been displaced from the rural to the urban areas, even though it is in the rural areas that the incidence of poverty and the more extreme forms of structural poverty remain the highest (Feres and León, 1990). Yet, in spite of faring relatively better in the 1980s, many smallholders are trapped in regions, activities and skills that have lost comparative advantage with adjustment, while the anti-employment bias of commercial farming has been reduced only modestly. Here too, a strategy of economic recovery based on agriculture can create new opportunities for effective rural development. We explore this possibility in this chapter, stressing the potential offered by democratic openings and the burgeoning of grass-roots movements.

We first characterise the highly uneven performance of the Latin American countries in stabilising their economies and restoring economic growth. We then analyse the determinants of the observed performance of agriculture, stressing the complementarity that exists between price incentives and the non-price determinants of the elasticity of supply response. We also analyse how agriculture is affected by the different instruments that have been used for stabilisation, namely exchange-rate devaluation, fiscal austerity, tight control of the money supply and wage repression. In the following section we consider the impact of the crisis and stabilisation policies on the welfare of different social groups and on rural poverty in particular. Finally, we extract the implications of this analysis to outline a strategy of agricultural and rural development for the 1990s.

Macroeconomic adjustment and agriculture

The heterogeneity of policies across countries and, over time, within the same country makes it difficult to characterise the way in which the Latin American countries have implemented stabilisation policies, and the effects of these policies on inflation, GDP growth and agricultural production. Policy implementation has often been quite unstable and the results have been blurred by external or unexpected events. In table 5.1, we nevertheless search for regularities and look at the four main policy options available for stabilisation: real exchange-rate depreciation, fiscal austerity directed at current and investment expenditures, restrictive monetary policy and wage control.

Taking inflation as the indicator of stabilisation, we can clearly distinguish three groups of countries (see also Selowsky, 1989, for a classification of Latin American countries by stages of the adjustment process). The first includes Argentina, Peru, and Brazil where stabilisation has so far been unsuccessful and where inflation in 1980–88 averaged 197 per cent. In the terminal period 1988–89 (table 5.2), average inflation raged to 1575 per cent. GDP growth has been negative in Argentina, stagnant in Peru and, though high in Brazil, that country's failure to control inflation signals that

Table 5.1. *Latin America: stabilisation and growth, 1970–88*

	Annual growth rates (%)						Economic outcomes		
	Stabilisation policies								
First period	Real exchange rate	Central govt deficit as % GDP	Current expenditure as % GDP	Capital expenditure as % GDP	Money supply as % GDP	Real minimum wage	Inflation	GDP	Agricultural production
	1970–80	1975–82	1975–82	1975–82	1975–82	1978–80		1970–80	1970–80
Group I									
Argentina	−3.9	−8.3	2.6	15.4	1.8	15.5	135	2.7	3.0
Peru	4.1	−8.0	−0.1	2.1	0.9	17.5	29	3.4	−0.1
Brazil	0.7	0.0[a]	−0.7	−5.2	1.4	1.0	34	5.8	3.5
Simple average	0.3	—	0.6	4.1	1.3	11.3	66	4.0	2.1
Group II									
Venezuela	−0.8	−20.7[a]	1.0	−8.6	1.0	21.0	8	4.9	3.0
Mexico	−0.2	4.4	3.9	−0.7	2.7	−4.6	17	5.9	3.3
Simple average	−0.5	—	2.5	−4.7	1.9	8.2	13	5.4	3.1
Group III									
Costa Rica	−2.1	2.3	−0.6	−1.2	7.5	2.0	11	2.6	3.7
Ecuador	−2.9	10.6	1.0	3.8	−0.8	46.3	13	7.7	2.4
Chile	−4.8	73.7[a]	8.0	10.8	7.8	−0.3	178	5.8	2.4
Colombia	−3.4	58.0[a]	6.0	2.0	−6.4	—	22	8.5	4.3
Simple average	−3.3	—	3.6	3.9	2.0	16.0	56	6.1	3.2

Second period	1980–88	1982–87	1982–87	1982–87	1982–87	1980–86		1980–88	
Group I: Failure to stabilise									
Argentina	8.0	−3.5	4.4	−10.6	3.1	2.7	286	−0.4	1.0
Peru	2.6	−8.9	−2.3	−4.9	−3.8	−7.8	120	1.1	2.8
Brazil	−0.7	375.0[a]	29.6	49.1	−0.8	−6.2	186	3.8	3.0
Simple average	3.3	—	10.6	11.2	−0.5	−3.8	197	1.5	2.3
Group II: Stabilisation without growth									
Venezuela	2.7	−45.0[a]	−1.5	−5.4	−0.7	0.4	14	0.4	2.0
Mexico	4.8	8.2	−6.7	−8.5	−3.3	−8.4	78	0.5	1.3
Simple average	3.7	—	−4.1	−7.0	−2.0	−4.0	46	0.5	1.6
Group III: Stabilisation and growth									
Costa Rica	1.1	−6.3	1.9	−5.9	−3.6	4.2	26	1.9	2.0
Ecuador	11.7	−71.7[a]	−6.7	−2.5	−4.1	−4.8	30	2.2	2.6
Chile	6.4	−55.1	−5.5	0.3	−2.8	−8.8	21	2.3	2.5
Colombia	5.2	−19.5	4.6	−3.0	8.6	2.2	22	2.9	1.9
Simple average	6.1	—	−1.4	−2.8	−0.5	−1.8	25	2.3	2.2

Note:
[a] Data include negative values; linear trend is calculated instead of growth rate, multiplied by 100.
Source: CEPAL, Statistical Yearbook for Latin America and the Caribbean, various issues.

Table 5.2. *Latin America: stabilisation and growth, 1988–89*

	Annual growth rates (%)		
	Inflation	GDP	Agricultural production
Group I: Failure to stabilise			
Argentina	1 711	− 3.7	− 1.6
Peru	2 032	− 9.6	2.5
Brazil	983	1.8	0.9
Simple average	1 575	− 3.8	0.6
Group II: Stabilisation without growth			
Venezuela	57	− 0.7	− 0.3
Mexico	67	2.2	− 3.2
Simple average	62	0.8	− 1.8
Group III: Stabilisation and growth			
Costa Rica	19	4.6	4.4
Ecuador	67	6.7	4.0
Chile	16	8.7	5.1
Colombia	27	3.5	3.7
Simple average	32	5.9	4.3

Source: Inter-American Development Bank (1990).

this growth is unstable and unlikely to be sustained, as seen in table 5.2. Venezuela and Mexico constitute a second group of countries that have been successful in stabilising their economies, with an average inflation of 46 per cent in 1980–88 and 62 per cent in 1988–89, but where growth has as yet failed to recover. Mexico, in particular, has applied a drastic orthodox stabilisation programme with monetary austerity and severe wage repression that cut real wages by more than 40 per cent between 1980 and 1987. The continuing debt burden – with interest payments on foreign debt claiming 57 per cent of total government expenditures in 1987 – and recurrent foreign exchange crises have severely limited public investment, dented confidence that reforms will be sustained and deterred the recovery of private investment. Finally, a third group of countries, including Costa Rica, Ecuador, Chile and Colombia, have been successful in controlling inflation and restoring some growth in GDP. Average inflation has been contained at 25 per cent in 1980–88 and 32 per cent in 1988–89. In Colombia, the effect of the crisis and the subsequent necessary adjustments have been small, with foreign exchange inflows continuing through the

1980s. In the other countries, large appreciations of the real exchange rate, fiscal austerity that effectively reduced the government deficit and restrictive monetary policies have all been applied. Wage repression has been severe in Chile and Ecuador but not in Costa Rica and Colombia. The fact that Chile was able to stabilise the economy under an authoritarian regime while Costa Rica, Ecuador and Colombia did so under democratic regimes indicates that democratic freedoms need not be restricted for stabilisation policies to succeed, as is sometimes implied by inspection of the Asian experience. On the contrary, democracy can aid the mobilisation of broad coalitions that make the burden of austerity politically more acceptable and shared more equitably among the population (Nelson, 1988).

It is interesting to note four common characteristics of those countries where stabilisation policies succeeded and some growth was resumed. Costa Rica, Ecuador, Chile and Colombia are all countries where the agricultural sector has a large share in the economy, where agrarian interests have significant political weight, where the formal urban labour sector created by import substitution was still relatively small and where the bureaucratic apparatus was not excessively bloated. As we will see later, agriculture is the main potential beneficiary of stabilisation through exchange-rate devaluation and restraint of current government expenditures. Thus, not only can agrarian interests back the State in implementing stabilisation policies, making it more politically feasible, but the economic gains for the agricultural sector can act as an engine of recovery for the economy as a whole.

Success in stabilisation was most notably associated with the ability to sustain fiscal austerity, while at the same time engaging in large depreciations of the real exchange rate and monetary austerity. By contrast, failure to stabilise the economy was associated with incapacity to sustain fiscal austerity (Brazil), monetary austerity (Argentina) and depreciation of the real exchange rate (Brazil), and failure to resist pressures for early real wage concessions (Argentina). These countries have a large formal sector workforce (Argentina and Brazil) and a large bureaucracy (Brazil), the two social sectors that would have been the main victims of a successful stabilisation programme. These groups also bore the brunt of stabilisation costs in Chile, Costa Rica, Ecuador and Colombia, but the political damage was less because the sectors were smaller.

Stabilisation instruments and agriculture

Agriculture tends to be affected in contradictory ways by the use of stabilisation instruments. As table 5.1 shows, in 1970–80, all but two countries had growth rates in GDP that were higher than in agricultural production. This situation was reversed in 1980–88 when all countries but two had higher growth rates in agriculture than in GDP. Agricultural growth performance has been uneven across country groups; the countries which stabilised and grew performed well, but so did Brazil and Peru in spite of failing to stabilise their economies. The superior performance of agriculture in the countries that have achieved stabilisation and recovery of GDP growth is clear in the terminal period 1988–89. When the annual growth of agricultural production averaged 0.6 per cent in the countries that failed to stabilise and − 1.8 per cent in the countries that failed to grow, it reached 4.3 per cent in the countries where stabilisation and GDP growth occurred.

Real exchange-rate devaluation can benefit the tradeable sectors of agriculture. In Latin America, most agricultural output is tradeable (Valdés, 1986). Liberalisation of trade, either by reducing export taxes on agriculture (Argentina, Uruguay) or by reducing import tariffs on industry (all countries), further contributes to depreciation of the real exchange rate. Fiscal and monetary instruments can benefit or hurt agriculture according to how they are applied and the structural context that determines the response to these policies. We explore these issues in this section.

Determinants of the aggregate supply response of agriculture

There has been intense controversy over the determinants of the aggregate supply response of agriculture (Mundlak, 1985). The outcome of this debate is fundamental in determining the production and welfare effects of stabilisation. While Timmer (1988) has argued that getting the prices right is the main determinant of supply response, Rao and Caballero (1990) maintain that response to price is weak and that structural factors and the delivery of public goods and services are the main determinants of production. We test these positions by using data for nine Latin American countries for the period 1970–88.

To capture the terms of trade effects of exchange-rate devaluation, we calculate the real effective exchange rate defined as the nominal exchange rate multiplied by the ratio of the United States wholesale price index (WPI) to the domestic WPI. Because there are no reliable data on public expenditures in agriculture for Latin America, we characterise this variable by real GDP. While there is a strong correlation between GDP and budgetary allocations to agriculture, GDP also captures the effective demand effect for agriculture and hence the price of non-tradeables. To assess the effect of stabilisation on production performance, we use as a proxy the rate of inflation. All three variables are lagged by one year. Finally, we introduce a partial adjustment mechanism by using as an additional exogenous variable agricultural output lagged by one year. With all variables in logs, the long-term elasticity of supply response is the short-run elasticity of the real exchange rate divided by one minus the elasticity of lagged output.

The results in table 5.3 indicate that the real exchange rate is generally a significant determinant of agricultural output but that the magnitude of the effect is small. Exchange-rate appreciation in the 1970s militated against agriculture while depreciation in the 1980s stimulated agricultural output. Without partial adjustment, the average elasticity for Argentina, Brazil, Costa Rica, Ecuador and Mexico, where the relation is significant, is 0.20. For Latin America as a whole, the elasticity is 0.07 and significant. While this is not large, it suggests that prices do indeed matter, even though total response is dominated by other effects, especially past overall economic growth. When a partial adjustment is introduced, the long-run elasticity of supply response is significant only in Brazil, Ecuador and Mexico, with an average value of 0.23. For Latin America as a whole, it is 0.07 and not significant.

The elasticity of lagged real GDP is highly significant; it is equal to 0.60 for Latin America as a whole with no partial adjustment and 0.16 with partial adjustment. This suggests that past overall economic growth, with its consequences for public investment and effective demand, is an important determinant of aggregate agricultural output. The slowdown in GDP growth in the 1980s thus contributed to the reduced growth of agriculture compared to the previous decade. Inflation, on the other hand, has an uneven effect on output and is not significant for Latin America as a whole. This suggests that, although inflation may be detrimental to GDP growth and hence indirectly to agriculture, it can be beneficial by reducing real interest rates. This explains the observation in table 5.1 of a strong relation between stabilisation and GDP growth but of an uncertain relation between inflation and agricultural growth. Clearly, the relation is more complex than can be captured in a simple regression analysis.

Agriculture's response to fiscal and monetary policies

To explain why some countries have been more successful than others in stabilising their economies and why agriculture has benefited from stabilisation in some cases and not in others, it is useful to establish a relation between the instruments used for stabilisation and their effects on the variables that determine the performance of the different sectors of the economy. Because we do not have enough degrees of freedom to do this econometrically, we use a computable general equilibrium (CGE) model for Ecuador (Fargeix, 1990; de Janvry, Sadoulet and Fargeix, 1991).

Table 5.3. *Determinants of aggregate agricultural supply, 1970–88 (endogenous variable: logarithm of agricultural output*

Countries	Intercept	Log of lagged real exchange rate	Log of lagged real GDP	Log of lagged inflation	Log of lagged agricultural output	R^2	Long-run supply elasticity
Argentina	−2.03	0.16*	1.25*	0.03		0.77	
w.p.a.[a]	−1.06	0.06	0.54*	0.01	0.63*	0.91	0.16
Brazil	1.89*	0.28*	0.24*	0.09*		0.97	
w.p.a.[a]	0.19*	0.29*	0.25*	0.09*	−0.03	0.97	0.28
Chile	1.44	0.02	0.70*	−0.03		0.73	
w.p.a.[a]	−0.74	0.01	0.31	0.02	0.84*	0.83	0.06
Colombia	2.07*	−0.08	0.64*	0.00		0.98	
w.p.a.[a]	0.53	0.02	0.22	0.01	0.64*	0.98	0.06
Costa Rica	0.66	0.16*	0.73*	−0.04*		0.94	
w.p.a.[a]	0.60	0.11	0.55*	−0.03*	0.23	0.94	0.14
Ecuador	1.51*	0.24*	0.48*	−0.07*		0.92	
w.p.a.[a]	1.51*	0.24*	0.48*	−0.07*	0.00	0.92	0.24
Mexico	1.10*	0.16*	0.63*	−0.03		0.96	
w.p.a.[a]	0.95*	0.13*	0.51*	−0.02	0.17	0.96	0.16
Peru	5.30*	−0.01	−0.18	0.06*		0.45	
w.p.a.[a]	2.90*	−0.01	−0.14	0.04	0.49*	0.55	−0.02
Venezuela	1.92	0.05	0.50*	0.07*		0.75	
w.p.a.[a]	−0.39	0.16	0.22	0.00	0.70*	0.85	0.53
All Latin America[b]	1.57*	0.07*	0.60*	−0.01		0.78	
w.p.a.[a]	0.50*	0.02	0.16*	−0.00	0.72*	0.89	0.07

Notes:

* Statistically significant at a 95 per cent confidence level.   [a] With partial adjustment.   [b] Country dummies were used.

The CGE model has both real and financial sectors. The real side of the model follows the standard specification given in Dervis, de Melo and Robinson (1982) and in de Janvry and Sadoulet (1987), with the following additional features which are important for the analysis of stabilisation and adjustment programmes.

Both private and public investment create productivity gains. Private investment responds negatively to the rate of interest and the rate of inflation and positively to the expected profitability of investment in the corresponding sector. Investment embodies new vintages of capital with higher productivity levels, thus raising the overall level of productivity of the capital stock. Public investment, particularly under the form of infrastructure, new technologies, and human capital formation, increases total factor productivity and hence also the profitability of private investment. It thus plays an important role in economic recovery in stimulating private investment. Fiscal austerity directed at public investment will thus have little growth effects in the short run but a strong impact in the long run. Current expenditures, by contrast, have little productivity effects but create strong losses in welfare for those who benefit from government subsidies and public health and educational services.

The financial side of the model adds two important features to standard real side models: a money market where money is supplied by the monetary authorities and demand originates from the households and firms. The general level of prices, and hence the rate of inflation, is determined by equilibrium in this market. The other additional market is for loanable funds, where total deposits supplied by households meet a demand for borrowing by firms and government. On this market, equilibrium determines the rate of interest.

Households make portfolio choices where savings are allocated, according to relative profitabilities to money, demand for housing, productive investment in informal sector activities, domestic bonds, and foreign assets (capital outflight). Capital outflight depends positively on both expected real devaluation of the exchange rate and on inflation which conveys information about likely future real devaluations and lack of confidence in successful stabilisation. When capital outflight increases, the domestic supply of loanable funds falls and interest rates rise. In addition, with limited ability to borrow on the international financial market, the balance-of-payments constraint imposes the need to increase the surplus in the balance of trade to make up for the fall in the balance of capital account, thus forcing a devaluation of the exchange rate.

The deficit between government expenditures and revenues can be made up in three ways: foreign borrowing (which is exogenously constrained by the debt stock), domestic borrowing that raises the rate of interest and crowds out private investment, and money creation that creates inflation and enhances capital outflight and reduces private investment. Fiscal policy is directed at reducing the public deficit by cutting either current or investment expenditures, or both. Monetary policy is directed at reducing money creation. Restrictive monetary policy increases the rate of interest which decreases demand and inflation. On the positive side, this lowers inflation and capital outflight. On the negative side, it creates disincentives to private investment. If monetary institutions are weak in inducing a savings response and in helping the repatriation of capital outflight, the interest rates will remain high, limiting the effectiveness of stabilisation through monetary policy as a component of economic reactivation.

In the model, the nominal wage is adjusted in each period to compensate for the inflation of the previous period. If inflation was accelerating, the real wage thus falls during the current period; if it was decelerating, the wage adjustment overshoots current inflation, and the real wage rises. There is surplus in all sectors of the economy and the wage level is also affected by the extent of unemployment in the economy.

In year one, the economy is affected by a foreign sector shock that originates in a fall in foreign borrowing by government and a drop in the price of oil, the main Ecuadorian export. With foreign borrowing constrained, four policy options remain for stabilisation:

(a) Exchange-rate devaluation with no reduction in government expenditures. Lower foreign borrowing has to be made up by government borrowing on the domestic market, which results in sharply rising interest rates and the crowding out of private investment.

(b) Fiscal austerity directed at reducing current expenditures. These expenditures are principally for health and education and their reduction implies a loss in public sector employment for skilled workers.

(c) Fiscal austerity directed at cutting not only current but also investment expenditures. The reduction in investment expenditures is detrimental to growth both directly through a smaller increase in the stock of capital and also indirectly because public investment enhances the productivity and hence the level of private investment.

(d) Restrictive monetary policy which results in rising interest rates but lower inflation. While higher interest rates deter private investment, lower inflation reduces capital outflight, wages growth and investment uncertainty. Lower capital outflight increases loanable funds and serves to put some downward pressure on interest rates.

We compare in table 5.4 and illustrate in figure 5.1 the effects of these four policies on the production of agricultural exports, food crops, industry and services. The first sector is fully tradeable, the second and third partially tradeable and the fourth wholly non-tradeable The four approaches to

Table 5.4. *Ecuador: impact of alternative stabilisation policies on agriculture*

	Changes relative to pre-shock year 1 unless indicated (%)							
	Exchange-rate devaluation		Fiscal austerity: cut current expenditures		Fiscal austerity: cut current and investment expenditures		Restrictive monetary policy	
	Year 2	Year 7	Year 2	Year 7	Year 2	Year 7	Year 2	Year 7
Exchange rate (growth rate)	75.3	39.8	79.9	37.5	81.1	38.0	54.3	24.0
Real interest rate (value)	22.5	43.0	1.1	4.0	−0.1	7.7	34.4	46.0
Inflation (growth rate)	46.7	40.3	47.9	38.1	48.3	38.8	32.4	24.5
Real GDP	−0.1	−1.8	−3.3	4.8	−3.0	2.8	−2.3	1.5
Sectoral value added at constant prices								
Agro exports	8.4	11.9	8.6	21.9	8.8	19.6	6.1	15.2
Food crops	4.1	−1.9	3.5	8.0	3.8	6.1	0.7	1.4
Industry	3.9	−3.6	3.7	8.9	3.9	6.1	0.7	0.6
Utilities, trade and services	1.1	−6.3	−0.2	6.5	−1.0	2.3	−2.6	−2.1

Source: Results from CGE model for Ecuador (de Janvry, Sadoulet and Fargeix, 1991).

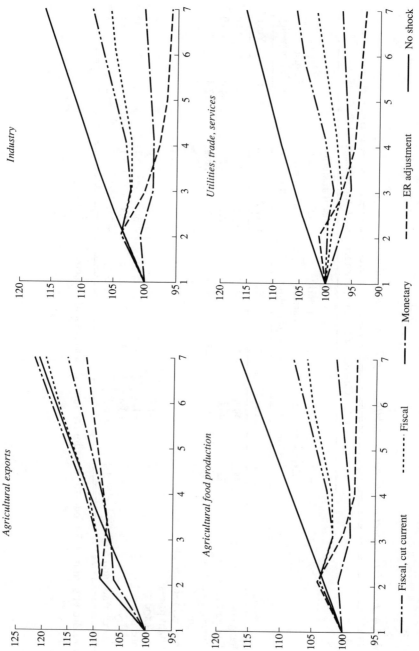

Agricultural exports

Industry

Agricultural food production

Utilities, trade, services

— · · — Fiscal, cut current   · · · · · · · Fiscal   — · — · Monetary

— — — ER adjustment   —— No shock

Figure 5.1 Ecuador: real sectoral value added under alternative adjustment policies.

stabilisation have different effects on the exchange rate, the real interest rate and the rate of inflation; all have powerful but different influences on GDP and sectoral growth.

The results show that agricultural exports are the main beneficiary of stabilisation policies in the short run because of the effect on the real exchange rate. Fiscal austerity leads to the greatest devaluation because it reallocates expenditures from government to private investment which has a higher import content and thus induces further devaluation. This effect is greatest when investment expenditures are cut: these relate mainly to labour-intensive public works projects which have a lower import content than current expenditures. In the long run, fiscal austerity further benefits agriculture by sharply curtailing interest rates. The result is that agricultural exports benefit from a fiscal approach to stabilisation, and do so even compared with their predicted growth performance without a foreign sector shock if fiscal austerity cuts current expenditures while protecting investment (figure 5.1). From table 5.1, we see that Ecuador and Chile, which have followed this approach, are the two countries which have stabilised with a strong growth performance of agriculture and of agricultural exports in particular.

Food crops, which are partially tradeable through import substitution, benefit in the very short run from exchange-rate devaluation without fiscal or monetary austerity because this has the least cost to GDP growth. By the same token, food crop production benefits most in the long run from the strategy that is most favourable to GDP growth, namely fiscal austerity directed at cutting current expenditures. Thus, while agricultural exports benefit from exchange-rate devaluation and low interest rates, food crops gain from strategies that maximise GDP growth.

Restrictive monetary policies seem to affect agriculture more adversely than fiscal austerity. This is because the high interest rates induced by monetary restraint to control inflation raise the costs of agricultural production and deter investment.

Turning to the other sectors of the economy, industrial products, like food crops, are only partially traded and are affected similarly by stabilisation policies. Services, which are wholly non-traded, are hurt by depreciation of the real exchange rate. As in the case of food crops, the best policy for the growth of services is that which most stimulates effective demand and GDP growth.

We conclude that the strong performance of agricultural production in countries that have stabilised their economies is associated with real exchange-rate devaluation and with fiscal austerity that preserves the role of public investment. These results thus strongly corroborate the historical observations in table 5.1 and the econometric estimates in table 5.3. While price incentives coming through exchange-rate changes are fundamental for agriculture, especially agricultural exports, public investment and overall economic growth are essential to agricultural performance during the process of structural adjustment. As Lipton (1989) correctly observed, agriculture can benefit through incentives from the market liberalisation effect of stabilisation but tends to be hurt by fiscal austerity that leads to a reduction in the role of the State. Both the econometric and simulation results reported above show that agriculture is highly sensitive to declines in public investment and moderately responsive to price incentives. The policy implication is that, if agriculture is indeed to play an important role in economic recovery, particular care must be given to preservation of or greater efficiency in public investment in agriculture (see also Commander, 1989).

Stabilisation and welfare

There are remarkably few data on the incidence of poverty in Latin America. A recent study by the Economic Commission for Latin America and the Caribbean (Feres and León, 1990) gives information on absolute poverty in 1980 and 1986, contrasting rural and urban households. To characterise changes in the satisfaction of basic needs, global indicators such as *per capita* government expenditures in health and education can be used. Until disaggregated data are available, estimates of how different types of households within the rural and urban sectors have been differentially affected by the crisis must be obtained by simulation. This is what we do later in this section, using income equations for Ecuador.

Changes in absolute poverty

There was a sharp rise in the incidence of poverty during the 1980s and this rise has been disproportionately located in the urban sector. As the data in table 5.5 indicate, for Latin America as a whole, the number of rural poor increased by 3.8 per cent and the number of urban poor by 50.1 per cent between 1980 and 1986, resulting in a total increase of 25.2 per cent. The incidence of poverty remained constant at 60 per cent in the rural sector while it rose from 30 to 36 per cent in the urban sector, with the total increase in incidence rising from 41 to 43 per cent.

Rising poverty levels should indeed be expected: while *per capita* GDP growth is the main source of poverty alleviation (Adelman, 1975; Stein, 1989), it fell in Latin America by an average annual rate of 1.1 per cent between 1981 and 1989. Real minimum wages fell quite precipitously between 1980 and 1989, with an average annual rate of decline of 2.6 per cent for Latin America as a whole (IDB, 1990). Open urban unemployment was 7.3 per cent in 1980, 10.5 per cent in 1985 and 8.3 per cent in 1989, showing an average annual increase of 1.3 per cent over the decade. With industry and services performing worse than agriculture, urban areas have been hit the hardest; formal sector workers in non-competitive import-substitution industries and the bureaucracy have lost most in employment and wages. As a result, while the incidence of rural poverty has not diminished, it has increased sharply in the urban sector.

The contrast between countries which have failed to stabilise with those which have stabilised and grown shows that urban poverty has increased much more in the first group (48 per cent) than in the second (17 per cent). In table 5.5, total poverty increased by 21 per cent in the first group of countries, 14 per cent in the second, and 13 per cent in the third. Clearly, uncontrolled inflation had devastating effects on the poor, particularly the urban poor.

The structure of poverty was thus sharply altered by the decade of crisis. A class of new poor created out of the middle class emerged and displaced the mass of absolute poverty from the rural to the urban sector. With impoverishment of the urban middle class, inequality increased sharply. While this suggests that the informal sector has in the short run become the new buffer for poverty alleviation, it is also the case that the new poor will be the first to be re-absorbed in productive employment as soon as economic growth picks up, as it is starting to do in the countries that have been successful at stabilisation and the renewal of growth. The rural areas will thus again be the locus of the greatest incidence of poverty and where the depth of poverty will remain by far the most extensive. For this reason, effective rural development will continue to be the fundamental component of any meaningful strategy of poverty reduction.

Turning to social expenditures, *per capita* expenditures on education and health had been rising rapidly during the 1970–82 period, faster than *per capita* GDP. While GDP *per capita* increased at the average annual rate of 1.9 per cent between 1970 and 1982 in the nine countries in table 5.6, *per capita* education expenditures rose at the rate of 3.9 per cent and health expenditures of 5.4 per cent. Indeed very significant improvements had been achieved in the 1970s in reducing the illiteracy rate, the infant mortality rate, and extending life expectancy. The distressing observation for the 1982–87 period is that these expenditures have been sharply reduced, not only across the board, but more extensively in the countries that have stabilised and grown, since recovery has been largely based on extensive fiscal austerity. In these countries, health expenditures have been reduced much more sharply than education expenditures. Even though the indicators of life expectancy, illiteracy, and infant mortality have continued

Table 5.5. *Latin America: population in poverty, 1980 and 1986 (numbers in thousands; incidence is percentage within the corresponding sector)*

	Group I: Failure to stabilise				Group II: Stabilisation without growth			Group III: Stabilisation and growth			Total		
	Argentina	Peru	Brazil	Sub-total	Venezuela	Mexico	Sub-total	Costa Rica	Colombia	Sub-total	Six countries[a]	Seven countries	Latin America
Rural poverty													
Numbers													
1980	960	4696	25768	31425	1457	13447	14958	343	4018	4361	37242	49211	73000
1986	1023	4722	23882	29626	1511			447	4180	4627	35764		75800
% change	6.5	0.5	−7.3	−5.7	3.7			30.5	4.0	6.1	−4.0		3.8
Incidence													
1980	19	80	68	64	43	51	50	28	48	45	60	56	60
1986	20	72	66	62	42			30	45	43	57		60
% points	1	−8	−2	−2	−1			2	−3	−3	−3		0
Urban poverty													
Numbers													
1980	1968	4150	25211	31329	2150	14628	18791	194	6895	7089	40569	73468	62900
1986	3707	5513	37151	46370	4164			279	8027	8307	58840		94400
% change	88.3	32.8	47.4	48.0	93.6			44.0	16.4	17.2	45.0		50.1
Incidence													
1980	9	38	34	29	20	30	30	18	40	39	29	34	30
1986	15	52	38	35	30			24	40	39	35		36
% points	6	14	4	6	10			6	0	0	5		6

Total poverty

Numbers													
1980	2929	8846	50979	62754	3607	26029	29637	536	10913	11450	77811	103840	135900
1986	4729	10234	61033	75997	5674	28075	33749	726	12207	12933	94604	122679	170200
% change	61.5	15.7	19.7	21.1	57.3	7.9	13.9	35.4	11.9	13.0	21.6	18.1	25.2
Incidence													
1980	10	53	45	39	25	40	37	24	42	41	38	39	41
1986	16	60	45	42	32	37	36	27	42	41	41	40	43
% points	6	7	0	2	7	−3	−1	3	0	0	2	1	2

Note:
a Excluding Mexico due to incomplete data.
Source: Feres and León (1990).

Table 5.6. *Latin America: social indicators, 1970–87* (average annual growth rate *per capita* (%))

		1970–82	1982–87
Group I: Failure to stabilise			
Argentina	Real GDP	−0.2	−0.2
	Education expenditures	4.8	0.1
	Health expenditures	1.1	14.8
Peru	Real GDP	0.3	−2.8
	Education expenditures	−2.6	−2.0
	Health expenditures	1.5	−0.9
Brazil	Real GDP	4.2	3.1
	Education expenditures	0.7	17.8
	Health expenditures	6.8	−6.8
Simple averages	Real GDP	1.4	0.0
	Education expenditures	1.0	5.3
	Health expenditures	3.1	2.4
Group II: Stabilisation without growth			
Venezuela	Real GDP	0.1	−3.2
	Education expenditures	3.6	−3.8
	Health expenditures	−0.6	−4.6
Mexico	Real GDP	3.2	−2.1
	Education expenditures	10.8	−7.2
	Health expenditures	4.7	15.8
Simple averages	Real GDP	1.7	−2.7
	Education expenditures	7.2	−5.5
	Health expenditures	2.1	5.6
Group III: Stabilisation and growth			
Costa Rica	Real GDP	1.6	1.2
	Education expenditures	1.6	1.5
	Health expenditures	8.8	−21.6
Ecuador	Real GDP	4.8	−1.3
	Education expenditures	10.7	−6.4
	Health expenditures	23.1	−20.1
Chile	Real GDP	0.2	2.3
	Education expenditures	−1.6	−2.6
	Health expenditures	0.7	−7.1
Colombia	Real GDP	3.1	2.2
	Education expenditures	7.1	3.7
	Health expenditures	2.2	0.0
Simple averages	Real GDP	2.4	1.1
	Education expenditures	4.5	−1.0
	Health expenditures	8.7	−12.2

Table 5.6. *contd*

	1970–82	1982–87
All nine countries		
Simple averages Real GDP	1.9	−0.1
Education expenditures	3.9	0.1
Health expenditures	5.4	−3.4

Source: Inter-American Development Bank (1989).

to improve during the 1980s due to lags in response, this suggests that recovery may have been obtained at a high cost in terms of long-run welfare, a cost that will become fully visible only in the next decade unless the levels of these expenditures are rapidly restored. Continued growth in health and education expenditures in the countries that have failed to stabilise only suggests future expected sharp falls. Recent hyperinflation indeed suggests that the need to impose fiscal austerity will be all the more stringent.

In many countries, notably Mexico and Bolivia, falling expenditures on food subsidies have been cushioned by targeting aid to the poorest social groups. While there was massive waste and inefficiency in food subsidy budgets before the crisis, the middle class has again been left aside by targeting the neediest.

Simulations with income equations

Although we do not have direct observations on household incomes before and after the crisis, we can simulate its effects on different groups from observed changes in the wage bill by type of employment, operating surplus (value added net of the wage bill) by economic sector and transfers. We propose here a simple methodology that can easily be applied to other countries using a household income survey and national accounts data. We start for this purpose from the sources of income that characterise each class. For Ecuador they are derived from a household survey carried out before the crisis in 1975 (see table 5.7).

We distinguish between seven social classes: three in the urban sector (low-, medium-, and high-education) and four in the rural sector (non-agricultural households, and small, medium and large farmers). The sources of income show the importance for small farmers of unskilled non-agricultural labour (37 per cent of total income) and of agricultural labour (22.5 per cent of total income). For large farmers, by contrast, domestic

Table 5.7. *Ecuador: sources of income by class, 1975*

Social classes	Class income (million sucres)	Labour income (%)				Unincorporated capital income (%)							Transfers (%)		
		Ag. labour	Non-ag. labour		Govt	Ag. exports	Other ag.	Cons. goods ind.	Prod. goods ind.	Util., const., transport	Trade	Services	Distributed profits	Other households	Govt
			Unskilled	Skilled											
Urban groups:															
Low-education	70910	1.4	41.4	5.2	6.8	2.1	0.6	10.2	1.5	7.9	7.5	4.5	1.3	6.0	3.8
Medium-education	55499	0.5	30.5	17.4	14.7	0.3	0.5	4.5	1.9	4.0	5.3	5.6	1.9	7.6	5.3
High-education	37893	0.3	4.4	37.7	27.3	0.6	0.3	0.4	0.4	1.7	1.2	8.3	2.6	9.7	4.9
Rural groups:															
Rural non-ag.	19254	3.2	36.9	5.7	6.8	8.9	0.2	7.3	1.4	6.9	11.6	6.4	0.5	3.6	0.6
Small farmers	33966	22.5	37.0	2.2	4.3	4.9	4.4	5.8	1.3	3.8	5.5	2.6	0.1	4.2	1.3
Medium farmers	11326	30.2	15.2	1.5	2.2	11.8	22.1	3.2	0.6	2.6	5.0	3.0	0.1	2.4	0.2
Large farmers	13093	22.5	8.4	2.3	2.3	16.5	29.7	1.8	0.4	4.2	6.2	3.1	0.4	1.7	0.4

market-oriented agriculture (other agriculture) and agricultural exports are the main sources of income, accounting respectively for 29.7 per cent and 16.5 per cent of total income. In the urban sector, the low-education households depend fundamentally on unskilled labour income (41.4 per cent of total income) but also on unincorporated capital income earned in the informal sector from consumer goods production, transport, trade and services (30.1 per cent of total income). High-education households, essentially formal sector workers and government employees, depend on skilled labour income (37.7 per cent of total income), government employment (27.3 per cent) and transfers (14.6 per cent).

From the national accounts data, we know the wage bills, the operating surplus, and the level of GDP for three important periods: rapid economic growth under 'Dutch disease' conditions in 1975–80; economic slowdown in 1980–82; and the debt crisis and implementation of stabilisation policies in 1982–87. The wage bill is available for agricultural labour, unskilled and skilled non-agricultural labour and government employment. Operating surplus is available for seven sectors that provide profit income to the seven household types: agricultural exports, other agriculture, consumer goods industry, producer goods industry, utilities, construction and transport, trade and services. Distributed profits and transfers from other households, foreign countries and government are assumed to change proportionately to GNP.

Price indexes for each of these sectors are also available from the national accounts. The GDP deflator is used for transfers. From knowledge of the consumption structure for each social class, a class-specific price index can be constructed. Using the observed changes in wage bills, operating surpluses and GDP, the sources of income for each social class and the class-specific price indexes, we can calculate the class-specific changes in levels of real income between the four years (table 5.8).

The simulation results show clearly how the oil and debt booms in 1975–80, combined with import-substitution industrialisation, boosted profits in industry and services while hurting those in agriculture. After 1980, and especially after 1982, with strong real exchange-rate depreciation and fiscal austerity, profits derived from the agricultural sector increased sharply while those in industry and services stagnated, the first because of trade liberalisation and the second because of real exchange-rate effects.

The wage bill rose very rapidly in industry and government services during the boom years 1975–80 while that in agriculture lagged behind. After 1982, the position reversed, with wages in agriculture falling less sharply than those in industry. In contrast to many other Latin American countries, the government wage bill in Ecuador fell only marginally after 1980.

140   **Alain de Janvry and Elisabeth Sadoulet**

Table 5.8. *Ecuador: simulation results, 1975–87*

	1975	1980	1982	1987	Change over the period (%)		
					1975–80	1980–82	1982–87
Wage bill							
Agriculture	100	127	101	71	27	−20	−30
Non-agriculture	100	153	147	103	53	−4	−30
Govt employees	100	138	134	134	38	−3	0
Operating surplus							
Agriculture	100	88	99	151	−12	13	53
Industry	100	175	224	276	75	28	23
Services	100	135	138	171	35	2	24
Real per capita *income (1975 = 100)*							
Urban groups:							
Low-education	100	131	116	92	31	−11	−21
Medium-education	100	131	116	89	31	−11	−23
High-education	100	131	118	81	31	−10	−31
Rural groups:							
Rural non-ag.	100	151	140	122	51	−7	−13
Small farmers	100	148	132	103	48	−11	−22
Medium farmers	100	129	115	99	29	−11	−14
Large farmers	100	123	111	104	23	−10	−6

Using data on the distribution of population between rural and urban areas over time, these effects are integrated in the calculation of class-specific real *per capita* incomes, y_k, by taking the total differential of the total income of each class in the following income equation:

$$y_k = \frac{\sum_l w_l L_{kl} + \sum_i \Pi_{ki} + \sum_z T_{kz}}{CPI_k}$$

where:

$w_l L_{kl}$ is the labour income derived by class k in labour category l, l = 1, ..., 4

Π_{ki} is the operating surplus derived by class k in sector i, i = 1, ..., 7

T_{kz} is the transfer income received by class k from source z, z = 1, ..., 4

CPI_k is the CPI for class k

The results (table 5.8) show that small farmers were the main beneficiaries during the boom years, followed by the urban classes, while the large farmers lagged behind. For the small farmers, this resulted from the high share in their total income of earnings from non-agricultural employment where the wage bill was rising rapidly. In Ecuador, as in much of Latin America, this was due to the growing integration of urban and rural labour markets and to employment of landless and small farmers in urban construction and services which were booming under 'Dutch disease' conditions. For the urban classes, rising incomes were due to a mix of a rising wage bill and operating surplus in industry. These results confirm that rapid economic expansion under 'Dutch disease' conditions is highly detrimental to agriculture and, within agriculture, to farmers producing a marketed surplus of tradeables.

Policy adjustments to the crisis after 1982, by contrast, hurt the larger farmers least. As we have seen in the previous section, this was largely due to strong depreciation of the real exchange rate and to the implementation of fiscal policies that cut current more than investment expenditures and served to preserve growth in agriculture. Worst hit were the urban and especially the medium- and high-education groups: wage bills fell in non-agriculture and operating surpluses declined in industry and services. Industry that had been recently created under import-substitution policies was not competitive with a liberalised equilibrium exchange rate, while the services sector was hurt by depreciation of the real exchange rate and stagnant effective demand.

Simulation through income equations thus confirms that, in relative terms, it is the urban classes that have been hit the hardest and, among them, the middle- and high-education groups. Farmers fared better, particularly larger farmers who are heavily involved in the production of agricultural exports and have a marketed surplus in food crops. The crisis thus reallocated poverty from the rural to the urban sectors, even though most poverty remains rural. It narrowed inequalities in the distribution of income in the urban sector and widened them in rural areas.

These observations suggest that rural development initiatives could be organised to capitalise on agriculture's better production performance compared to other sectors of the economy, and to help small farmers benefit from agricultural growth as large farmers have done. Linking rural poverty alleviation to agricultural growth opens new development possibilities, which we explore in the next section.

Adjustment and rural development

Though still in the making and poorly evidenced, there has been a significant rethinking of the 1970s' approach to rural development as stabilisation and adjustment have proceeded. This approach, which was pioneered by the World Bank after 1973, focused on integrated development projects where state agencies actively managed the delivery of subsidies and services to peasant communities or to individual households. The Puebla project in Mexico and the Colombian DRI are archetypal examples.

Changes in thinking on rural development stem from several sources. First, there was widespread acknowledgement of the failure of the 1970s' approach and corresponding fatigue of the sponsoring governments and agencies (Leonard, 1984). Second, the approach was largely based on plentiful government budgets and the use of rural development schemes to transfer resources to weaker sectors of society. The massive Mexican Food System (Sistema Alimentario Mexicano, or SAM) project is typical: with oil rents appropriated by the stronger sectors and the benefits of rapid growth under 'Dutch disease' conditions accruing largely to the urban populations, the project was used as a compensatory mechanism and to achieve non-economic objectives such as a greater degree of national food self-sufficiency. After the early 1980s, fiscal resources were no longer available for transfer and the project had to be massively scaled down.

Third, the role of the State in economic development came in for fundamental reconsideration (Fishlow, 1990). The State had been prominent in promoting Latin American economic growth, most importantly through the strategy of import-substitution industrialisation. But the 1980s have seen a rapid process of trade liberalisation, privatisation and reduced government expenditures. This was prompted by the necessary adjustments to the economic crisis of the 1980s as well as by the successful examples of Asian development, an ideological shift away from the teachings of dependency theory and pressure for policy reform in the conditions set for new loans by the international lending agencies. While the debate is far from settled, the new Latin American consensus does not appear to be one of undirected free trade but of a stronger State with a reduced but more efficient presence in those areas complementary to private activity: the delivery of public goods, the correction of externalities and monopolies, the provision of public investments when social discount rates differ from private ones, and the management of social justice. For rural development, this signals a State less directly involved in the management of projects and more in the provision of favourable policy and structural conditions for rural development to take place under the aegis of other institutions.

Fourth, the special role of agriculture as a leading sector of economic growth in the recovery period has created opportunities for some smallholders to participate in the production of agricultural exports and import substitutes. Often, however, terms of trade effects have not been passed through to them because of inadequate policy interventions or monopolistic merchants, and state compression and institutional discrimination have not allowed them to reallocate their resources to the newly favoured activities.

Fifth, the rise of democracy and the widespread decentralisation of government have allowed the rural poor to make new claims on their political representatives. With limited fiscal resources for welfare, these claims have often been answered by transferring productive assets to the poor, as in the north-east of Brazil (Tendler, 1988). In other situations, rural development schemes have been managed by non-governmental organisations using resources transferred by central (Ecuador) or local (Brazil) governments.

Sixth, the 1970s and 1980s have witnessed the massive rise of grass-roots organisations, in part as a response to the suppression of traditional centralised social organisations by military governments. These organisations take the form of Christian community groups, neighbourhood associations, social clubs, producer associations, etc. They provide new channels for the transfer of resources and for the management of rural development schemes.

Finally, growing environmental concerns arising from massive deforestation in the humid tropics, deforestation and soil erosion in the watersheds and depletion of underground water tables, has increased interest in rural development strategies which internalise some of the externalities created by poverty. The debt crisis has further increased the cost of these externalities (e.g., the need to import food and oil as water reservoirs are rapidly silted by soil erosion in the watersheds). The possibility of using rural development to promote environmental protection, transferring resources by taxing those who would benefit from reducing the externalities of poverty, has opened up new approaches. A rapidly growing number of ecologically motivated rural development organisations and projects throughout Latin America is symptomatic of the spread of these new approaches.

These new approaches to rural development are only beginning to emerge, but some of their main traits can be discerned. They will become more heterogeneous with decentralisation and better tailored to the great heterogeneity of rural poverty (de Janvry and Sadoulet, 1990). They will rely to a large extent on a new partnership between government and grass-roots organisations. They will be based less on the transfer of resources (e.g., subsidised credit) than on the promotion of new institutions able to mobilise local resources (e.g., the Grameen Bank model). They will have a strong non-agricultural component to capture the linkage effects of agricultural development; these activities will be located as far as possible in the rural areas to provide complementary sources of income for peasant households and reduce the external costs of excessively rapid urban migration. And they will have a strong environmental purpose, involving the transfer of resources as payment for the reduction of increasingly costly national and international externalities of poverty.

Conclusion

We have shown in this chapter that agriculture has made important contributions to economic recovery in Latin America and that the countries that have been most successful are also those where agriculture has an important weight. This is due both to the foreign exchange contribution of agriculture and to the political support for stabilisation generated by an agrarian coalition. Agriculture itself has benefited from the most effective instruments used for stabilisation: depreciation of the real exchange rate and fiscal austerity directed at current expenditures. On balance, however, the growth of agriculture has been determined more by non-price factors such as public investment and overall economic growth than by the incentives provided by real exchange-rate depreciation.

Rural poverty remains pervasive throughout Latin America and poverty increased as *per capita* GDP fell through the 1980s. It is not, however, the agricultural poor who have borne the main cost of the crisis, but the urban classes, particularly workers in the formal sector and government employees. Since these sectors embody an important share of national human capital, special retraining and credit programmes need to be set up to reincorporate them productively in a restructured economy. Many of the rural poor depend for employment on urban labour markets and their real incomes have fallen alongside those of urban unskilled workers.

Improved incentives for agriculture and proper management of fiscal austerity to preserve public investment in agriculture have provided new possibilities for rural development and rural poverty reduction. But much remains to be done to define and implement a new approach to rural development adapted to the situation of market liberalisation, state contraction, newly recovered democratic rights and a burgeoning of grass-roots organisations, new social actors and new social movements. We have identified a number of features of this new model. They include a redefined role for the State that confines it to the areas where it has a unique role; use of grass-roots organisations, often in partnership with the State, to provide access to resources; promotion of enabling conditions to ease poverty that stress development of human capital, local institutions and new employment opportunities, especially in non-agricultural activities; and internalisation of environmental externalities that failed rural development imposes on the rest of society.

References

Adelman, I., 1975. 'Growth, income distribution and equity-oriented development strategies', *World Development*, vol. 3, nos. 2–3, February–March, pp. 67–76.

Commander, S. (ed.), 1989. *Structural Adjustment and Agriculture: Theory and Practice in Africa and Latin America*, London: James Currey and Heinemann.

Dantwala, M. and V. Dandekar (eds.), 1989. *Indian Society of Agricultural Economics, Golden Jubilee Volume*, Delhi.

de Janvry, A. and E. Sadoulet, 1987. 'Agriculture price policy in General Equilibrium Models: Results and comparisons', *American Journal of Agricultural Economics*, vol. 69, no. 2, May, pp. 230–46.

1990. 'Rural development in Latin America: Relinking poverty reduction to growth', in M. Lipton and J. van der Gaag (eds.), *Proceedings of the Poverty Research Conference*, Washington, DC: International Food Policy Research Institute and World Bank.

de Janvry, A., E. Sadoulet and A. Fargeix, 1991. *Adjustment and Equity in Ecuador*, Paris: OECD.

Dervis, K., J. de Melo and S. Robinson, 1982. *General Equilibrium Models for Developing Countries*, New York: Cambridge University Press.

Fargeix, A., 1990. 'Stabilization policies and income distribution: A computable general equilibrium model for Ecuador', Ph.D. dissertation, Department of Agricultural and Resource Economics, University of California, Berkeley.

Feres, J.C. and A. León, 1990. 'The magnitude of poverty in Latin America', *CEPAL Review*, no. 41, August, pp. 133–51.

Fishlow, A., 1990. 'The Latin American State', *Journal of Economic Perspectives*, vol. 4, no. 3, pp. 61–74.

Inter-American Development Bank, 1986. *Economic and Social Progress in Latin America, 1986 Report*, Washington, DC: Inter-American Development Bank.

1989. *Economic and Social Progress in Latin America, 1989 Report*, Washington, DC: Inter-American Development Bank.

1990. *Economic and Social Progress in Latin America, 1990 Report*, Washington, DC: Inter-American Development Bank.

Leonard, D., 1984. 'Disintegrating agricultural development', *Food Research Institute Studies*, vol. 19, no. 2, pp. 177–86.

Lipton, M., 1989. 'State compression: Friend or foe of agricultural liberalization?', in Dantwala and Dandekar (eds.) (1989).

Mundlak, Y., 1985. *The Aggregate Agricultural Supply*, Working Paper, no. 8511, Center for Agricultural Economic Research, Rehovot, Israel.

Nelson, J., 1988. 'The politics of pro-poor adjustment policies', Symposium on Poverty and Adjustment, Washington, DC: World Bank.

Rao, J.M. and J.M. Caballero, 1990. 'Agricultural performance and development strategy: Retrospect and prospect', *World Development*, vol. 18, no. 6, June, pp. 899–913.

Selowsky, M., 1989. *Preconditions Necessary for the Recovery of Latin American Growth*, Washington, DC: World Bank.

Stein, L., 1989. 'Third World poverty, economic growth, and income distribution', *Canadian Journal of Development Studies*, vol. 10, no. 2, pp. 225–40.

Tendler, J., 1988. *Northeast Brazil Rural Development Evaluation: First Impressions*, Department of Urban Studies and Planning, Massachusetts Institute of Technology, December, mimeo.

Timmer, P., 1988. *Getting the Prices Right*, Baltimore: Johns Hopkins University Press.

Valdés, A., 1986. 'Impact of trade and macroeconomic policies on agricultural growth: The South American experience', in Inter-American Development Bank (1986).

Part II

6 Alternative development strategies and the rural sector

AMIT BHADURI

Supply-side potentials and alternative development strategies

In many ways a development strategy can be regarded as an attempt to short-circuit economic history. Today's developing countries might have been content with their 'natural' pace of historical evolution, if it were not for unacceptably large disparities in *per capita* income and output between rich and poor nations. Not only do these huge disparities exist but developing countries are more acutely aware of them than ever before. For most of these countries this creates an overwhelming political compulsion to hasten the pace of economic development. The essence of economic development becomes the speed with which *per capita* income and output can be raised in a sustained manner.

Differences between nations in *per capita* income and output are indeed enormous. *Per capita* income is about twenty times higher in the developed market economies than the average for all developing countries. It is about fifty times that for the low-income developing countries and about five times the average for the upper-middle-income developing countries (see Appendix, pp. 172–4, table 6A.1).

However, *per capita* output or income is a composite statistic and needs to be decomposed in order to understand the origins of such large differences. The three components which statistically must account for the differences are:
(a) the participation ratio (the share of economically active in total population);
(b) the sectoral composition or occupational distribution of the active population; and
(c) sectoral labour productivities.

Sectoral labour productivities weighted by sectoral composition of active population and adjusted for the participation ratio yield *per capita* output according to the formula:

$$\frac{X}{N} = \frac{X_a + X_i + X_s}{L} \cdot \frac{L}{N} \equiv \left[\frac{X_a}{L_a} \cdot \frac{L_a}{L} + \frac{X_i}{L_i} \cdot \frac{L_i}{L} + \frac{X_s}{L_s} \cdot \frac{L_s}{L} \right] \cdot \frac{L}{N}$$

or, more compactly,

$$\frac{X}{N} \equiv y = r \sum_j x_j w_j; \ \sum_j w_j = 1; \ j = a, i, s \qquad (6.1)$$

where X = output (GDP)
       N = population
       L = labour force

       y = X/N = *per capita* income or output (GDP)
       r = L/N = participation ratio
       x_j = labour productivity in sector j
       w_j = proportion of labour force in sector j

and subscripts a, i and s stand for agriculture (primary), industry (secondary) and services (tertiary) sectors respectively.

The statistical decomposition in (6.1) helps to identify the main sources for increasing *per capita* output in a developing country. Any development strategy must exploit these three sources of output growth in combination to initiate and sustain economic development.

First, and in the case of some labour-surplus economies most importantly, *the participation ratio* (r) may be raised through a reduction in open and disguised unemployment.

Second, the very different *occupational distribution* (w_j) of the labour force in developed and developing countries (table 6A.2, p. 173) probably accounts for the biggest part of the gap in *per capita* output. Because industry typically has much higher labour productivity than agriculture (see Appendix), any shift in the occupational distribution towards industry tends to increase overall labour productivity as well as *per capita* output. Conversely, a higher share of the labour force in agriculture depresses *per capita* output. Thus, in the developed market economies, roughly 7 per cent of the labour force works in agriculture, contributing about 4 per cent of GDP. In contrast, the developing economies have 62 per cent of their labour force in agriculture, contributing only about 16 per cent of GDP (table 6A.2, p. 173).[1] This demonstrates, in simple and dramatic terms, why developing countries typically feel compelled to industrialise. Their compulsion can be even better understood by a more detailed analysis of occupational distribution in relation to sectoral labour productivity (see Appendix). Although labour productivity in the agricultural sector (x_a) is lower than the national average in both developed and developing countries, the gap is much greater in developing countries and thus the economic advantage in terms of average labour productivity gain from transferring labour from agriculture to industry is much higher (see Appendix). Consequently, the exploitation of *intersectoral labour productivity differentials* through intersectoral labour transfer provides a central justification for an industrialisation-led development strategy.

Third, it should be pointed out that differences in labour productivity are actually largest within the agricultural sector itself. Output per worker in agriculture is 40 times higher in the developed than in the developing countries while output per worker in industry is about ten times higher (see Appendix).[2] This suggests that there may be considerable scope for raising labour productivity in agriculture in many developing countries. Thus, quite apart from questions of intersectoral balance in any development strategy, the potential for raising labour productivity through reorganisation of agriculture must not be overlooked.

These broad comparisons of occupational distribution and sectoral labour productivity also help us to schematise three *types or variants of development strategy* in terms of the emphasis placed on exploiting each of the three supply-side potentials for raising *per capita* output.

In the *first variant*, the main emphasis is on utilising surplus labour and raising the participation rate (r). This is sometimes described as the *strategy for extensive growth*, which is especially relevant for labour-surplus economies. However, whether the surplus labour should be absorbed mostly within agriculture and the rural sector or through a gradually expanding industrial and urban sector remains a debatable issue. Suffice it to mention here that much of the influential earlier literature on development economics (e.g., Lewis, 1954; Mahalanobis, 1953; Ranis and Fei, 1961) viewed the problem of surplus labour absorption as essentially one of intersectoral labour transfer through industrialisation. In this respect, it fused the concepts of extensive and intensive growth,[3] because transfer of labour from agriculture to industry would entail typically not only labour absorption ('extensive' growth) but also higher average labour productivity ('intensive' growth).

One of the main intellectual attractions of the *industrialisation-led development strategy* derives from this analysis. Extensive growth and surplus labour absorption are seen as two aspects of the same problem of intersectoral labour transfer through rapid industrialisation. Thus, instead of directly raising the participation ratio (r), this *second variant* of the development strategy assigns the central role to the exploitation of intersectoral labour productivity differentials through transfer of labour from agriculture to industry. Surplus labour absorption within the agricultural or rural sector receives little attention; instead, rising *per capita* output through a changing occupational structure in favour of industry becomes the main source of productivity growth, broadly in the image of the historical development of today's advanced market economies (see table 6A.3, p. 174).

Nevertheless, the range of labour-intensive industries and techniques is far too limited in general to absorb surplus labour at a sufficiently high rate. The experience of most developing countries has shown that industrialisation is primarily a process of *intensive* growth, where some increase in average labour productivity is achieved through intersectoral labour transfer but the industrial sector itself has relatively little ability to absorb labour. The *third variant* of the development strategy thus emphasises the need to modify the pace and content of industrialisation so as to pay greater attention to the rural/agricultural sector not merely as the traditional reservoir of labour for industrialisation, but as the sector which may have greater flexibility to absorb labour and generate extensive growth. It would, however, be misleading to describe this as an 'agriculture-first' strategy. Its main thrust is not the 'priority' of agriculture over other sectors, but an attempt to combine the advantages of industrialisation and intensive growth with extensive growth in agriculture achieved mainly through better labour absorption and a higher participation ratio.

To sum up, supply-side potentials for increasing *per capita* output exist in developing economies due to intrasectoral differences in labour productivity, extremely low productivity of labour in agriculture (compared to industry) by international standards and the possibility of raising the participation ratio. Development strategies need to exploit these three supply-side possibilities to the full. However, the most effective combination will vary from country to country depending on the specific situation. The purpose of economic analysis is to highlight the main economic linkages in particular contexts for judging the appropriateness of a particular development strategy, without claiming falsely that any particular development strategy is the most appropriate under all circumstances.

Sectoral autonomy in characterising alternative development strategies

The three major supply-side potentials for raising *per capita* output mentioned in the last section (see (6.1) above) are interlinked in various ways, reflecting the various demand and supply relations between sectors in developing economies. At the macroeconomic level, probably the most important and the most studied relation is the link between industry and agriculture. To avoid misunderstanding, two rather obvious points need to be mentioned. First, sectoral interlinkages deserve special attention when an economy operates under a serious balance-of-payments constraint with rather limited import capacity. This is because imbalances in demand or supply arising from the neglect of links between sectors cannot be met, by assumption, from sustained imports over time. Second, the agriculture–industry link is especially important in economies trying to industrialise because of the need to analyse the role agriculture can play in industrialisation. In what follows, we shall concentrate mostly on the situation of a predominantly agrarian economy trying to industrialise with a persistent foreign exchange constraint as the broad context for formulation of a development strategy.

The crux of a development strategy is to assess the extent to which expansion of a particular sector can be treated as an *exogenous* policy variable. This would mean that exogenous changes could be activated deliberately as a matter of development policy in that sector, while the other major sectors of the economy adjusted to it more or less passively and endogenously. In short, underlying a development strategy and its associated policies is an assumption (often implicit) of the degree of autonomy of a sector.

This distinction between exogenous and endogenous variables is a general feature of economic policy formulation and does not relate only to problems of development. Thus, the Keynesian theory of short-period income determination rests on the crucial assumption that expenditure – more specifically public investment as a component of aggregate expenditure – is the exogenous policy variable to which income and saving adjust as endogenous variables.[4] Similarly, the separation of 'targets' from 'instruments' in the design of economic policy (Tinbergen, 1952) also rests on a prior classification of economic variables into exogenous (instrument) and endogenous (target) variables.

Like all policy-oriented economic models, the formulation of a development strategy also needs to distinguish between exogenous and endogenous variables.[5] However, development strategies differ in the sectors identified as relatively exogenous. The classification of sectors into exogenous and endogenous variables for policy formulation has at least three important implications. *First*, the degree of exogeneity or autonomy of a sector may sometimes reflect considerations of administrative feasibility, rather than the intrinsic macro-economic properties of the model. For instance, massive development of small-scale irrigation or land consolidation sponsored by the State may be ruled out as administratively infeasible which, in turn, may reduce the autonomy or exogeneity of the agricultural sector for policy purposes.

Second, the debate over the 'priority' of agriculture *vis-à-vis* industry in a development strategy reduces essentially to the question of the relative autonomy of the two sectors. For instance, 'agriculture-first' can be easily justified if agriculture is assumed to be a relatively autonomous sector, so that its performance is not constrained by the performance of industry or industrial performance is assumed to adjust endogenously to agricultural performance. However, without such assumptions, it would be difficult to sustain the arguments in favour of an 'agriculture-first' strategy.

Third, all industrialisation-led development strategies assume, explicitly or implicitly, a significant degree of autonomy or exogeneity of the industrial sector, with the rural–agricultural sector adjusting more or less endogenously to the requirements of industrialisation. If it fails to adjust, the process of industrialisation runs into difficulties. The Lewis model (Lewis, 1954) can be used to illustrate this point. The assumption of an 'unlimited supply of labour' at a given real wage implies that the agricultural sector will adjust endogenously so that labour transfer from agriculture to industry will not hamper agricultural production. On the other hand, as Lewis himself argued, if agricultural prices rise because agricultural output fails to adjust to the demand from industry, the shift in the terms of trade in favour of agriculture will thwart the process of industrial accumulation by reducing industrial profit. With hindsight, an interesting innovation of the Lewis model was to 'break up' the agricultural (rural) sector, treating labour supply as endogenously adjustable but output supply as exogenously given.

In contrast to the Lewis model, which treated the agricultural sector as partly endogenous and partly exogenous in the above sense, the more extreme variants of industrialisation-led development strategies tend to treat the agricultural sector as almost completely endogenous, i.e., as a sector which would adjust more or less passively to the requirements of industrialisation. Although not explicitly stated, the Feldman–Mahalanobis model of 'heavy industrialisation' (Domar, 1957; Mahalanobis, 1953, 1955) falls into this category. The model, which provided some intellectual justification for rapid development of heavy industries in the context of early Soviet industrialisation and the Indian Second Five-Year Plan (1956–61), underplayed the constraints which such a process of industrialisation may face when the agricultural sector fails to adjust endogenously. In contrast, Kalecki (1972) presented a picture of industrialisation constantly threatened by lack of adequate wage goods, mostly 'food', because he treated the rate of growth of agricultural output as exogenous, almost the obverse of the Feldman–Mahalanobis model.

Viewed from this perspective, the appropriateness of the industrialisation-led development strategy depends on the viability of the assumption that the agricultural sector will adjust endogenously in response to industrialisation. This postulated adjustment process has several aspects of which the most important are: (i) generation of *marketed surplus*, intersectoral resource flow and terms of trade; (ii) the *real wage rate*; (iii) *incentive to invest*; and (iv) intersectoral *labour transfer* involving rural–urban migration. Both the viability of the assumption of endogeneity in agriculture and the limits to the industrialisation-led development strategy can be appreciated more clearly if we examine these different aspects of the adjustment process.

Limits to an industrialisation-led development strategy

Industrialisation-led development strategies in a *closed* economy can be classified into two broad categories according to the type of supply-side constraint envisaged. One class of models (e.g., Lewis, 1954; Kalecki, 1972) emphasises the role of limited availability of agricultural marketed surplus or production as the binding constraint on the process of industrial development. The other class of models (e.g., Domar, 1957; Mahalanobis, 1953, 1955) directs attention to the problem of limited capacity of the domestic capital goods sector for physically transforming savings (in terms of agricultural surplus) into a corresponding flow of investment goods. The latter problem and the strategy to overcome it are described succinctly by the Feldman–Mahalanobis model. In this model the role of the traditional agricultural sector is not even incorporated explicitly on the assumption that the level or rate of growth of agricultural surplus (cf. Kalecki, 1972) is not the binding constraint on the pace of industrialisation. Instead, by using the Marxian two-department scheme of a capital goods sector (Department 1) and a consumption goods sector (Department 2), the model elaborates a strategy for rapid development of the capital goods sector. Without going into details, in essence it identifies the rate of growth of the capital goods sector (Department 1) as the variable which is determined exogenously (irrespective of other macroeconomic relationships) by fixing the proportion of investment devoted to that sector (λ) and its capital–output ratio (u_k). Thus, additional capacity created in the capital goods sector (ΔI) is given by

$$\Delta I = \frac{\lambda I}{u_k} \tag{6.2}$$

from which it immediately follows that the growth rate of that sector (g_k) is governed by

$$g_k \equiv \frac{\Delta I}{I} = \frac{\lambda}{u_k} \tag{6.3}$$

Since by assumption the capacity of the capital goods sector operates as the binding constraint on the process of industrialisation, it follows that the relaxation of this constraint over time requires a high rate of growth of 'heavy' industries (g_k) which can be achieved by devoting a consistently high proportion (λ) of investment to that sector.

Several implicit and controversial macroeconomic assumptions are embodied in this model to make 'heavy' industrialisation a viable development strategy, even in a closed economy. As already pointed out, the model is non-committal on whether the rapid growth of heavy industries will be associated with increased extraction of agricultural surplus sufficient to maintain the real wage (in terms of 'food') of the industrial sector. Alternatively, the industrial sector itself may be expected to 'finance' the process of heavy industrialisation through a lower industrial real wage rate, without significant net resource transfer from agriculture.[6]

In political terms a heavy industrialisation strategy involves an awkward choice which tends to create major difficulties when pursued over a long period of time, as was recognised partly even in the early debates on Soviet industrialisation. If the real wage rate of industrial workers is maintained during 'heavy' industrialisation by forcibly extracting marketed surplus at an increasing rate from agriculture, then the peasantry and the agricultural sector bear disproportionately the burden of industrialisation. Thus they tend to become alienated politically under policies of massive net resource transfers from agriculture to carry out 'forced' industrialisation, a strategy which was articulated intellectually by Preobrazhensky and, to some extent, carried out ruthlessly by Stalin. As Preobrazhensky argued, the exchange (terms of trade) of agricultural products for essential industrial consumer goods can be made so unfavourable for the peasants that they are *forced* to part with the amount of agricultural surplus required for industrialisation. This can be brought about by administratively holding down agricultural prices or by imposing heavy indirect commodity taxes on essential industrial consumer goods bought by the peasants, policies which, with some variations, were pursued recently in an attempt to industrialise at a forced pace in several African countries. Almost invariably, such State-sponsored industrialisation in the African context ran into grave difficulties, as the peasantry in these predominantly agrarian economies gradually began to lose rather than gain from industrialisation (cf. Saith, 1990).

In contrast to the strategy of forcible extraction of agricultural surplus, the process of industrialisation may be 'financed' by voluntary exchange. In the context of the Soviet debate on industrialisation, this strategy is usually associated with the name of Bukharin and it has an important political dimension in so far as it tries to forge an alliance between the peasantry and industrial workers. The idea is to induce, rather than force, the peasantry to exchange voluntarily the required quantum of agricultural surplus against industrial (consumer) goods on reasonably favourable terms of trade for agriculture. The problem is that the level and rate of growth of industrial consumption goods (Department 2) will be determined by the requirement for generating agricultural surplus and so, as a result, will the proportion of investment devoted to consumer goods industries (i.e., $1 - \lambda$, see (6.2) and (6.3) above). Thus, the ability to fix *independently* the growth rate of the heavy industrial sector (by freely choosing the value of λ, see (6.3)) has to be surrendered in order to generate adequate agricultural surplus. In short, it becomes difficult to reconcile analytically the generation of agricultural surplus voluntarily (*à la* Bukharin) with the freedom to choose a high rate of growth of heavy industries as the exogenous variable of the model.

However, a development strategy concentrating on heavy industries along Feldman–Mahalanobis lines emerges in a different light if the *real* wage rate of urban industrial workers is treated as flexible. Although in the theoretical debate on early Soviet industrialisation the option of depressing the real wage of industrial workers was never considered seriously,[7] there is some evidence to suggest that the urban real wage did fall during some phases of that industrialisation. The implication is that the industrial sector itself bore part of the burden of 'financing' the cost of industrialisation (cf. Ellman, 1975). Consequently, orthodox models which stipulate that the *entire* cost of industrialisation would be met by net resource transfer from agriculture to industry may be oversimplistic both in theory and in the light of historical experience. Cross-country empirical studies of industrialisation experiences suggest that in fact there is no unique pattern of net resource transfer between industry and agriculture. The study by Karshenas (chapter 7 in this volume), which considers intersectoral resource transfer in five countries, points out that '"the net finance contribution" of agriculture to the growth of other sectors appears to have been negative in most of the economies in the sample and for much of the observation period' (p. 219). Thus, rigid industrialisation-led development strategies which rely explicitly or implicitly on the assumption of a passive agricultural sector adjusting endogenously to the requirements of industry, especially in terms of net intersectoral resource transfer, seem mostly not to work in practice. And, to the extent that the agricultural sector fails to adjust by providing adequate surplus, this will be reflected typically in terms of *either* a slower pace of industrial accumulation *or* downward pressure on the industrial real wage rate.

Many 'dual economy' models following Lewis' seminal work (Lewis, 1954, 1958) highlight the mechanism by which industrial accumulation may slow due to inadequate provision of agricultural surplus. The logical core of the model consists of the assumption that the real wage in terms of 'food' (i.e., agricultural product) is given so that the *real* wage in industry is inflexible by assumption. However, the *product* wage of industry, i.e., the wage in terms of industrial goods, is flexible in so far as the terms of trade between agriculture and industry are also flexible because, by definition,

$$\frac{w}{P_a} \equiv \frac{w}{P_i} \cdot \frac{P_i}{P_a} \tag{6.4}$$

where P_a = price level of agricultural products
   w/P_a = real wage in terms of 'food' (assumed constant)
   P_i = price level of industrial products and
   w/P_i = product wage in terms of industrial products

As the faster pace of industrialisation increases the demand for food, inadequate provision of agricultural surplus manifests itself in the movement of the terms of trade in favour of agriculture which lowers (P_i/P_a). With a constant real wage in terms of agricultural product (i.e., (w/P_a) constant), it is evident from (6.4) that the product wage in industry (w/P_i) must rise. This implies lower profit margins in industry and, under the usual neo-classical assumption of profit maximisation (i.e., product wage equals the marginal product of labour), the levels of employment, profit, saving and investment all fall in the industrial sector to slow down the pace of industrial accumulation. More formally, using linear approximation for the marginal productivity of labour in the industrial sector, we have from (6.4) and the first-order profit maximisation condition,

$$\frac{w}{P_i} \equiv \frac{w}{P_a} \cdot \frac{P_a}{P_i} = a - bL_i, \ a, \ b > 0 \tag{6.5}$$

or

$$L_i = \frac{1}{b}\left[a - T \cdot \frac{w}{P_a}\right], \ T = P_a/P_i \tag{6.6}$$

It follows from (6.6) that industrial employment (L_i) decreases as the relative price of agricultural goods (T) increases. Further, the real profit of the industrial sector, which is assumed to be saved and invested back in industry, is given as

$$R_i = \frac{bL_i^2}{2} = \frac{1}{2b}\left[a - T \cdot \frac{w}{P_a}\right]^2 \tag{6.7}$$

Consequently, both industrial profit and saving fall as the terms of trade move in favour of agriculture, i.e., T rises, resulting also in a fall in industrial investment in so far as it can be assumed to be governed by the saving of that sector.[8]

If the rate of industrial accumulation does not slow down despite inadequate provision of agricultural surplus, then the Lewis-type assumption of a constant real wage rate in terms of 'food' must be deemed to be untenable. Without additional net resource transfer from agriculture to industry, additional industrial investment can be financed only by depressing the real wage rate, resulting in 'forced saving' on the part of workers through an inflationary rise in the price of food and/or other consumer goods in relation to money wages (cf. Keynes, 1930; Kaldor, 1955–1956).

The magnitude of this problem of depressed real wages, as a result of an exogenously given rapid expansion of capital goods industries, can be seen by assuming that the industrial real wage consists entirely of industrial consumption goods. Alternatively, we may assume a *constant* exchange ratio between industrial consumption goods and agricultural products ('food') which remains sufficiently high (*à la* Bukharin) to obtain the necessary agricultural products. Suppose:

P = general price level
x = average labour productivity

and assume for algebraic simplicity[9]

$Px = P_k x_k = P_c x_c$ (i.e., uniform nominal labour productivity)

where subscripts k and c stand for the capital goods ('heavy') and consumer goods ('light') industrial sectors.

Since the total industrial labour force is divided between the two sectors, i.e., $L_k + L_c = L$, the investment-saving equality or the initial balance between demand and supply of consumption goods entails

$$PxL_k = sh\, PxL,$$

or

$$L_k/L = sh \text{ and } L_c/L = (1 - sh) \tag{6.8}$$

where s ($1 > s > 0$) is the constant fraction of profit saved (all the wage is consumed by assumption) and h ($1 > h > 0$) is the fraction of profit in value added of either sector. From (6.8) we obtain:

$$\frac{\Delta L_k}{L_k} = \frac{\Delta h}{h} + \frac{\Delta L}{L} \tag{6.9}$$

i.e., any increase in employment of the 'heavy' industrial sector must be matched *either* by an increase in consumer goods output and total employment ($\Delta L/L$) *or* by a lower real wage rate and a higher share of profit ($\Delta h/h$) in the economy. Further, by definition,

$$Px\,(1 - h) = w$$

where w = uniform money wage rate and, consequently,

$$\frac{\Delta h}{h} = \left[\frac{1-h}{h}\right] \cdot \left[\frac{\Delta P}{P} + \frac{\Delta x}{x} - \frac{\Delta w}{w}\right] \tag{6.10}$$

Using (6.8), (6.9) and (6.10), we obtain the extent of the depression in the real wage as a result of faster growth of 'heavy' industries (the K-sector) as

$$\frac{\Delta P}{P} - \frac{\Delta w}{w} = \left[\frac{h(1-sh)}{1-h}\right] \cdot \left[\frac{\Delta L_k}{L_k} - \frac{\Delta L_c}{L_c}\right] - \frac{\Delta x}{x} \tag{6.11}$$

Since in the Feldman–Mahalanobis model we have (see also equation (6.3))

$$\frac{\Delta L_k}{L_k} - \frac{\Delta L_c}{L_c} = \frac{\lambda}{u_k} - \frac{(1-\lambda)}{u_c} \cdot \frac{I}{C} = \frac{\lambda}{u_k} - \left[\frac{(1-\lambda)}{u_c} \cdot \frac{L_k}{L_c}\right]$$

equation (6.11) can also be rewritten as

$$\frac{\Delta P}{P} - \frac{\Delta w}{w} = \left[\frac{h(1-sh)}{1-h}\right]\left[\frac{\lambda}{u_k} - \frac{(1-\lambda)}{u_c} \cdot \frac{sh}{(1-sh)}\right] - \frac{\Delta x}{x} \tag{6.12}$$

Thus, if $s = 0.5$, $h = 0.8$, $u_k = 3:1$ and $u_c = 2:1$, then $\lambda = 0.6$, so that a 20 per cent growth in the heavy industry (K-) sector (see equation (6.3)) implies a 16 per cent reduction in the *real* wage in terms of industrial consumption goods, assuming no growth in labour productivity (i.e., $\Delta x/x = 0$).

The distinction between capital goods (K-sector) and consumption goods (C-sector) within industry in the Feldman–Mahalanobis model, or the industry–agriculture classification in the Lewis-type model, highlights the interaction between important macroeconomic variables to show various possibilities such as: how the level of industrial investment adjusts through changes in the terms of trade between industry and agriculture (e.g., the Lewis model); the key role played by expansion of the capital goods sector if wage goods present no constraint (e.g., the original Feldman–Mahalanobis model); and the problem of inflation leading to 'forced saving' through depressing the real wage (see equation (6.12)) or its rate of growth, if wage goods are a bottleneck in the industrialisation process. However, the industry–agriculture or the capital goods–consumption goods distinction is far too aggregated to capture the crucial problem of interindustrial balance in the Leontief sense. Indeed, this may be a serious limiting factor to the feasible pace of industrialisation, especially when some of the raw materials have to be imported but availability of foreign exchange is limited. When such modifications are examined within the Feldman–Mahalanobis framework (see Bhaduri, 1989, Appendix B), another weakness of concentrating on heavy industries (the K-sector) becomes apparent. Since capital goods require raw materials, investment is needed simultaneously not only in the capital goods sector but also in the sector which produces raw materials for it. As a result one needs to examine the investment required per unit of final output in the vertically integrated capital goods (K-) sector in relation to that in the vertically integrated consumption goods (C-) sector. When this vertically integrated capital goods sector is significantly more investment-intensive as well as import-intensive compared to the consumption goods sector, it may begin to operate in extreme cases as a 'black hole' which sucks in limited import and investible resources on an increasing scale without promoting the longer-term growth and consumption potential of the economy. This would suggest some moderation of any oversimplistic emphasis on heavy industries, even if agricultural surplus is not the immediate bottleneck.

The theoretical economic literature tends to emphasise mainly the problem of demand-and-supply balance *either* of *final* goods (e.g., the question of marketed surplus and capacity to supply capital goods domestically) *or* of *intermediate* raw materials. But there is an overwhelming *incentive problem* which is seldom acknowledged in debates on development strategy. This incentive problem relates on the one hand to *capitalists' incentive to invest* in a mixed or not fully centrally planned economy, and on the other to the *incentive to migrate* on the part of the working population, i.e., a pattern of migration mainly from rural to urban areas associated with industrialisation. It is perhaps a valid generalisation to say that the failure of many industrialisation-led development strategies to deal with this two-sided incentive problem manifests itself in too weak an incentive for industrial accumulation on the part of domestic capitalists combined with too strong a tendency to migrate from rural areas on the part of the labour force. It is this broader incentive problem, rather than simply the conventional issue of price incentives, that needs to be examined when considering some of the other macroeconomic constraints (apart from the demand–supply balance) on an industrialisation-led development strategy.

The obvious but important point that the pace of industrialisation may be limited, not by any *supply-side* constraint like limited availability of marketable surplus or limited capacity of the domestic capital goods sector, but by a weak incentive to invest by private capitalists, finds little recognition in the Lewis-type or Feldman–Mahalanobis models. Thus, they fail to emphasise that the *demand for capital goods* rests on an *independent investment function*; a weak incentive to invest reflecting a low demand for capital goods may impose a fundamental *demand-side constraint* on the pace of industrialisation, which is further magnified by the multiplier mechanism to generate a low level of aggregate demand in the economy. By following the classical Ricardian assumption (cf. Pasinetti, 1959–1960; Bhaduri and Harris, 1987) that saving out of industrial profit is automatically ploughed back as industrial investment, the Lewis-type model fails to deal satisfactorily with this problem of an *independent* investment function. Alternatively, by concentrating implicitly or explicitly on a *totally* centrally planned economy, the Feldman–Mahalanobis model and other important discussions (e.g., Kalecki, 1972) by and large ignore the problem altogether.

The incentive to invest in industry is influenced strongly by the size of the market through some version of the 'acceleration relation' and the income of the agricultural sector is a critical determinant of the size of the home market in a predominantly agrarian economy. Thus, not merely as a provider of agricultural surplus, but also as a demander of industrial goods, the agricultural or the rural sector may constrain the pace of industrialisation. By overemphasising the supply-side problem of limited availability of agricultural surplus, the classical debate on industrialisation has frequently missed the point that the *method* of agricultural surplus extraction may influence strongly the level of demand generated by agriculture for industrial goods. For instance, in an extreme case, a higher direct or indirect tribute extracted from agriculture (e.g., tax or land revenue or a lower administered agricultural price) may provide the necessary agricultural surplus for industrialisation, but may still constrain the pace of industrialisation by reducing the domestic *demand* for industrial goods. Analytically, this may be one of the characteristic features of a 'colonial' agricultural policy whose legacy seems to be sadly present even in post-colonial industrialisation strategies in some African countries (cf. Saith, 1990).

By underemphasising the demand-generating role of agriculture, industrialisation-led development strategies are often forced to rely on demand from the 'foreign' as opposed to the 'home' market. While there are many advantages of a strategy of export-led industrialisation, including the discipline of international cost efficiency that it imposes on the exporting country, it is seldom recognised that this very process of export-led growth has to be initiated typically in the 'home' market, which may even be protected for a time (e.g., the 'infant industries' argument). Serious constriction of the home market due to failure to recognise the demand-generating role of agriculture may thwart this initiation. Conversely, a sufficiently large and growing home market generated by demand from a dynamic agricultural sector in predominantly agrarian economies would seem the ideal pre-condition for export-led growth.

Agrarian reform also has this double-sided role in development strategies. The role of agrarian reform in raising agricultural production or marketed surplus is frequently emphasised (cf. Sobhan, 1989).[10] But how agrarian reform can provide a crucial impetus to industrialise by expanding the size of the home market remains a relatively unexplored issue, despite its role in several successful cases of export-led industrialisation (e.g., Japan, Republic of Korea and Taiwan, China). There may also be much to learn by comparing this experience with the experience of agrarian reforms in socialist countries which tried to 'internalise' the same demand impetus without seeking simultaneously to promote exports.

The fact that the agricultural or rural sector can provide an important home market during industrialisation should caution against treating agriculture as a 'passive' sector which merely needs to provide the required quantum of marketed surplus to industry. There is even greater need for caution when practical experience teaches that migration from rural to urban areas can become a dominant, autonomous process. The rising problems and costs of urbanisation have reached overwhelming proportions in many developing countries to thwart the very process of industrialisation. Paradoxically, migration into cities occurs alongside large-scale open and disguised unemployment in the urban areas and despite extremely limited job opportunities in industry. Its conventional theoretical explanation is given in terms of the 'pull' of the earnings differential between the *expected* urban wage and rural income (e.g., Todaro, 1969, 1976; Harris and Todaro, 1970). Since migration into urban areas at a rate faster than expansion of urban employment opportunities reduces the probability of finding urban employment and, therefore, *expected* earnings from urban employment, the 'pull' explanation suggests that migration into urban areas would tend to stabilise as expected urban income falls towards the level of rural earnings.

Although this line of argument has the virtue of identifying open and disguised urban unemployment as a causal factor in migration, one of its central weaknesses is to understate the dynamic link between migration and the pace of industrialisation itself. This link cannot be understood simply through the pull of wage differentials, without also recognising the role which the rural sector plays or fails to play in the survival strategies of potential migrants. Recent Latin American experience shows that the relative size of the peasantry in the economically active population assumes a residual role: 'When pull factors are weak, migration opportunities are reduced, and the relative size of the peasantry increases as a refuge sector of surplus population' (de Janvry, Sadoulet and Wilcox, 1986, p. 3). By the same token, industrialisation can become almost self-destructive by reinforcing the pull factors which lead to migration. The problem does not lie with industrialisation but with the treatment of the rural sector as a 'refuge sector'.

The destabilising effects of migration are likely to be less powerful in countries where labour markets are more segmented. Research suggests at least two important reasons for the segmentation of urban and rural labour markets, especially in India (cf. Bharadwaj, 1989, pp. 2, 13, 34). First, with the *family as the basic production unit* in peasant agriculture, the decision to migrate is frequently a family rather than an individual decision – for example, some members of the family (usually adult males) migrate on the assumption that others will stay and continue with farming. Indeed, remittance income from the urban sector may help in maintaining otherwise unviable family farms, thus reinforcing the segmentation of the urban–rural labour market (cf. Bhaduri, 1983, ch. 6). Second, migration occurs frequently through kinship, caste or village networks which supply information, reduce search cost and provide essential support systems in urban areas. The degree of labour market segmentation increases in areas where such networks are weaker.

The effect of labour market segmentation on the industrialisation process is often misunderstood. It is believed, wrongly, that development of the wage labour market will facilitate industrialisation through a smooth process of intersectoral labour transfer. However, this view oversimplifies the migration issue when agriculture is allowed to become a 'refuge sector'. In that case, segmentation of the labour market may actually reduce the problems of industrialisation by keeping net migration rates from the rural sector within manageable limits. The lesson to draw from this is not that segmentation of the labour market is a desirable objective, but that any development strategy which in its enthusiasm for industrialisation assigns to agriculture the role of a mere 'refuge sector' is bound to be beset with intrinsic difficulties and self-contradictions.

The role of the rural sector in the development process

An appropriate role for the rural sector in a development strategy can emerge from examining the *interactions* between the generation of marketed surplus and intersectoral labour transfer. As discussed earlier these interactions are very wide-ranging, taking in the pace and pattern of industrialisation, as well as affecting the supply-side potentials which need to be exploited effectively during the development process.

From a broad analytical viewpoint, the mechanism of intersectoral labour transfer cannot be isolated from the *method* of extraction and utilisation of agricultural surplus. Forcible extraction of agricultural surplus at an exceedingly high rate may strengthen the factors which 'push' the rural population to migrate to urban areas. Despite generating the required amount of agricultural surplus, such a process of industrialisation could become unsustainable over time by destroying the livelihood of many more people in the rural economy than benefit from urban industrial jobs created. Similarly, shifts in the terms of trade between industry and agriculture could affect in a complex way the urban–rural earnings differential which exerts its 'pull' on intersectoral transfer of labour. Thus, relatively prosperous 'surplus farmers' who are net sellers of foodgrains in the market would gain as the terms of trade moved in favour of agriculture. But agricultural labourers, marginal and small 'deficit farmers', who are net buyers from the market, would tend to lose, thereby strengthening the 'push' factor from agriculture.[11] Further, in so far as the 'deficit farmers' dominate in numbers, such a push factor could have a disproportionately large impact on migration to the urban areas. This example shows that the generation of agricultural surplus, even if it is based on the price (i.e., terms of trade) mechanism, affects intersectoral labour transfer in different ways depending on the class composition of the peasantry.

The mode of extraction of agricultural surplus, including changes in the terms of trade, will also affect both the level and the composition of demand for industrial goods. This will affect the level of capacity utilisation in industry, as well as the level of industrial investment through the 'acceleration relation', to influence the rate of expansion of job opportunities in the urban sector. Since both the *supply* of agricultural surplus as well as the *demand* for industrial goods depend on the agricultural–rural sector, it should be evident that this sector will exert a dominant influence in shaping the course of industrialisation of large, predominantly agrarian economies. Any development strategy would be faulty in so far as it fails to reckon with this factor and treats industrialisation as an exogenous process.

It is hardly surprising, therefore, that attempts to industrialise by careless extraction of agricultural surplus have frequently run into difficulties. Several examples of recent African experience illustrate this problem. Industrialisation, grafted on to export-oriented colonial agriculture, was to be carried out by the State using agricultural export taxes and/or low administered prices for agricultural goods. On the supply side, such a strategy hindered the growth of adequate agricultural surplus by draining the agricultural sector of its essential resources. On the demand side, it led to inadequate expansion of the home market and forced the industrial sector to rely prematurely on the world market. This had the disastrous consequence that only a continued inflow of foreign aid could sustain the process of industrialisation, which was therefore extremely vulnerable to adverse movements in the international terms of trade, a growing debt servicing burden and a drop in the flow of net external finance in real terms. One response was 'withdrawal from the market': as the profitability of export crops declined due to adverse movements in both the internal and the external terms of trade, the monetarised agricultural sector began to retreat. In an extreme case like Uganda, even urban groups turned to subsistence farming, 'producing some of their food requirements on their own garden plots' (Jamal, 1988, p. 698).

These abortive attempts at industrialisation point up an important lesson for the formulation of development strategies. In predominantly agrarian economies it is a common mistake – encouraged by 'dual' economy models and undue concentration on 'heavy' industries – to attempt to detach economically and administratively the process of industrialisation from development of the rural–agricultural sector. Instead it is necessary to think of the interaction between the two sectors in an organic way. An essential criterion for the sustainability of a development strategy is the *net* addition of earning opportunities on an economy-wide scale. Rather like the Schumpeterian process of 'creative destruction' (Schumpeter, 1947), the mode of extraction and utilisation of agricultural surplus in a development strategy needs to be 'creative' – that is, it should be able to create more income-earning opportunities (jobs and livelihoods) than it destroys.

In terms of the preceding discussion five interrelated *guidelines* can be identified as necessary (not sufficient) for generating a process of 'creative destruction' through the interaction of industry and agriculture:

(a) An undue burden should not be placed on the rural–agricultural sector to 'finance' industrialisation. This requires restraint of both the *pace* of industrial accumulation and the *growth in the industrial real wage* to be compatible with the availability of agricultural surplus (see previous section).

(b) The *composition* of industrial growth must take into account the need to increase production of industrial consumer goods for which the agricultural sector would voluntarily exchange part of its produce (*à la* Bukharin; see previous section). In this area the price mechanism should be strengthened to reduce forcible extraction of agricultural surplus and ensure *compatibility of incentives* between industrialisation and agricultural growth, rather than relying exclusively on State-sponsored industrialisation.

(c) State-sponsored industrialisation can result in rapid growth of the *bureaucracy* which, in turn, has to be sustained by increased extraction from agriculture. This growth of State bureaucracy rather than growth in the real wage rate of industrial workers leads to an unsustainable increase in claims on the rural–agricultural sector. It is important to avoid ideological overtones in this context. In most developing countries the State has to play an active economic role in many areas, such as infrastructural development, reorganisation of agrarian relations, public investment for the development of strategic industries and sectors, and so on. The central problem is to ensure that the State plays this active role without disproportionate growth in the bureaucratic-administrative sector as a claimant on resources for development.

(d) *Decentralisation* in decision-making and geographical decentralisation of industrial development can be effective in reducing disproportionate growth of the bureaucratic–administrative sector. It is also probably a more efficient way of implementing a development strategy in certain areas. Two crucial sources of development potential already identified (see pp. 150–1) require increasing labour productivity, especially in agriculture, and creating 'extensive growth' through a higher participation ratio. This typically involves reorganisation of agriculture through consolidation of fragmented landholdings, and rapid expansion of small-scale irrigation and rural infrastructure through mobilisation of rural (surplus) labour, etc. Major obstacles to implementing these measures are the administrative problems, and information and other costs involved in centralised operations. Genuine decentralisation can be especially effective in developmental activities related to 'extensive growth'.

(e) Finally, *geographical decentralisation* in industrial development that also involves spreading of economic and social overheads is essential for handling the problem of intersectoral labour transfer and migration, on the one hand, and reducing the extraction of surplus from agriculture for industrialisation, on the other. The greater the spread of industrialisation in the rural areas the wider would be supplementary income opportunities; this could even make small farms viable, diluting the strength of the 'push' factor in migration from rural to urban areas. At the same time, it could also weaken the 'pull' factor by reducing urban–rural earning differentials. Indeed it may be forcefully argued that the success of a development strategy does not depend on adopting an 'agriculture-first' or an 'industry-first' approach.[12] Rather than *counterposing* industry against agriculture, the need is for a pattern of industrialisation whose scope extends organically to the rural sector as well. Development strategies must break out of the orthodox mould which treats industrialisation as virtually synonymous with urbanisation.

Macroeconomic policies for development with special reference to agriculture and the rural sector

The guidelines for the rural sector in a development strategy suggested in the preceding section also provide a longer-term perspective within which to formulate short-term macroeconomic policies, so as to minimise *conflict* between policies aimed at short- and long-term objectives.

A fundamental reason for this conflict is the *asymmetry* of adjustments on the demand and supply sides. Management of demand using traditional fiscal and monetary policies along Keynesian lines usually works quite rapidly, whereas supply-side adjustments involving reallocation of resources, net investment for capacity expansion and so on typically involve structural changes which take longer to effect. Thus the *speed of adjustment* is typically much slower on the supply than on the demand side, especially in a developing economy.[13] Minimising this zone of conflict between short- and long-term economic policy requirements necessitates paying special attention to the 'fast dynamics' of demand management compared to the 'slow dynamics' of increasing supply. Neither simple-minded reliance on 'market solutions' nor dogmatic reliance on central planning can avoid this problem.

The distinction between *stabilisation programmes* and *structural adjustment loans* (SAL), made by the IMF and the World Bank respectively in recent years, is based upon some recognition of this asymmetry in speed of adjustment. Chronic balance-of-payments difficulties or inflationary price rises can often be traced back to a relatively slow increase in domestic supply compared to rapid expansion in demand, which forces countries to undergo stabilisation programmes directed primarily at short-period management of the international payments position. However, SALs often reinforce the short-term bias of IMF 'conditionality' in stabilisation programmes instead of modifying them from a longer-term development perspective. This underlines the common perception of many developing countries that 'stabilisation' can be attempted only at the cost of the longer-term growth potential of the economy.

Embedded in a general philosophy in favour of 'market solutions' and a 'small public sector', the 'conditionality' practised by the IMF has three main components:[14]

(a) *monetary programming*, designed to control domestic credit by imposing a ceiling either on the level or on the rate of growth of some (usually narrow) definition of 'money supply';

(b) *financial liberalisation*, which involves raising the real interest rate (and is thus compatible with monetary programming *provided* the demand for 'money' is unchanged) in the hope of encouraging savings; and

(c) *import liberalisation*, accompanied usually by devaluation, which is intended primarily to shift resources in favour of tradeable commodities in order to improve the balance-of-payments position.

The main defects of IMF conditionality have, analytically, two main causes:

(i) a tendency to confuse the nature of demand- and supply-side adjustments, with the result that the link between short-term 'stabilisation' and long-term 'structural adjustment' is often misspecified; and

(ii) inadequate attention paid to *asymmetrical* speeds of adjustment of demand and supply.

To take the first issue of confusing demand- and supply-side adjustments,

INTERNATIONAL LABOUR OFFICE
BUREAU INTERNATIONAL DU TRAVAIL
OFICINA INTERNACIONAL DEL TRABAJO

Geneva, 8 December 1993

With the compliments of

Samir Radwan
Chief
Policies and Programmes for Development Branch
Employment and Development Department

4, route des Morillons, CH-1211 GE
Télégramme INTERLAB GE

the main impact of monetary programming through the imposition of a credit ceiling, especially on the public sector borrowing requirement, is usually to reduce government investment expenditure and, therefore, aggregate demand through the Keynesian multiplier mechanism. At the same time, a credit ceiling may also reduce aggregate supply, particularly through a reduction in the availability of working capital (cf. Blinder, 1987). Consequently, due to the credit ceiling, the level of output may be either demand- or supply-constrained.[15] To describe it more formally in the simplest of models:

let

I = aggregate exogenous investment (including public investment), $S = sY$ = savings, $1 > s > 0$

so that

$Y_d = I/s$ = demand-determined level of output (through the multiplier mechanism)

On the other hand, if

c = credit (working capital) required per unit of output

and

D = credit advanced by the financial sector (related to 'high-powered' narrow definition of 'money'), then
$cY_s = D$ or $Y_s = D/c$ which is the supply-determined level of output

Thus actual income $= Y$, where $Y = \min (Y_d, Y_s) = \min (I/s, D/c)$.

If output is supply-constrained in the above sense, i.e., $Y = D/c$, a squeeze in credit would result in reduced aggregate *supply* without a corresponding fall in aggregate demand. In general, if investment also depends on the availability of credit then the reduction in aggregate demand due to a marginal credit reduction would be:

$$\frac{dY_d}{dD} = \frac{1}{s} \cdot \frac{dI}{dD} = \frac{\alpha}{s} \text{ where } \alpha \equiv \frac{dI}{dD}, \text{ i.e.,}$$

α measures the sensitivity of investment to credit availability. Reduction in aggregate supply due to a marginal reduction in credit is given by:

$$\frac{dY_s}{dD} = \frac{1}{c}$$

Hence, if $1/c$ is greater (less) than α/s, excess demand would increase (decrease) in the economy as a result of a credit squeeze. Greater excess demand is likely to worsen the balance-of-payments and the inflationary situation in general. In this case, monetary programming may fail even in its short-period objective of 'stabilisation'[16] while reduced aggregate supply may also be detrimental to the longer-term growth potential of the economy.

Taking into account the asymmetrical speeds of adjustment in demand and supply strengthens this line of argument. A credit squeeze leading to a faster fall in output supply than in output demand, due to lack of working capital, would widen the excess demand gap over time and upset 'stabilisation' objectives.[17]

Many of the specific recommendations frequently made by the IMF, especially regarding the agricultural sector, under a typical 'stabilisation programme' reflect the error of *not* separating carefully the process of reduction in aggregate demand from that in aggregate supply. Inspired by the philosophy of 'market solutions', the IMF frequently recommends raising agricultural prices to provide supply incentives to farmers. However, this recommendation cannot be sustained, even analytically, if the higher agricultural price leads to an overall net reduction in demand for agricultural goods through lower industrial real wages. Agricultural prices being largely 'demand-determined' (cf. Kalecki, 1971; Okun, 1981), this would produce conflicting policies that deliberately raise agricultural prices while allowing the demand for agricultural commodities to drop sharply. The IMF policy recommendation may thus turn out to be oversimplistic, precisely because it fails to take into account the impact of agricultural price changes on demand.

There is also an international aspect to this problem which the IMF typically ignores. Even if higher agricultural prices are maintained by subsidising domestic agriculture and result in higher domestic supply, the lower domestic demand for agricultural goods would force producers to build unwanted inventories and/or export (especially for exportable cash crops). This may lead to a sharp deterioration in the international terms of trade. Thus, the *domestic* terms of trade between agriculture and industry may move in the *opposite direction* to the *international* terms of trade, resulting in confusing price signals to producers and traders in the economy. The essential point of this discussion is *not* to oppose or support higher agricultural prices, but to indicate the lacuna of ignoring demand considerations while emphasising simplistically only the supply incentives provided by higher agricultural prices.

An almost blind emphasis on the price mechanism-based 'market solution' to agriculture also demonstrates ignorance of the complex interrelation between short-term economic management and longer-term development objectives, especially in agriculture. The price mechanism

performs reasonably well in agriculture *provided* certain prior conditions
are fulfilled (cf. Sobhan, 1989). As already mentioned, higher agricultural
prices may depress the standard of living of agricultural workers, marginal
farmers and artisans who are *net buyers* of foodgrains, only to accelerate
migration from rural to urban areas by strengthening the 'push' factor.
Thus, the price 'incentive' could have an unintended impact on migration
depending on the class situations and the degree of forced involvement of a
highly differentiated peasantry in the 'market' (cf. Bhaduri, 1983, ch. 2).
This may even jeopardise longer-term development in cases where higher
prices increase the volume of marketed surplus from a minority of 'surplus
farmers' while, at the same time, increasing rural destitution and stimulating accelerated migration to urban areas. Thus, the issue of price incentives
should not be separated from that of the class composition of the peasantry
in recommending policies, particularly in situations where the peasantry is
known to be highly differentiated as an intrinsic 'initial condition' of the
agricultural sector.

Similarly, higher prices may not provide adequate supply incentives to all
agricultural producers if minimum irrigation, drainage, land consolidation
and improvement, and so on, are not ensured beforehand. Several econometric studies have shown (Krishna, 1963; Narain, 1965) that, in densely
populated agriculture with little scope for extending the margin of cultivation, the 'price response' of farmers operates mostly through changing crop
composition (assuming a given yield per acre) induced by relative price
changes for different crops. However, this flexibility on crop composition is
known to depend critically on water control. Various problems including
the 'free rider' problem make it difficult to control water without active
public irrigation programmes (major and minor). IMF-style 'monetary
programming', with its bias against public investment (including irrigation
investment), could be incompatible with the supply incentives provided
through higher agricultural prices, especially for smaller farmers. It is
therefore necessary to examine carefully the *composition* of public investment, rather than imposing sweeping restrictions on it, in order to make
short-term policies more compatible with the longer-term rural development perspective.

Ultimately, any development strategy which places improvement and
expansion of rural livelihood along with industrialisation as its core
objective cannot rely blindly on the price mechanism alone. The need for
adequate public action must be recognised, especially for the restructuring
of the rural sector. This often calls not for 'economic austerity' but for an
expanded programme of public investment, with its composition more
thoughtfully geared towards the requirements of the rural sector. Only then
will reasonably high growth in agriculture also expand opportunities for

earning on- and off-farm income and thus provide supplementary income to an otherwise economically marginalised rural population. It is this challenge which the development strategies in predominantly agrarian, large economies must meet through an imaginative blend of public action and the 'market solution'. Neither can meet the challenge alone.

Appendix: Statistical tables and notes

Comparative levels of income

Table 6A.1 illustrates the orders of magnitude involved in the comparison of levels of income between groups of countries (referred to on p. 149).

Differences in labour productivity

Let L_j = the number of workers in sector j, x_j = labour productivity in sector j, m_j = proportion of total labour force in sector j and n_j = proportion of GDP contributed by sector j (j = a, i, s). Without subscript, the relevant variables stand for total labour force and average labour productivity. Definitionally, we then have

$$L_j x_j = n_j.x.L$$

or

$$x_j/x = n_j/m_j, \text{ where } m_j = L_j/L \tag{6A.1}$$

Relevant data referring to 1980 are provided in table 6A.2. They show three things:

(a) Labour productivity in agriculture is 51 per cent of average labour

Table 6A.1. *Comparative levels of income by country group, 1988*

	GNP per capita (US$)	Ratio (developed to developing economies)
Industrial (developed) market economies	17 470	1
Low- and middle-income (developing) economies	750	23
Low-income (including India and China)	320	55
Middle-income	1 930	9
Lower-middle-income	1 380	13
Upper-middle-income	3 240	5

Source: World Bank (1990), table 1, pp. 178–9.

Table 6A.2. *Sectoral distribution of GDP and labour force, 1980*
(% except for ratio figures)

Sector	Developed market economies			Developing economies		
	GDP n_j	Labour force m_j	Ratio of labour productivity in sector to average labour productivity $\dfrac{x_j}{x} = \dfrac{n_j}{m_j}$	GDP n_j'	Labour force m_j'	Ratio of labour productivity in sector to average labour productivity $\dfrac{x_j'}{x'} = \dfrac{n_j'}{m_j'}$
Primary/ agriculture	3.6	7	0.51	15.9	62	0.26
Secondary/ industry	38.7	35	1.11	40.9	16	2.56
Tertiary/ services	57.7	58	0.99	43.2	22	1.96
Total	100.0	100	1.00	100.0	100	1.00

Source: For GDP shares, UNCTAD (1989), table 6.3, p. 438, and for labour force shares, World Bank (1988), table 31, pp. 282–3.

productivity in the developed economies; agricultural labour productivity is only 26 per cent of average labour productivity in developing countries. This establishes the *first* proposition on p. 150 that *agricultural labour productivity is lower than the national average in both developed and developing countries.*

(b) In the developed economies, *intersectoral* differences in labour productivity range from 51 per cent (in agriculture) to 111 per cent (in industry) of average labour productivity; in developing countries, they range from 26 per cent (in agriculture) to 256 per cent (in industry) of average productivity. This establishes the *second* proposition on pp. 150–1 that *intersectoral labour productivity differences are much wider in the developing than in the developed economies.*

(c) The ratio of average labour productivity in developed to developing economies (x/x') is of the same order of magnitude as the *per capita* income ratio (around 20, see table 6A.1) since the difference in participation rates is not huge (67 per cent for developed and 58 per cent for developing countries in 1985, see World Bank, 1988, table 31, pp. 282–3). Since $x_j/x_j' = [(x_j/x)/(x_j'/x')] (x/x')$, using the results in table 6A.2 and the above ratio of average labour productivities, it can be seen

Table 6A.3. *Percentage of labour force in agriculture for selected countries and years*

	1870	1910	1979–80
France	—	41.0	8.8
Japan	85.8	—	11.2
Sweden	—	46.1	5.8
United Kingdom	—	8.8	2.6
United States	54.0	31.6	2.5
Portugal	—	57.4	30.3
Spain	—	56.3	19.6
Brazil	—	70.5^a	44.2
Egypt	—	69.1	42.1
India	74.4	—	63.9
Mexico	—	63.7	40.1
Philippines	—	72.9^b	50.1

Notes:
[a] 1920 figure.
[b] 1939 figure.
Source: Figures from United Nations sources adjusted for comparison.

that *intrasectoral* differences in labour productivity (x_j/x_j', where $j = a, i, s$) are highest in agriculture; agricultural productivity is about forty times higher in the developed than in the developing economies. In industry (and services) labour productivity in developed countries is only about ten times greater than in developing economies. This establishes the *third* proposition on p. 151 that *the relative potential for labour productivity increases in developing countries is considerably larger in agriculture than in industry.*

Finally, it may be added that the method used is general. The numbers generated are only illustrative but the qualitative conclusions remain, even when data from other sources or years are used.

Trends in the share of labour force in agriculture

Table 6A.3 illustrates the long-term trends in the share of labour force in agriculture for selected countries (p. 152).

Notes

1 These figures relate to 1980. See Appendix, pp. 172–4 for details of calculation and methods used.

2 The Appendix explains the analytical basis for these three propositions, which remain qualitatively valid even if a different source of data or base year is used.
3 Extensive growth arises from an increase in the level of employment (L), whereas intensive growth arises from an increase in labour productivity, i.e.,

$X = xL = xrN$ (notations as in (6.1), p. 150) or,

$\frac{\Delta X}{X} = \frac{\Delta x}{x} + \frac{\Delta r}{r}$, if N = constant,

i.e., the first term of a labour productivity increase ($\Delta x/x$) causes 'intensive' growth, whereas an increase in the participation ratio ($\Delta r/r$) causes 'extensive' growth.
4 To take another example, the *real* wage is *endogenously* determined in the model of the *General Theory* (Keynes, 1936), where investment determines effective demand, effective demand determines output and the marginal product of labour at *that level of output* must equal the real wage rate to satisfy the first-order profit maximising condition. In contrast, in orthodox neo-classical theory, the real wage is treated as an *exogenous* variable which can be manipulated for influencing the employment level. Also note that, by eschewing the difference between exogenous and endogenous variables, one will be forced to the general equilibrium theorist's position that 'everything depends on everything else', so that nothing meaningful in terms of policy intervention can be said!
5 The distinction between endogenous and exogenous variables is fundamentally a way of imposing 'causation' on an economic model for policy purposes. A policy model can therefore be misleading either because the causation/classification is wrongly specified or because the economic model itself is wrongly specified. But no policy prescription can be derived from a model without the prior distinction between endogenous and exogenous variables (see also n.4 above).
6 It is the rate of *growth* of real wage rather than the *level* of real wage which may have to be depressed, if we take into account growth in labour productivity over time.
7 This is politically understandable in so far as the urban working class provided the main political base of the Russian revolution. See the 'Introduction' by Nove in Preobrazhensky (1965) for a succinct summary of the debate.
8 This pre-Keynesian assumption of 'saving governs investment' is a feature of both the Ricardian and the neo-classical growth models. The weakness of this assumption is discussed later, when we consider the 'incentive to invest' as an independent variable.
9 The assumption of uniform nominal productivity of labour is made to keep the algebra simple. This assumption can be relaxed without modifying qualitatively the argument in the text. Bhaduri (1986, ch. 2) provides a more general analysis without this simplifying assumption.
10 It has also been argued that more equal income and asset distribution following agrarian reform may actually *reduce* agricultural surplus by increasing the level of grain consumption by the rural poor as an immediate short-run effect.

11 Saith (1990, p. 218) points out that in India 'the incidence of rural poverty was directly related to inflation (measured in a manner appropriate for the classes of rural labourers and food-deficit market-dependent marginal farmers who together constitute most of the poor)'.

12 Such debates usually centre around the question of investment allocation (or government expenditure allocation) between the sectors. But they seldom point out that within a centralised administrative structure it is almost impossible to achieve a geographically decentralised pattern of development which provides supplementary income in rural areas on a wide scale.

13 With a binding foreign exchange constraint, the supply of 'tradeable' goods through imports cannot be increased rapidly in a developing country. Indeed, the 'foreign exchange crisis' is often a reflection of this disparate speed of adjustment on the demand and supply side.

14 Avramovic (1988) provides a useful summary and critical assessment of IMF conditionality.

15 One problem with the quantity theory $Y = K.M$ and the 'money multiplier', i.e., $\Delta Y/\Delta M = K$, is the failure to identify whether they are demand or supply relations. This is related to the debate about the 'transmission mechanism' from a change in the money supply to a change in output. The quantity theory can also be interpreted simply as a demand equation for money. Polak (1957) provides the classic IMF framework, made more explicit by Khan, Montiel and Haque (1990), for the use of the quantity theory of money in 'conditionality' discussions.

16 This is logically the worst case against 'monetary programming', when it fails in short-term stabilisation as well. Less extreme cases (of demand-constrained output) may be worked out.

17 *Faster* supply-side adjustment compared to demand-side adjustment is quite plausible in the case of a *reduction* in output due to a credit squeeze. The reverse may hold typically in the case of a credit expansion, i.e., the *increase* in output supply is slower than the increase in aggregate demand.

References

Avramovic, D., 1988. 'Conditionality: Facts, theory and policy – Contribution to the reconstruction of the international financial system', *Working Paper*, no. 37, Helsinki: World Institute for Development Economics Research.

Bhaduri, A., 1983. *The Economic Structure of Backward Agriculture*, London: Academic Press.

  1986. *Macroeconomics: The Dynamics of Commodity Production*, London: Macmillan and Armonk, New York: M.E. Sharpe.

  1989. 'Alternative development strategies and the rural sector', paper presented at the ILO/SAREC Workshop on the 'Interrelationship between Macroeconomic Policies and Rural Development' (Geneva, 11–13 December 1989).

Bhaduri, A. and D.J. Harris, 1987. 'The complex dynamics of the simple Ricardian system', *Quarterly Journal of Economics*, vol. 102, no. 4, November, pp. 893–901.

Bharadwaj, K., 1989. 'The formation of rural labour markets: An analysis with special reference to Asia', paper presented at the ILO/SAREC Workshop on the 'Interrelationship between Macroeconomic Policies and Rural Development' (Geneva, 11–13 December 1989).

Blinder, A.S., 1987. 'Credit rationing and effective supply failures', *Economic Journal*, vol. 97, no. 386, June, pp. 327–52.

de Janvry, A., E. Sadoulet and L. Wilcox, 1986. 'Rural labour in Latin America'. World Employment Programme, *Research Working Paper*, WEP 10–6/WP79, Geneva: ILO.

Domar, E., 1957. 'A Soviet model of growth', in E. Domar, *Essays in the Theory of Economic Growth*, New York: Oxford University Press.

Ellman, M., 1975. 'Did the agricultural surplus provide the resources for the increase in investment in the USSR during the First Five Year Plan?', *Economic Journal*, vol. 85, no. 340, December, pp. 844–63.

Harris, J.R. and M.P. Todaro, 1970. 'Migration, unemployment and development: A two-sector analysis', *American Economic Review*, vol. 60, no. 1, March, pp. 126–42.

Jamal, V., 1988. 'Coping under crisis in Uganda', *International Labour Review*, vol. 127, no. 6, pp. 679–701.

Kaldor, N., 1955–1956. 'Alternative theories of distribution', *Review of Economic Studies*, vol. 23, pp. 83–100.

Kalecki, M., 1971. 'Costs and prices', in M. Kalecki, *Selected Essays on the Dynamics of the Capitalist Economy*, Cambridge: Cambridge University Press.

1972. 'Problems of financing economic development in a mixed economy', in M. Kalecki, *Selected Essays on the Economic Growth of the Socialist and the Mixed Economies*, Cambridge: Cambridge University Press.

Keynes, J.M., 1930. *A Treatise on Money*, vol. 1, London: Macmillan.

1936. *The General Theory of Employment, Interest and Money*, London: Macmillan.

Khan, M.S., P. Montiel and N.U. Haque, 1990. 'Adjustment with growth: Relating the analytical approaches of the IMF and the World Bank', *Journal of Development Economics*, vol. 32, no. 1, pp. 155–79.

Krishna, R., 1963. 'Farm supply response in India-Pakistan: A case study of the Punjab region', *Economic Journal*, vol. 73, no. 291, September, pp. 477–87.

Lewis, W.A., 1954. 'Economic development with unlimited supplies of labour', *Manchester School of Economic and Social Studies*, vol. 22, no. 2, May, pp. 139–91.

1958. 'Unlimited labour: Further notes', *Manchester School of Economic and Social Studies*, vol. 26, no. 1, January, pp. 1–32.

Mahalanobis, P.C., 1953. 'Some observations on the process of growth of national income', *Sankhya: The Indian Journal of Statistics*, vol. 12, pp. 307–12.

1955. 'The approach of operational research to planning in India', *Sankhya: The Indian Journal of Statistics*, vol. 16, nos. 1–2, pp. 3–130.

Narain, D., 1965. *Impact of Price Movements on Areas under Selected Crops in India 1900–1939*, Cambridge: Cambridge University Press.

Okun, A.M., 1981. *Prices and Quantities: A Macroeconomic Analysis*, Washington,

DC: Brookings Institution.

Pasinetti, L.L., 1959–1960. 'A mathematical formulation of the Ricardian system', *Review of Economic Studies*, vol. 27, pp. 78–98.

Polak, J.J., 1957. 'Monetary analysis of income formation and payments problems', *IMF Staff Papers*, vol. 6, no. 1, pp. 1–50.

Preobrazhensky, E., 1965. *The New Economics*, Oxford: Oxford University Press.

Raj, K.N. and A.K. Sen., 1961. 'Alternative patterns of growth under conditions of stagnant export earnings', *Oxford Economic Papers*, vol. 13, no. 1, February.

Ranis, G. and J.C.H. Fei, 1961. 'A theory of economic development', *American Economic Review*, vol. 51, no. 4, September, pp. 533–65.

Saith, A., 1990. 'Development strategies and the rural poor', in *Journal of Peasant Studies*, vol. 17, no. 2, January, pp. 171–244.

Schumpeter, J., 1947. *Capitalism, Socialism and Democracy*, London: George Allen & Unwin.

Sobhan, R., 1989. 'Agrarian reform and its alternatives', paper presented at the ILO/SAREC Workshop on the 'Interrelationship between Macroeconomic Policies and Rural Development' (Geneva, 11–13 December 1989).

Tinbergen, J., 1952. *On the Theory of Economic Policy*, Amsterdam: North-Holland.

Todaro, M.P., 1969. 'A model of labor migration and urban unemployment in less developed countries', *American Economic Review*, vol. 59, no. 1, March, pp. 138–48.

1976. 'Urban job expansion, induced migration and rising unemployment: A formulation and simplified empirical test for LDCs', *Journal of Development Economics*, vol. 3, no. 3, pp. 211–25.

UNCTAD (United Nations Conference on Trade and Development), 1989. *Handbook of International Trade and Development Statistics 1988*, New York: United Nations.

World Bank, 1988. *World Development Report*, New York: Oxford University Press.

1990. *World Development Report*, New York: Oxford University Press.

7 Intersectoral resource flows and development: lessons of past experience

MASSOUD KARSHENAS

Introduction

This chapter investigates the direction and pattern of intersectoral resource transfers in the process of development on the basis of empirical evidence from selected countries. In the economic development literature it is often assumed that the growth of agrarian economies, at least in the early stages, requires a net transfer of 'surplus' from the agricultural sector to maintain high rates of industrial investment. This proposition seems to be almost tautological if one considers that the growth process is necessarily accompanied by a differentiation in demand and increased division of labour in the economy. However, a variety of definitions of 'agricultural surplus' exists in the literature, and there is a wide gulf between different authors' interpretations of the optimum magnitude and direction of resource flow and the appropriate transfer mechanisms. This variety arises from differences in theoretical perspectives as well as the specific empirical conditions which furnish their underlying assumptions. Before considering the empirical evidence, therefore, it is essential to examine the theoretical arguments so as to highlight the underlying assumptions and single out the themes that guide our empirical investigation.

The chapter is divided into three main sections. The first classifies theories according to their treatment of the role of agriculture in the growth process and their notion of agricultural surplus. This section also examines the interrelationships between different definitions of 'agricultural surplus' within a consistent accounting framework, and discusses different measurement methodologies. The section concludes with an overview of the determinants of intersectoral resource flows and possible policy recommendations derived from different theoretical perspectives. In the second section we examine the patterns and processes of intersectoral resource flows in five countries and areas for which estimates are available, namely, China, India, the Islamic Republic of Iran (hereafter Iran), Japan and

179

Taiwan, China. The following section investigates the implications of different patterns of intersectoral resource flows for economic growth on the basis of the experiences of these five economies. The limited number of countries and areas in the sample (they are also all in Asia), which is dictated mainly by the availability of data, necessitates a certain caution in making generalisations. The sample is, nevertheless, wide-ranging enough in terms of initial conditions, resource availabilities and development strategies to allow useful conclusions to be drawn. Some of the main conclusions of the study, and possible areas for further research, are discussed in the final section.

Theoretical and methodological considerations

Development theory and intersectoral resource flows

The contribution of the agricultural sector to the growth process in an underdeveloped economy can take different forms. Agricultural output constitutes an important wage good, and the growth of agricultural marketed surplus is normally an important pre-condition for non-inflationary growth of employment in other sectors of the economy. In the early stages of industrialisation, when comparative advantages in international trade are inevitably determined by natural resource endowments, agricultural marketed surplus may also make a significant foreign exchange contribution. The degree of market participation of the agricultural sector is also important on the demand side as it dictates the extent and structure of the home market, at least in the early stages of development. The agricultural sector may also make a factor contribution to the growth process. This could take the form of a net transfer of capital for investment in other sectors of the economy, or a transfer of labour through various forms of labour migration.

The different contributions of agriculture to the growth process are obviously interdependent and cannot be analysed in isolation. It is nevertheless helpful to make a conceptual distinction between them. The contribution of agriculture within different theoretical perspectives depends on what is assumed to be the main constraint to the growth of the economy (see the discussion in chapter 6 in this volume). The existing development literature may be classified on the basis of closeness to one of two extremes.

At one extreme lie the neo-classical theories with their common substitution and continuity assumptions and reliance on the price mechanism to bring about the necessary supply adjustments. In a neo-classical model all resources simultaneously and continuously act as a bottleneck to growth along the equilibrium growth path. Within this framework, sectoral distinctions between agriculture and non-agriculture lose their significance and the analysis is shifted to the project level. Given the assumed perfect mobility of labour and capital any shortages or slack which result in deviations from the equilibrium growth path are removed by the operation of the market mechanism. The main thrust of policy recommendations emerging from neo-classical theories is the removal of barriers to the mobility of factors of production and the correction of instances of market imperfection.

At the other extreme are the structuralist or bottleneck models in which industrial accumulation at any particular time is constrained by the scarcity of specific resources which, given the 'structural' rigidities of less developed economies, cannot be resolved through neo-classical substitution mechanisms. In this literature, the major scarcities which hinder industrial accumulation fall into three major groups: (a) the supply of domestic savings, (b) the supply of key goods and services and (c) the supply of human resources. In principle, bottlenecks in the supply of key goods and services – such as capital goods, food, raw materials and intermediate products – could be overcome through imports. This would not be feasible, however, if the rate of growth of foreign exchange earnings is also constrained by structural obstacles to the diversification and expansion of exports. This also suggests a further possible constraint to industrial accumulation, namely, the limitation of the domestic market and lack of effective demand.

In the structuralist literature the timing and direction of agriculture–industry transfers of surplus, as well as the definition of the relevant concept of agricultural surplus, depend on what is assumed to be the binding constraint. Where the savings constraint is assumed to be binding, accelerated industrial accumulation calls for a net transfer of resources from agriculture to other sectors of the economy. Here, agriculture makes a factor contribution in the form of net financial surplus for investment in non-agricultural sectors (see, e.g., Johnston and Mellor, 1961; Fei and Ranis, 1966; Owen, 1966). Lewis' dual economy model, with its surplus labour and fixed price assumptions, is a good example of the structuralist-type models where industrial accumulation is savings-constrained (Lewis, 1954).

Others assume that industrial accumulation is mainly constrained by a shortage of foodstuffs and agricultural raw materials. Thus in an open but balance-of-payments-constrained economy the growth process encounters inflationary wage spirals due to a shortage of food supplies in urban areas. The central concept of agricultural surplus here is the marketed surplus. Under these circumstances, it is argued that acceleration of industrial accumulation may necessitate an initial net capital transfer to agriculture to alleviate the food supply constraint (see, e.g., Sen, 1957; Nicholls, 1961, 1963; Dobb, 1964; Kaldor, 1967; Ishikawa, 1967a; Kalecki, 1976, ch. 5). In this approach the relative returns on investment in the agricultural and non-agricultural sectors are immaterial for determining the direction of optimum resource flows.

Another possibility is that, rather than being supply-constrained, industrial accumulation might be hindered by a lack of investment opportunities arising from the limitation of the home market. This case of demand-driven accumulation in the industrial sector figured prominently in the early debates on balanced growth (see Rosenstein-Rodan, 1943; Nurkse, 1953; Hirschman, 1958; Streeten, 1959). The thesis has also been put forward more recently in the context of sluggish industrial investment and excess capacity in the Indian industrial sector since the mid-1960s by Bagchi (1975), Raj (1976), Rangarajan (1982) and Mundle (1981, 1985). According to Mundle this phenomenon is due largely to the overextraction of agricultural surplus which, on the one hand, has hindered commercialisation of agriculture and growth of demand for intermediate goods from industry and, on the other, has led to sluggish growth of agricultural incomes and hence of final demand for manufactured consumer goods. These arguments may suggest that, in a predominantly agrarian economy where lack of demand is the main constraint to industrial growth, acceleration of industrial accumulation would require a net transfer of resources to the agricultural sector. While this conclusion may be valid under some circumstances, it should be noted that a major proportion of demand for industrial products often comes from the growth of government investment and services in the urban areas and, as pointed out by Kuznets (1964), the significance of agriculture's demand for industrial output declines over the process of industrialisation. Thus the mere fact that industrial growth may be constrained by the limitations of the home market does not necessarily imply that the optimum direction of intersectoral resource transfer should be towards agriculture.

A related, and perhaps more important, argument on the demand side emphasises the nature of intersectoral resource flows and the structure of the home market rather than aggregate demand. According to this view the method and direction of intersectoral resource extraction may lead to a lopsided structure of domestic demand, and hence industrial output, through its income distributional and employment effects. This may result in what Kalecki (1970) has referred to as a process of 'perverse growth', geared to the luxury consumption of the rich, which may endanger the long-term viability of the growth process (see, e.g., Karshenas, 1990). The policy recommendations resulting from this view require a disaggregated treatment of surplus transfer and the analysis of the impact of different mechanisms of resource transfer on income distribution and employment. Finally, there is the case of a labour-constrained economy. In the structuralist literature, the labour constraint facing developing economies relates mainly to a shortage of skilled labour and managerial know-how. Such economies are usually portrayed as surplus-labour economies, where the main problem is to find productive employment for the pool of unskilled labour rather than a general labour constraint as such. Consequently, the case of a labour-constrained economy has not figured prominently in the debate on intersectoral resource transfer and economic development. This is not to deny the important role of the agricultural sector in the provision of labour to other sectors of the economy. But from a policy standpoint the main issue is the impact of different intersectoral resource flow mechanisms on employment generation rather than the alleviation of labour shortages.

Definitions and mechanisms of surplus transfer

The measurement of intersectoral resource flows involves a multitude of conceptual and data problems which are not always adequately addressed in the literature. The best way to comprehend these problems is to represent the flows within a Social Accounting Matrix framework (SAM). Table 7.1 shows a SAM with the minimum number of entries adequately to represent intersectoral resource flows. As usual, columns represent expenditures and rows show receipts. Sectors or activities produce goods and services by using intermediate products (A) and factor services (F) provided by institutions. Factor incomes received by institutions (Y) are spent on current consumption (C), invested in physical assets (I) or saved (S). Table 7.1 also shows current transfers between institutions (T), e.g., government taxes and subsidies, migrant workers' remittances, gifts, etc., and capital transfers (K), e.g., government investment in agriculture and changes in the financial assets of institutions. Accounting consistency requires that row totals be equal to the corresponding column totals. Two activities or sectors (agriculture, non-agriculture) and three institutions (farm households, government, and others) are distinguished. The category 'others' also includes the rest of the world. For ease of presentation, factors of production have been consolidated into one category. Transactions or transfers *within* sectors and institutions are excluded.

A quick glance at table 7.1 reveals immediately a major conceptual problem with measuring intersectoral resource transfers, namely that consumption, investment and current and capital transfers take place within and between institutions, while production takes place in sectors. As Ishikawa (1967a) has pointed out, resource transfer is meaningful only in

Table 7.1. *A social accounting framework for intersectoral resource flows*

	Activities		Factors	Institutions (current account)			Institutions (capital account)		
	Agriculture (1)	Non-agriculture (2)	(3)	Farm households (4)	Government (5)	Others (6)	Farm households (7)	Government (8)	Others (9)
Activities									
Agriculture		A_{an}		C_{af}	C_{ag}	C_{ao}	I_{af}	I_{ag}	I_{ao}
Non-agriculture	A_{na}			C_{nf}	C_{ng}	C_{no}	I_{nf}	I_{ng}	I_{no}
Factors									
Factors	F_a	F_n							
Institutions (current account)									
Farm households			Y_f		T_{fg}	T_{fo}			
Government			Y_g	T_{gf}		T_{go}			
Others			Y_o	T_{of}	T_{og}				
Institutions (capital account)									
Farm households				S_f				K_{fg}	K_{fo}
Government					S_g		K_{gf}		K_{go}
Others						S_o	K_{of}	K_{og}	

the context of institutions, but production sectors should be so chosen as to incorporate the activities of the respective institutions. For example, if the resource transfer between the farm sector and non-farm sector is of interest (as in table 7.1), then the activity referred to as 'agriculture' should incorporate all the production activities of the farm sector, including their non-agricultural activities. Failing this, the resource flow measure would be a hybrid measure where, for example, the flow of intermediate products referred to agricultural/non-agricultural activities, and consumption to farm/non-farm households. This point has not been adequately addressed in the empirical literature (see, e.g., Lee, 1971; Mundle, 1981). One reason may be lack of data. Often it is not possible to find accurate data on non-agricultural activities of the farm sector. However, as Karshenas (1990) has shown, it may be possible to assess the magnitude of error by examining the different sources of income of agricultural households from household budget surveys.

A second conceptual issue is the appropriate choice of institutions or sector boundaries. Various divisions such as farm/non-farm, subsistence/ commercial, rural/urban, etc. have been suggested. The choice obviously depends on the purpose of the study and its theoretical starting point, as well as on the availability of data.[1] Once a particular institutional categorisation has been chosen, the production activities must be reclassified accordingly.

The analysis of different notions of agricultural surplus and the mechanisms of surplus transfer may proceed in a straightforward manner by utilising the accounting identities implicit in the SAM presented in table 7.1. In what follows, the institutional boundaries are defined in terms of the farm/non-farm dichotomy (as in table 7.1), and the agricultural sector is redefined correspondingly. We shall therefore use agriculture/non-agriculture and farm/non-farm surplus transfers interchangeably.

An important concept of surplus transfer in the literature is the 'net finance contribution' of the agricultural sector to accumulation in other sectors of the economy. As we saw above, this is important where the savings constraint is believed to be the main bottleneck to industrial accumulation. On the real side it is defined as the difference between commodity exports (sales) to and imports (purchases) of the agricultural or farm sector from the rest of the economy – what Millar (1970) has called the 'net product contribution' of the agricultural sector. If we denote agricultural exports by X_a, imports by M_a, and the net finance contribution of agriculture by R, we have, from table 7.1:

$$X_a = A_{an} + C_{ag} + C_{ao} + I_{ag} + I_{ao} \tag{7.1}$$

$$M_a = A_{na} + C_{nf} + I_{nf} \tag{7.2}$$

and

$$R = X_a - M_a = F_a - (C_{af} + C_{nf}) - (I_{af} + I_{nf}) \qquad (7.3)$$

that is, the net finance contribution of the agricultural sector is the value added in the farm sector minus total consumption and investment in the sector. These formulae are often used to measure the intersectoral resource flows from the real side. They clearly show the source of error due to the misclassification of sectors and institutions referred to above. While consumption categories refer to households as institutions, intermediate and investment demands are normally measured on the basis of sectoral or activity demands.

This concept of intersectoral resource flow can also be looked at from the financial side. A net export surplus of the agricultural sector corresponds to a net outflow of funds from the sector. To derive the financial counterpart of this concept of agricultural surplus, we utilise the accounting identities of column (4) and row 4 and column (7) and row 7 in table 7.1 (i.e., the current and capital accounts of the farm sector) to transform (7.3) into:

$$X_a - M_a = (F_a - Y_f) - (K_{fg} - K_{gf}) - (K_{fo} - K_{of}) - (T_{fg} - T_{gf}) - (T_{fo} - T_{of}) \quad (7.4)$$

The right-hand side of (7.4) gives the financial counterpart of the surplus transfer: $(F_a - Y_f)$ is the outflow of net factor incomes from the agricultural sector, mainly comprising rent payments to absentee landlords, interest on loans and net labour income of the farm sector from non-agricultural activities (with a negative sign); $(K_{fg} - K_{gf})$ is the net government investment in the agricultural sector; $(K_{fo} - K_{of})$ represents net private capital transfers into the farm sector, mainly lending to and borrowing from formal and informal financial institutions, hoarding/dis-hoarding of money, acquisition of financial assets, etc.; $(T_{fg} - T_{gf})$ is the net inflow of government taxes/subsidies; and $(T_{fo} - T_{of})$ is the net current private transfers, e.g., remittances of migrant members of farm households. Combining the factor payments and current transfers into one term V, and the capital transfers into K, gives the famous formula

$$R = X_a - M_a = V + K \qquad (7.5)$$

discussed first by Ishikawa (1967a) and often quoted in the later literature. The presentation of intersectoral resource flows from the financial side, particularly in decomposed form, illuminates the various mechanisms through which resource transfer from agriculture can take place. The financial characterisation of surplus flow may also be useful in empirical estimation when data on the real side is incomplete (see Karshenas, 1990), or for double-checking the accuracy of real side measures.

The SAM framework shown in table 7.1 can be used to derive other notions of agricultural surplus discussed in the literature. For example, marketed surplus is the total sales of the farm sector to the non-farm sector (X_a). The 'net agricultural surplus', following Millar (1970), is the value added in the farm sector minus the consumption of farm households which may be written, in the notation of table 7.1, as:

$$NS_a = F_a - C_a = (I_a + X_a - M_a) \qquad (7.6)$$

where $C_a = C_{af} + C_{nf}$ and $I_a = I_{af} + I_{nf}$ are total consumption and investment of the farm sector respectively. The difference between this notion of agricultural surplus and the net finance contribution of agriculture ($X_a - M_a$) is total investment in agriculture. Net agricultural surplus is a useful notion, as it refers to resources made available by the agricultural sector for investment within the sector itself and for utilisation in other sectors, including exports. It also refers to the maximum possible outflow of resources from the agricultural sector, which may be useful in estimating the direction of resource flows in situations where resource outflows cannot be measured due to data problems. Other definitions of agricultural surplus given by Millar (1970) and Ellman (1975) can also be easily derived from table 7.1.

Terms of trade effect

So far we have been considering intersectoral resource flows at current prices. But from a developmental point of view the contribution of agriculture to economic growth depends on the real value of the resources made available. Denoting real magnitudes by lower-case letters, and the prices of the agricultural sector's sales and purchases by P_x and P_m respectively, the real net product contribution of the agricultural sector (r) can be written as:

$$r = x_a - m_a = (X_a/P_x) - (M_a/P_m) \qquad (7.7)$$

This is the real product contribution of the agricultural sector from the viewpoint of the economy as a whole. Here, what matters is the net real value of resources made available by a sector or an institution; the intersectoral relative prices are immaterial. From a sectoral point of view, however, the real value of the net financial surpluses depends on the terms of trade between the sales of that sector and its purchases. A rise in relative prices in favour of the farm sector, for example, implies an income gain for that sector at the expense of others. The magnitude of this gain depends on the price index which is assumed appropriate for deflating the net financial surpluses/deficits of the sector. Let us assume P to be such a price index, so that the real value of the financial surplus of the agricultural sector, viewed from the point of view of the sector itself (i.e., inclusive of terms of trade gains), can be written as:

$$r' = (X_a/P) - (M_a/P) = (V + K)/P = R/P \tag{7.8}$$

The difference $(r' - r)$ represents the income terms of trade gains of the agricultural sector, denoted by TT. Using (7.7) and (7.8), the general formula for the terms of trade gains for the farm sector may be obtained as:

$$TT = x_a(P_x/P - 1) + m_a(1 - P_m/P)$$

The choice of an appropriate price index (P) has been subject to an old and as yet unresolved controversy in the literature (see, e.g., Stuvel, 1956; United Nations, 1968; Kurabayashi, 1971; and Gutmann, 1981). Ishikawa (1967a) has suggested the use of P_x for an export surplus and P_m for an import surplus. Assuming $P = P_x$ we can write the following expression for the real net finance contribution of the agricultural sector:

$$r = x_a - m_a = (V + K)/P_x - TT$$

where $TT = m_a(1 - P_m/P_x)$. As can be seen, in addition to the current and capital transfers discussed above, the real net finance contribution of agriculture includes the terms of trade effect. The variety of intersectoral resource flow mechanisms underlines the importance of a disaggregated analysis of resource transfer from a policy perspective.

Determinants of surplus transfer and policy constraints

In recent years, intersectoral resource transfer has become a central issue in the growing criticism of the industrialisation policies pursued in developing countries over the past four decades. It has been argued that the 'industriali-sation bias' of government, mainly characterised by the pursuit of import-substitution industrialisation policies, has squeezed investible funds out of the agricultural sector. This allegedly has retarded the growth of both agriculture and industry. The argument has sometimes taken a political turn, with 'urban bias' blamed for the distortion of resource allocation processes (see, e.g., Lipton, 1977). The rationale for the criticism in both cases has been the seemingly much higher rate of return on investment in the 'capital-hungry' agricultural sector. While the issue of intersectoral resource transfer is central to such arguments, little has been done to substantiate them empirically, except to make the general point that import-substitution industrialisation policies, by turning the terms of trade against agriculture, must have led to an outflow of resources.

This is not an entirely satisfactory argument. As the above discussion revealed, there are various mechanisms of intersectoral resource transfer, of which the terms of trade mechanism is only one. It may, for example, be argued that import-substitution industrialisation policies, by increasing government revenues in the form of import duties, can contribute to the growth of government investment in agriculture or the provision of subsidies on strategic inputs such as fertilisers. The empirical evidence also seems to suggest that the response of agricultural output to such strategic inputs is more important than to relative prices (Taylor and Arida, 1988). Furthermore, import-substituting industrialisation need not necessarily lead to worsening terms of trade against agriculture. Productivity growth in the industrial sector, combined with greater demand for food arising from higher industrial investment, may produce the opposite result. This raises the important issue of the constraints imposed by the empirically-given structure of the economy on the government's ability to enforce particular patterns of intersectoral resource flow.

The best way to approach this problem is to analyse the determinants of intersectoral resource flows, under given initial conditions and development patterns, and subsequently to examine the possibilities of government to influence these determinants. This requires a complete multisectoral dynamic model based on the Social Accounting Matrix discussed earlier, and simulation exercises under different policy assumptions. Such an exercise is beyond the scope of the present study but it is possible to examine the major determinants of intersectoral resource transfers on the basis of partial equilibrium analysis of the disaggregated formulae presented earlier. Here we shall mainly concentrate on the notion of net resource transfer or the 'net finance contribution' of agriculture. Other notions of agricultural surplus could be analysed in a similar manner, and their determinants turn out to be much the same.

Consider the following formula of net intersectoral resource flow, based on (7.3), where all variables are measured in real terms:

$$r = x_a - m_a = f_a - (c_{af} + c_{nf}) - (i_{af} + i_{nf}) \qquad (7.9)$$

Abstracting from price changes and assuming that necessary adjustments are made by the government to ensure equilibrium in financial and goods markets, this equation can be used to investigate the main determinants of surplus transfer from the agricultural sector.

As can be seen, for given levels of value added and investment in agriculture, the net finance contribution of the sector will be higher the lower its total consumption. But higher population pressure on land implies a higher level of total agricultural consumption from any given level of agricultural output. Where agricultural land is scarce, diminishing returns to labour prevail and technological progress in agriculture is independent of population pressure, the higher the rate of growth of population the lower will be the net financial contribution of agriculture to economic growth. In countries with significant surplus labour in agriculture and high population pressure on land, the ability of the government to extract investible resources from agriculture may be extremely limited. If agricultural output is dependent on the level of consumption of agricultural workers, as in the efficiency wage theories (see, e.g., Bardhan, 1979), this ability will be even more constrained.

In countries experiencing high growth of labour productivity in agriculture, resulting from rapid absorption of agricultural surplus labour in industry or technological change, the net finance contribution of agriculture to economic growth could be higher. In this case of dynamic interaction between agriculture and manufacturing, ever-larger surplus transfer can go hand in hand with increased agricultural consumption in a continuing 'natural' process. In these circumstances, the government has ample possibilities to increase the outflow of surplus by controlling the growth of agricultural consumption.

A further determinant of surplus flow on the consumption side is the distribution of agricultural incomes. A more skewed distribution implies a lower level of aggregate consumption and hence a higher net surplus outflow for a given level of agricultural output. The increase in the surplus outflow through income distribution mechanisms, however, is not a 'natural' process, in the sense that it has a one-off effect and is not the result of expansion in the productive potential of the economy. By reducing the productivity of agricultural workers, as emphasised by the efficiency wage theories, it may even have a negative effect on surplus flow in the long run.

The second major determinant of agricultural surplus from (7.9) is the level of agricultural investment relative to output. For given levels of consumption in the farm sector, a higher incremental capital–output ratio implies a lower net finance contribution of agriculture to economic growth. Ishikawa (1967a) emphasises this factor as a major determinant of surplus flow in selected Asian countries, where the need for heavy investment in irrigation implies a net resource flow into agriculture. To the extent that the capital intensity of agricultural production can be varied, the possibility exists of government influencing the magnitude or direction of net resource flow through choice of technique. Again, a more important factor is technical progress. The introduction of new inputs such as improved seeds and fertilisers, and the application of other modern cultivation techniques, could substantially reduce the incremental capital–output ratio in agricultural production. In most cases, however, this is predicated upon prior investment in irrigation facilities.

Another important aspect of technological progress is the reorganisation of agricultural production. Such reorganisation can on the one hand reduce the incremental capital–output ratio and lead to a higher net finance contribution of agriculture to economic growth, by increasing the effectiveness of capital investment in agriculture. On the other hand, it can help increase on-farm production components of agricultural investment (i_{af}) and consumption (c_{af}), by more effective utilisation of surplus labour and other internal resources of the agricultural sector. As can be seen from (7.9) this latter factor would have the effect of concomitantly increasing agricultural output (f_a) together with consumption and investment in the sector, and hence increasing the net resource outflow by reducing the purchases of the agricultural sector from outside for any level of agricultural output.

These determinants of agricultural surplus define the possibilities of and limits to government intervention to influence the direction and magnitude of net intersectoral resource flows. They are rooted partly in the initial conditions inherited from the historical experience of growth, and partly in the development strategies adopted and the political constraints to government intervention in each country. Some policies, e.g., reorganisation of agricultural production or choice of technique for government investment projects in agriculture, are immediately transparent from analysis of intersectoral resource flows on the real side. For other, more indirect policies it would be more appropriate to look at the financial side of the resource flow equation.

The financial side of the agricultural resource flow equation can be written as:

$$r = x_a - m_a = (f_a - y_f) - (k_{fg} - k_{gf}) - (k_{fo} - k_{of}) - (t_{fg} - t_{gf})$$
$$- (t_{fo} - t_{of}) - TT \tag{7.10}$$

where the right-hand-side variables, that is, the financial flow variables, are denoted in real terms (deflated by the agricultural sales price index), and TT is the income gain in the agricultural sector arising from terms of trade improvements. To analyse the financial mechanisms of resource transfer we have to remove the assumptions of fixed prices and passive financial equilibria made above, and instead begin with the assumption of a fixed magnitude of net resource flows determined on the real side. This of course is a simplistic assumption, as financial flows may have an important impact on the real side as well, but it is necessary at the outset for clarity of exposition.

As can be seen from (7.10), a given level of agricultural surplus (r) can be extracted through various mechanisms. Government policy can strongly affect the relative magnitude of the flows through different channels with important consequences for the process of development. For example, a land reform programme which reduces ($f_a - y_f$) by removing absentee landlordism, may be accompanied by an equal amount of land taxes to maintain the same level of surplus transfer – but the result, in terms of the utilisation of agricultural surplus, would be far-reaching. Similarly, a change in the magnitude of surplus transfer through the terms of trade effect (TT) should have its counterpart with opposite sign in other financial items, for a given level of r. An attempt to increase the surplus flow through taxation of the farm sector or terms of trade changes, in the face of constraints set on the real side, would lead to a compensating reduction of surplus flow through voluntary savings and financial channels ($k_{fo} - k_{of}$).

The interdependence of financial flows characterises the limits which the given level of real resource flow (r) sets for policy – a rise in one item should be compensated by a decline in another financial flow. Of course, the assumption of a given level of r, entirely determined on the real side of the economy, is not realistic. Different patterns of financial flow have different implications for agricultural development and hence the magnitude of resource flow. For example, an increase in the flow through the terms of trade effect would change the supply of agricultural products, income distribution and probably even the choice of technique in the sector. This would in turn affect the magnitude of total resource flow as discussed above. The significance of these interactions is a matter for empirical research, but it should not be difficult to see that in the absence of dynamic forces such as growth of productivity of labour and capital arising from technical progress, other types of influences would have a short-run and limited effect.

In the above analysis we have mainly focused on the agricultural side of intersectoral resource flow accounts, assuming that other sectors respond passively to maintain equilibrium in the financial, commodity and factor markets. This could give rise to misleading conclusions. As discussed above, the dynamic interactions between agriculture and industry could play an important role in the resource flow processes. For example, the absorption of surplus agricultural labour by industry is an important determinant of the finance contribution of agriculture to economic growth. However, as long as the possible implications of such interactions are kept in mind, short of a full multisectoral dynamic model, the above framework should be adequate for the analysis of empirical case studies that follows.

Empirical evidence on intersectoral resource flows

This section examines the empirical evidence on intersectoral resource flows for China, India, Iran, Japan and Taiwan, China. This evidence is considered in the context of the specific agricultural growth paths and agrarian development processes in each economy, in order to identify some of the factors determining resource flow. The broader issues of the interrelationship between intersectoral resource flows and economic growth will be discussed in the next section. The central concept of resource flow used here is the 'net finance contribution' or 'net product contribution' of agriculture, as defined previously. This has formed the central concept in the classical debate on resource transfer, where savings mobilisation is considered to be fundamental to the growth process. As we shall see below, however, other concepts such as marketed surplus, net surplus and labour surplus are strongly linked to this concept. In the first subsection, we briefly discuss the characteristics of the five countries and areas in terms of their initial conditions and development strategies. This is followed by empirical evidence on resource flows in each economy. The concluding subsection sums up the parallels and differences between them.

Country and area characteristics

Estimates of intersectoral resource flows are considered for the following reference periods: India for 1951–70, Iran for 1963–77, China for 1952–80, Japan for 1888–1937 and Taiwan, China for 1911–60. In the case of Japan, estimates for the period after the Second World War are also available but its earlier experience is of most relevance to present-day developing countries.

Though the choice of countries and areas has been mainly dictated by the availability of estimates on intersectoral resource flows, they nevertheless form a varied sample in which each could be taken as representative of a distinct type of economy with similar characteristics. Taiwan, China belongs to the group of newly industrialising economies where, starting from a resource-poor agrarian economy, relative success in modernisation of agriculture and diversification of the industrial base has been achieved. Iran is an example of resource-rich oil exporting economies which, during the 1960s and 1970s, benefited from rapid growth of foreign exchange revenues from the oil sector. China and India have various similarities in terms of initial conditions and economic structure, but differences in their development strategies allow instructive comparisons regarding the respective roles of policy and initial conditions in resource transfer processes. The experience of resource transfer in pre-war Japan, where resource outflow from agriculture is believed to have financed a major part of industrial accumulation, has often been quoted as an example to be followed by present-day developing economies. However, in drawing useful conclusions from the experiences of different economies, it is necessary to take into consideration the initial conditions which helped shape the experience of resource transfer in each.

In terms of resource endowments, all the economies in the sample, with the exception of Iran, had similar initial conditions. They could be broadly characterised as densely populated, with limited new agricultural land frontiers and no significant endowments of exportable natural resources. Iran is distinguished by its large oil exports. Revenues from the oil sector financed more than 70 per cent of gross investment in Iran over the period. However, in common with the others, Iran's economy was also character-ised by labour surplus, as reflected in the relatively large share of agriculture in the labour force at the start of the reference period: 54 per cent in Iran (1960), 72 per cent in India (1951), 83 per cent in China (1952), 70 per cent in Japan (1888) and 70 per cent in Taiwan, China (1911).

With regard to *per capita* national income and, in particular, the productivity of labour in agriculture, there were important differences. *Per capita* national income in 1960 was below US$400 (1975 US dollars) in India and China, while in Iran it was about US$750 (Kravis *et al.*, 1982). Excluding oil revenues, however, Iran's *per capita* national income falls to just over US$400, which is a more appropriate indicator of labour productivity in the domestic economy. In the case of Japan and Taiwan, China, *per capita* national income, even at the beginning of the period (1888 in Japan and 1911 in Taiwan, China), was more than twice that prevailing in the other sample countries (excluding oil export revenues in the case of Iran) in the 1960s (Ishikawa, 1967a). Since the majority of the labour force was in agriculture, these differences are also indicative of agricultural labour productivity differences in these economies. In fact, considering that industrial labour productivity in India, China and Iran in the 1960s must have been well above the levels prevailing in Japan and Taiwan, China in the last century, the *per capita* national income differences are indicative of even more glaring disparities in agricultural labour productivity. Such differences have major implications for the ease with which the savings ratio may be raised and the net financial surplus from agriculture extracted in different countries.[2]

Another important difference in initial conditions relates to population growth, where the experience of Japan stands out. The annual rate of growth of population in Japan from 1888 to 1937 was 1.2 per cent, compared to 2.5–3.0 per cent for the other economies in their respective reference periods. Thus to match Japan's rate of growth of labour productivity in agriculture, the other countries and areas would have had to maintain considerably higher rates of growth in land yields than Japan, or achieve higher rates of labour absorption in non-agricultural activities. This points to another important difference in the initial conditions which arises from the difference in the timing of industrialisation. The fact that the other economies in the post-war period had to use a much more advanced industrial technology than Japan in its reference period, implies that they had, *inter alia*, a lower rate of labour absorption in their non-agricultural sectors.

Institutional factors also affect the nature of policy intervention by government and organisational possibilities in each economy. In all the sample, government played a major role in mobilising and allocating resources. In pre-war Taiwan, China, a major determinant was the policy of the Japanese colonial government to turn the island into Japan's granary. The post-colonial government inherited a low-wage, and highly productive, agricultural sector. The ability of the government to maintain a low-wage economy, while extracting the agricultural surplus through taxation after the land reform of the 1950s, played an important role in mobilising and directing national savings into industrial accumulation in the early decades of the post-war period (see below). In China, the government faced the task, through central planning, of mobilising and channelling national savings in a poor agrarian economy with an extremely low degree of commercialisation. A large part of savings was channelled into heavy industry. New organisational forms were also introduced, particularly in agriculture, which were instrumental in making productive use of surplus labour in the economy, as well as achieving a rapid diffusion of new technology.

The post-independence Indian economy confronted the government with tasks similar to China's, but different development strategies were adopted. As in China, the State played an important role in allocation of investible funds and initially great emphasis was put on heavy industry. Industrial priorities were modified somewhat in the mid-1960s but the government continued to play an important role in the sectoral allocation of investment. In contrast to China, however, government intervention in agriculture has been indirect and market-mediated, though in technological research and infrastructural investment the government's role has been important. In the case of Iran the government has played a dominant role in the economy through its control over oil revenues. In contrast to India, China and Taiwan, China, mobilisation of savings has not been a major preoccupation in Iran; the main task was rather the allocation of already centralised funds in the form of oil revenues. This was attempted through direct investment by the government as well as provision of finance to the private sector through investment banks, within a mixed economy framework. In Japan, too, the State played an important role through provision of finance, infrastructural investment, and science and technology research. As the agricultural sector had already achieved a high degree of commercialisation during the period under consideration, the main channels of intersectoral resource transfer were market-mediated, though government taxation also played a part. An important aspect of the agrarian organisation of Japan in this period was the existence of an influential rural-based cultivating landlord class, which was receptive to new innovations introduced by government initiative.

Evidence on intersectoral resource flows

This section reviews the existing evidence on the direction and magnitude of intersectoral resource flows, with reference to both the financial and real sides of the surplus transfer mechanisms. As the methodologies adopted in different case studies are varied, and since processes of resource transfer in each economy require specific explanations, we shall consider the evidence for each country or area separately and compare their experiences subsequently.

India, 1951–70

There are various partial studies of agricultural resource transfer for India.[3] The only consistent time-series study of intersectoral commodity flows is that of Mundle (1981) for the period 1951–70. Mundle's estimates of real exchanges between agriculture and non-agriculture for consumer and producer goods are given in table 7.2. An important shortcoming of the estimates is that agricultural purchases and sales are both evaluated at purchasers' prices.[4] This substantially overestimates agricultural sales and incomes, as it assigns the income of households involved in transportation and trade of agricultural goods to agricultural producers. We have therefore presented a set of 'revised estimates' as well in table 7.2 which involve a downward adjustment of sales by 20 per cent as a conservative estimate for transport and traders' margins.[5]

Mundle's estimates indicate a net inflow of resources into agriculture in the early 1950s, turning into an outflow from the mid-1950s and increasing to a relatively large drain of resources from agriculture by the early 1960s. This trend is again reversed from the mid-1960s and by the end of the decade there is a relatively large inflow to agriculture. By contrast, the revised estimates show a negative financial contribution of agriculture throughout the period, with the exception of 1962/63 and 1963/64 when the resource outflow was negligible. The revised estimates are also supported by independent estimates of net resource transfers from the financial side, all of which show a net resource transfer into agriculture on both the private and government current and capital transfer accounts (see, e.g., Krishna and Raychaudhuri, 1980; Mody, 1981; Shetty, 1971). Considering that the terms of trade movements also implied substantial net income gains for the agricultural sector (table 7.3), there is enough evidence to cast serious doubt on the accuracy of direction of resource flows indicated by Mundle's estimates.

Table 7.2. *India: commodity purchases and sales of agriculture, 1951/52–1970/71 (billion rupees, 1960/61 prices)*

Year	Agriculture's purchases			Agriculture's sales					Agriculture's net sales	
				Mundle's estimates			Revised estimates		Mundle's estimates	Revised estimates
	Consumer goods (1)	Producer goods (2)	Total (3)	Consumer goods (4)	Producer goods (5)	Total (6)	Total (7) = 0.8 × (6)[a]		(8) = (6) − (3)	(9) = (7) − (3)
1951/52	23.3	4.1	27.4	15.2	7.3	22.5	18.0		−4.88	−9.38
1952/53	29.1	3.6	32.7	16.7	7.6	24.3	19.4		−8.40	−13.26
1953/54	27.9	3.0	30.9	19.0	8.2	27.2	21.7		−3.76	−9.19
1954/55	25.1	3.3	28.4	19.0	9.2	28.2	22.5		−0.17	−5.81
1955/56	27.1	3.4	30.6	20.6	10.4	31.0	24.8		0.41	−5.78
1956/57	26.0	3.5	29.5	21.1	11.5	32.7	26.1		3.15	−3.38
1957/58	27.0	2.9	29.9	20.6	12.3	33.0	26.4		3.05	−3.54
1958/59	28.6	2.9	31.5	21.3	13.6	34.9	27.9		3.34	−3.63
1959/60	28.7	2.7	31.4	21.6	14.9	36.5	29.2		5.18	−2.13
1960/61	29.3	2.6	31.9	23.0	16.8	39.8	31.9		7.95	−0.03
1961/62	30.2	3.5	33.7	23.8	17.2	41.0	32.8		7.27	−0.93
1962/63	29.7	3.5	33.2	24.0	17.7	41.6	33.3		8.46	0.12
1963/64	29.6	4.1	33.8	25.2	18.1	43.3	34.7		9.58	0.90
1964/65	33.8	5.0	38.8	24.9	18.5	43.4	34.7		4.51	−4.16
1965/66	34.1	5.0	39.1	24.5	18.3	42.8	34.2		3.63	−4.91
1966/67	34.9	6.0	40.9	24.8	18.0	42.8	34.3		2.32	−6.24
1967/68	41.8	7.0	48.8	27.0	17.9	44.9	35.9		−3.89	−12.88
1968/69	41.9	7.9	49.8	27.3	17.9	45.2	36.1		−4.59	−13.64
1969/70	43.8	9.3	53.1	28.3	17.8	46.1	36.9		−6.96	−16.18
1970/71	43.9	10.7	54.6	29.4	17.3	46.7	37.4		−7.84	−17.19

Note: [a] Transport and traders' margins assumed to be 20 per cent of agricultural sales. *Source:* Mundle (1981).

Table 7.3. *India: terms of trade of agriculture, 1951–70* (1951 = 100)

Year	Price indices of agricultural:		Net barter terms of trade (P_a/P_n)	Income terms of trade (billion rupees, 1951 prices)
	Sales (P_a)	Purchases (P_n)		
1951	100.00	100.00	100.00	0.00
1952	86.40	87.78	98.43	− 0.52
1953	91.00	88.35	103.00	0.90
1954	82.63	85.77	96.33	− 1.08
1955	77.36	82.21	94.10	− 1.91
1956	90.07	88.54	101.73	0.50
1957	92.19	94.31	97.75	− 0.69
1958	97.12	96.22	100.93	0.29
1959	100.44	99.49	100.95	0.30
1960	104.78	105.53	99.29	− 0.23
1961	105.21	105.23	99.97	− 0.01
1962	106.83	108.59	98.38	− 0.55
1963	113.42	117.30	96.70	− 1.15
1964	132.90	123.18	107.89	2.84
1965	144.78	127.38	113.66	4.70
1966	168.83	138.17	122.19	7.43
1967	187.15	150.77	124.13	9.49
1968	183.20	158.70	115.44	6.66
1969	198.85	159.30	124.83	10.56
1970	208.07	164.59	126.41	11.41

Source: Mundle (1981).

Leaving aside the possible error in the direction of resource flow, and disregarding the cyclical movement of the early 1950s,[6] Mundle's estimates point to a sharp reversal of the secular trend in net resource flows in the mid-1960s. In order to distinguish more clearly the factors that were responsible for this reversal, table 7.4 shows the growth rates of intersectoral commodity flows in real terms for the 1955–64 and 1964–70 subperiods. As can be seen, the deceleration in the growth of agricultural sales and the acceleration in the growth of agricultural purchases were equally responsible for the trend reversal.

These results may at first seem paradoxical, particularly in view of the fact that there was a slight decline in the rate of growth of agricultural output in the latter period.[7] The changing trends of intersectoral commodity flows are the result of complex forces working on both the demand and

Table 7.4. *India: growth of intersectoral commodity exchanges, 1955–71 (%)*

	Real average annual growth rates:	
	1955/56–1964/65	1964/65–1970/71
Agriculture's purchases (imports)	2.7	5.8
Consumer goods	2.5	4.4
Producer goods	4.4	13.5
Agriculture's sales (exports)	3.8	1.3
Consumer goods	2.1	2.9
Producer goods	6.6	−1.1

Source: Based on data in table 7.2.

the supply side. Given the more or less elastic supply of industrial goods, it may be safely assumed that agricultural purchases are largely demand-determined. The acceleration in the purchase of producer goods in the latter period largely reflected the spread of biochemical technology and the consequent increase in the demand for non-agricultural inputs per unit of agricultural output.[8] However, as producer goods had only a small share in total purchases early on, consumer goods played a more important role in the acceleration of the agricultural sector's purchases from the mid-1960s. Though total agricultural output may have been growing more slowly in the latter period, it is the growth of output per agricultural worker which is more relevant in explaining the acceleration of the growth of consumer goods imports into agriculture. The available evidence points to a slightly higher growth of output per agricultural worker during the 1960s than in the 1950s and the early 1960s. While during 1950–61 this measure of labour productivity declined by about 31 rupees (in 1970 prices), over the 1961–71 period it rose by about 25 rupees. The improvement was not due to a faster decline of surplus labour in the latter period,[9] but rather resulted from greater application of new biochemical land-saving technology from the mid-1960s. This increase in labour productivity, however, is not significant enough to explain the rapid acceleration in the growth of agriculture's demand for non-agricultural consumer goods. A more important factor is the income gains in agriculture arising from rapid improvement in the terms of trade from the mid-1960s (see table 7.3) These gains amounted to 8.6 billion rupees (in 1951 prices) between 1964 and 1970 and were nearly twice as much as the income gains attributable to normal growth of agricultural output.

As regards the decline in the rate of growth of agricultural sales from the

Table 7.5. *India: financing of net agricultural resource outflow, 1968/69* (billion current rupees and % of agricultural income)

		Mundle's estimates		Revised estimates	
			(%)		(%)
Net resource outflow	(R)	7.54	(5)[a]	−8.13	(−6)
Agriculture's sales	(X)	78.77	(54)	63.10	(43)
Agriculture's purchases	(M)	71.23	(49)	71.23	(49)
Financing items					
Net outflow of factor income[b]	$(F_a - Y_f)$	14.75	(10)	−0.92	(−1)
Net outflow of current transfers[c]	$(T_{fg} - T_{gf})$	3.95	(3)	3.95	(3)
Net outflow of capital transfers		−11.16	(−8)	−11.16	(−8)
Private	$(K_{fo} - K_{of})$	−6.46	(−5)	−6.46	(−5)
Public	$(K_{fg} - K_{gf})$	−4.70	(−3)	−4.70	(−3)

Notes:
[a] Figures in brackets are percentage shares of agricultural income.
[b] Including current private sector transfers.
[c] Refers only to government's net transfers.
Source: Mundle (1981); Mody, Mundle and Raj (1985).

mid-1960s, the explanation may be sought in various demand- and supply-side factors. Mody, Mundle and Raj (1985) have emphasised the demand side. According to them, consumer goods sales grew more slowly because of the slower growth of the non-agricultural sector and the negative income and price effects of the shift in the terms of trade. In the case of producer goods sales, they point to the additional factor of a relative decline in the share of agri-based industries in industrial output (Mody, Mundle and Raj, 1985, p. 283). These demand-side explanations, however, are not entirely satisfactory in view of the sharp acceleration in agricultural imports from abroad[10] and the growth of agricultural prices since the mid-1960s. Other independent studies have also emphasised the food supply constraint to industrial growth in India over the same period (see, e.g., Sen, 1981).

The intersectoral commodity flows have their counterpart in the financial flows, as stressed earlier. Table 7.5 shows the different financial flows which sum to the balance of commodity exchanges at current prices. These should be regarded as tentative estimates based on partial studies by different authors. Since no independent study of net factor payments is available, this item is estimated as a residual, using both Mundle's estimates and the revised estimates. All independent estimates indicate a net financial inflow into agriculture on both private and official accounts. For Mundle's estimates to be correct, a relatively large countervailing net factor income outflow $(F_a - Y_f)$ is implied, which does not seem plausible.On the other hand, the revised estimates indicate a net factor income inflow of about 1 per cent of total agricultural income; in other words, labour income plus net private current transfers are greater than the rent paid to non-farming landlords and interest payments.[11] Though intercountry comparisons with regard to net factor income flows may be problematic, the revised estimates are much closer to the experiences of China, Iran, Japan and post-colonial Taiwan, China, discussed later.

To sum up, the existing evidence strongly suggests a net resource flow into Indian agriculture during the 1951–70 period. This is brought out by independent estimates both on the real side, i.e., the intersectoral flow of commodities, and on the financial side, namely the private and public current and capital transfers and the terms of trade effect. We have also seen the varying trend of net resource transfer in different stages of agricultural growth and development strategies. From the mid-1960s, with the virtual exhaustion of new cultivable land frontiers and growing population pressure on land, greater resort was made to modern land-saving biochemical technology. This was embodied in the New Agricultural Strategy which involved a greater inflow of modern producer goods from the non-agricultural sector into agriculture. The resulting output response, however, was not commensurate with the increased use of inputs and the food supply constraint became binding, as evidenced by a noticeable decline in the growth of agricultural marketed surplus and a rapid increase in the agricultural terms of trade. The outcome was an intensification in the net resource inflow to agriculture throughout the post-1965 period.

Taiwan, China, 1911–60

A detailed analysis of intersectoral commodity flows and capital transfers for Taiwan, China between 1911 and 1960 is provided by Lee (1971). These estimates, which stretch over the pre- and post-colonial periods, reveal a number of interesting features of changing intersectoral relations in the process of development.

The flow of real commodity exchanges between agriculture and non-agriculture is given in table 7.6. A striking feature is the extremely large resource outflow from agriculture throughout the 1911–60 period. In net terms the outflow amounted to about 40–50 per cent of the sector's gross sales during 1911–30, declining to about 30 per cent in the 1930s and

Table 7.6. *Taiwan, China: real intersectoral commodity flows, 1911–60* (million T$, 1935–37 prices)

Year	Real value of agricultural sales			Real value of agricultural purchases			Net balance
	Consumer goods	Producer goods[a]	Total	Consumer goods	Producer goods	Total	
1911–15	30.0	61.7	91.7	32.9	9.6	42.5	49.2
1916–20	27.6	96.5	124.1	37.0	15.9	52.9	71.2
1921–25	40.2	111.8	152.0	59.6	32.5	92.1	59.9
1926–30	46.6	151.4	198.0	84.5	54.3	138.8	59.2
1931–35	60.0	200.0	260.0	105.8	64.0	169.8	90.2
1936–40	68.3	233.4	301.7	137.4	74.8	212.2	89.5
1951–55	138.2	159.6	297.8	119.4	65.6	185.0	112.8
1956–60	168.1	221.0	389.1	165.6	127.4	293.0	96.1

Note:
[a] Sales of producer goods includes overseas exports.
Source: Lee (1971).

remaining more or less at this level thereafter. Surplus extraction on such a scale was made possible by rapid growth of agricultural productivity, but the actual magnitudes were determined by government policy and institutional factors which were reflected in the changing financial mechanisms of resource transfer over time. Labour productivity in agriculture grew at an annual average rate of 1.8 per cent during 1911–60, despite high population growth (2.5–3.0 per cent per annum) and the limited possibilities of increasing land under cultivation. The agricultural labour force grew more slowly, however, as non-agricultural sectors absorbed the surplus labour.[12] Employment in non-agricultural sectors grew by more than 3.0 per cent per annum between 1911 and 1960, while the agricultural labour force increased by 0.7 per cent each year. Nevertheless, given the limited possibilities of expanding the cultivated area, population pressure on land continued. Before 1930, cultivated land per unit of labour grew somewhat, as population growth was low and possibilities of extending the agricultural land frontier still existed. During the 1930s cultivated land per unit of labour began to decline, but in the 1950s it stabilised at about 0.5 hectares. The rapid growth of agricultural labour productivity was sustained through the constant introduction of land-saving technological innovations, and efficient use of capital investment in the sector.

Technological progress in agriculture during the first three decades of this century was mainly the result of Japan's colonial policy of fostering Taiwan, China, as its granary. In the few years before 1920 the colonial government financed a major land infrastructure and irrigation programme which paved the way for the introduction of seed-fertiliser technology, making possible sustained increases in land and labour productivity. The introduction of new varieties of rice and sugar cane, destined for the Japanese market, had a major impact on improving agricultural productivity up to the late 1920s. From that date, increasing use of modern chemical inputs and a constant diversification of agricultural production helped maintain the momentum of agricultural productivity growth. In addition, investments in irrigation, flood control and drainage made possible more intensive multiple cropping, thereby effectively increasing the land–labour ratio despite the shortage of cultivable land (Kikuchi and Hayami, 1985).

The significance of fixed investment in irrigation, land reclamation and flood control in increasing agricultural productivity has been emphasised in various studies (see, e.g., Rada and Lee, 1963; Lee, 1971, 1974; Hayami and Ruttan, 1985). An interesting aspect of the experience of Taiwan, China, however, is that the share of fixed investment goods in the flow of producer goods into agriculture was very small up to the late 1950s – less than 10 per cent of producer goods and less than 3 per cent of total goods purchased by agriculture. This reflected the significant use for investment of internal resources of the farm sector, especially surplus labour, and the extremely efficient use of capital investment in agriculture. More than 90 per cent of the inflow of producer goods was land-augmenting, seed-fertiliser technology which, being perfectly divisible, particularly suited the small operational farm units in Taiwan, China.

Despite the rapid growth of labour productivity in agriculture, *per capita* consumption of the agricultural population grew at the relatively modest rate of 0.9 per cent per annum. This was due partly to the faster growth of agricultural population than labour, and partly to the siphoning-off of a large part of agricultural value added through rents paid to non-farming landlords, government taxation and adverse terms of trade movements. Table 7.7 shows the financial channels of surplus transfer from agriculture in two representative periods of the colonial and post-colonial eras. As can be seen, in the colonial period land rents constituted about 90 per cent of the net resource outflow from agriculture. Up to the 1930s, these were mainly invested in financial assets in Japan. During the 1930s, and particularly in the post-war period, the financial surplus of agriculture was increasingly utilised to finance industrial investment in Taiwan, China itself.

Government taxes formed the second most important source of resource extraction from agriculture in the colonial period.[13] After the war

Table 7.7. *Taiwan, China: financing of net agricultural resource outflow,
1931–60* (million current T$, annual averages)

		1931–35	1956–60
Net resource outflow	(R)	63	948
Agriculture's sales	(X)	208	9 665
Agriculture's purchases	(M)	146	8 716
Financing items			
Net outflow of factor income	$(F_a - Y_f)$	47	−813
Land rents		56	739
Labour income		−9	−1 552
Net outflow of current transfers[a]	$(T_{fg} - T_{gf})$	17	1 446
Net outflow of capital transfers		−1	316
Private	$(K_{fo} - K_{of})$	0	381
Public	$(K_{fg} - K_{gf})$	−1	−65
Errors and omissions[b]		—	−1

Notes:
[a] Refers only to government's net transfers.
[b] Mainly consists of private transfers $(T_{fo} - T_{of})$.
Source: Lee (1971).

agricultural taxes replaced rents as the main mechanism of surplus extraction (table 7.7) and took the form of compulsory sale of rice and high
fertiliser prices in obligatory barter exchange with the government.[14] The
share of rents in the post-war period declined from an average of about 50
per cent to a maximum of 37 per cent, after land rents were reduced by
legislation and land reform increased the proportion of land under owner
cultivation.[15] Another major post-war change in financial flows was the
significant increase in the farm labour income from non-farming activities.
This amounted to more than twice the rent payments and easily offset all the
taxes paid by the farm sector to the government (table 7.7).

A further mechanism of resource transfer was through terms of trade
changes. During the colonial period agricultural terms of trade fluctuated,
mainly as a result of Japanese government policies regarding imports and
pricing of rice in the domestic Japanese market. The overall trend, however,
was in favour of agriculture (table 7.8). In the post-war period there was a
sharp deterioration in agriculture's terms of trade which, as we have already
observed, was due to government pricing policies effected through compulsory rice collections and fertiliser sales. This amounted to an important
source of surplus outflow from agriculture in the 1950s.[16]

Table 7.8. *Taiwan, China: terms of trade of agriculture, 1911–60*
(1935–37 = 100)

Year	Price indices of agricultural: Sales (P_a)	Purchases (P_n)	Net barter terms of trade (P_a/P_n)
1911–1915	60	73	82.19
1916–1920	92	119	77.31
1921–1925	102	114	89.47
1926–1930	103	103	100.00
1931–1935	80	86	93.02
1936–1940	120	123	97.56
1951–1955	141	177	79.66
1956–1960	248	298	83.22

Source: Lee (1971).

Iran, 1963–77

Estimates of intersectoral resource flows for Iran have not been available until very recently. The predominant assumption in the literature, however, has been that in view of the industrialisation bias of the government and the relative neglect of agriculture, the direction of net resource flow must have been away from agriculture during 1960–77 (see, e.g., Katouzian, 1978; Ashraf and Banuazizi, 1980). Karshenas (1990) has estimated intersectoral resource flows for 1963–77. Since the results, contrary to what has hitherto been believed, indicate a substantial net flow of resources into agriculture, care has been taken to show the most conservative estimates of the inflow.

Accurate data for estimating the magnitude of resource flows from the real side are not available for all the years 1963–77, so estimation was attempted from the financial side. Table 7.9 shows the sources of the flow of funds into and out of Iranian agriculture during this period. Row 1 of the table shows the inflow of funds through government development expenditure. Since land taxes were absent, and other indirect taxes and subsidies are taken into account in measuring the resource flow through the terms of trade mechanism, this could be taken as the resource inflow through official current and capital transfer accounts. Of course, this is a conservative estimate: the inflow of government current administrative expenditure in agriculture and interest subsidies on cheap official loans have not been included. The former has been omitted because of possible objections to its inclusion, and the latter because of estimation problems and the

Table 7.9. *Iran: major categories of inflow and outflow of funds in agriculture, 1963–77* (billion rials)

	1963–67	1968–72	1973–77
Inflow			
Government development expenditure	36.6	73.6	244.0
Gross credit inflow by:			
Specialised banks	23.4	48.9	285.2
Commercial banks	20.0	54.9	185.5
Informal institutions	41.7	99.7	201.7
Total[a]	*121.7*	*277.1*	*916.4*
Outflow			
Maximum possible outflow[b]	*97.8*	*271.4*	*606.7*

Notes:
[a] Excludes transfers due to interest rate subsidies by the government and administrative budgetary expenditures on agriculture.
[b] Refers to net agricultural surplus, i.e., value added minus consumption expenditure of direct producers.
Source: Karshenas (1990), table 6.5, p. 150.

ambiguities regarding the 'correct' or equilibrium market interest rate in Iran over this period.

The second row of table 7.9 shows the gross inflow of funds through formal and informal credit institutions. These, together with government development expenditure, add up to a substantial gross inflow of funds into Iranian agriculture, which particularly increases during the oil-boom years of 1973–77. Since accurate data on the outflow of funds through the credit system and private factor incomes and transfers are not available, we have compared the sum of the gross inflows with a measure of maximum possible outflow of funds which is given in the last row of the table. The latter is the 'net agricultural surplus' as defined previously and equals the agricultural income minus the consumption of direct agricultural producers. Since part of the net agricultural surplus is expected to have been invested in the sector itself, this gives a measure of the maximum possible outflow of funds from the sector. Even with this qualification in mind, the comparison between the last two rows of the table gives a clear indication of the large, and rapidly increasing, net inflow of financial resources into Iranian agriculture over this period.

The estimates in table 7.9 are at current prices and do not show the effect

Table 7.10. *Iran: terms of trade of agriculture, 1963–77* (1963 = 100)

Year	Price indices of agricultural:		Net barter terms of trade (P_a/P_n)	Income terms of trade (billion rials, 1963 prices)
	Sales (P_a)	Purchases (P_n)		
1963	100.0	100.0	100.0	0.0
1964	110.4	102.0	108.2	5.2
1965	110.6	100.5	110.1	6.7
1966	109.5	100.0	109.5	7.1
1967	109.1	100.9	108.1	6.5
1968	110.6	102.6	107.8	7.1
1969	114.6	104.3	109.9	9.6
1970	116.7	105.8	110.3	10.7
1971	131.3	110.5	118.8	17.4
1972	137.9	114.4	120.5	21.6
1973	159.0	126.4	125.8	30.3
1974	211.4	139.7	151.3	57.5
1975	205.9	145.3	141.7	53.3
1976	237.7	161.2	147.5	65.7
1977	283.7	180.4	157.3	81.7

Source: Karshenas (1990), tables A1.5, p. 249 and A1.6, p. 250.

of terms of trade changes on resource flows. These are shown in table 7.10. There was a sustained terms of trade movement in favour of agriculture throughout 1963–77, which particularly accelerated during the oil-boom years of the 1970s. The income gains of agriculture due to terms of trade improvements were by 1977 equal to about 82 billion rials (in 1963 prices), a sum higher than the income gains arising from the normal growth of value added in the sector. Added to resource inflows through the budgetary and credit mechanisms, this implies a substantial net resource inflow into agriculture, made possible by the existence of substantial surpluses in the oil sector and the rapid growth of labour productivity in the manufacturing sector.

These financial flows have their counterparts in commodity flow accounts on the real side. In fact, to understand why such substantial gross financial inflows through the development budget and the credit system have not over time created a commensurate rate of financial outflow, we must examine the real side, in particular with respect to the productivity of investment in agriculture and consumption of the farm sector. A comparison of the experiences of Iran and Taiwan, China is instructive. Similarities include rapid population growth (close to 3 per cent per annum), a relatively slow growth of the agricultural workforce (below 1 per cent per annum) as a result of high rural-to-urban migration and the rapid absorption of labour in other sectors, moderate growth of agricultural value added (3–4 per cent per annum) and a labour productivity growth rate of 2–3 per cent. The completely opposite direction of net resource flows in the two economies resulted from differences in the efficiency of capital use and in the consumption behaviour of the agricultural sector. The main thrust of agricultural policy in Iran over this period was towards the encouragement of highly capital-intensive mechanised farming. Apart from giving encouragement to the private sector for land consolidation and mechanisation through various forms of subsidies (see Nowshirwani, 1976), the government also intervened directly to hasten the mechanisation process by creating new forms of production units such as farm corporations and agri-business enterprises. Government development expenditure by and large benefited only the newly created large-scale mechanised farms which made little contribution to the growth of output and were created by the displacement of thousands of peasant households.[17] More than 30 per cent of the credit granted by the specialised banks was also absorbed by large, State-sponsored agri-business concerns. A large body of research on Iranian agriculture testifies to a lack of commensurate response of agricultural production – and particularly production in the new government-sponsored projects – to the considerable human and financial resources allocated to the sector. Of course, the medium and large peasant cultivators who received land under the land reform programme of the 1960s also benefited from the provision of subsidised new inputs and credits by the government. The favourable output response of this group, which formed the mainstay of Iranian agriculture, accounted for the major part of output growth in this period (Karshenas, 1990, ch. 6). But the 60 per cent of agricultural households composed of poor peasant farmers and landless labourers had extremely low productivity and living standards. Unlike in Taiwan, China, where fixed capital investment played a crucial role in setting in motion a chain of land-augmenting technical progress by increasing the efficiency of the new seed-fertiliser technology, in Iran fixed capital investment in agriculture was directed towards highly mechanised extensive farming which accounted for much of the 40 per cent growth of land under cultivation between 1960 and 1974 resulting from government land infrastructure investment.

Inefficient capital investment was not the sole reason for the divergence in the direction and pattern of resource flows in Iran and Taiwan, China. Another important factor was the rapid growth of consumption in the

Table 7.11. *Iran: urban demand, marketed surplus and imports of food, 1963–77* (billion rials, 1963 prices)

	1963	1970	1977	Trend growth rates 1963–70	Trend growth rates 1970–77
Real food consumption by non-agricultural sector	74.2	130.7	238.2	8.3	9.3
Real food imports	2.0	2.9	32.1	1.9	28.0
Food import ratio (%)	2.7	2.2	13.5	—	—
Real marketed surplus of food	51.4	60.8	114.0	8.3	5.5
Real value added of agricultural sector	98.4	140.2	177.3	3.9	4.3

Source: Karshenas (1990), table 6.8, p. 157.

agricultural sector in Iran. During 1963–72 real consumption per agricultural household grew by 2.3 per cent per year, more or less in line with the growth of labour productivity. Between 1972 and 1977, however, consumption per household grew by more than 7 per cent per annum in real terms. Such a phenomenal rate of growth in the oil-boom period was made possible by substantial increases in the labour income of farm households from non-agricultural activities, large subsidies received by agriculture and major improvements in the terms of trade. The resulting increase in the net resource flow into agriculture was manifested in the increasing inflow of consumer goods and slower growth of agricultural marketed surplus. The slowdown, at a time when food consumption in Iran was sky-rocketing, led to a jump in the food import ratio (table 7.11). It is this jump which has been wrongly attributed to the poor performance of agriculture in the 1970s.

Japan, 1888–1937

Estimates of commodity flows between agriculture and non-agricultural sectors over the 1888–1937 period are available at current prices in Mundle and Ohkawa (1979). These estimates were deflated by appropriate price indices and the results, at 1888–92 prices, are presented in table 7.12. A surprising observation is that, contrary to what is generally believed, there appears to have been a net flow of resources into Japanese agriculture over much of the period under consideration. The popular notion that Japanese agriculture financed industrialisation over the period is largely based on the substantial agricultural taxes during the Meiji era. However, two further important influences, namely the relatively large

Table 7.12. *Japan: real intersectoral commodity flows, 1888–1937* (annual averages, million yen, 1888–92 prices)

Year	Real value of agricultural sales	Real value of agricultural purchases			Net balance
		Consumer goods	Producer goods	Total	
1888–92	188.0	104.0	84.0	188.0	0.0
1893–97	208.8	127.4	99.7	227.1	− 18.3
1898–1902	268.2	189.0	118.4	307.4	− 39.2
1903–07	294.2	194.9	133.7	328.6	− 34.4
1908–12	382.7	264.5	166.0	430.5	− 47.8
1913–17	389.9	172.2	178.7	350.9	39.0
1918–22	544.8	510.5	232.1	742.7	− 197.9
1923–27	583.6	621.5	256.0	877.5	− 293.9
1928–32	637.7	569.3	250.3	819.6	− 181.9
1933–37	684.5	605.3	274.9	880.2	− 195.6

Sources: Mundle and Ohkawa (1979); Ohkawa and Shinohara (1979); Mody, Mundle and Raj (1985).

factor income inflows and the terms of trade effect, have also to be taken into account. To see the effects more clearly we shall consider the estimates of intersectoral resource transfers in conjunction with different financial mechanisms.

The different financing items of net resource transfer for 1918–22 are shown in table 7.13. These items are representative of the 1888–1937 period as a whole, with the exception of agricultural taxes. Direct agricultural taxes, mainly land taxes, took a much higher share of agricultural income in the late 19th century. This share stood at about 20 per cent in the 1890s and then gradually declined to less than 10 per cent in the 1920s.[18] The share of land taxes in total tax revenues in early Meiji Japan was about 90 per cent. As table 7.13 shows, however, the net inflow of factor incomes to agriculture more than compensated for the outflow through taxation. Though data for the earlier periods are scanty, this is believed to have been true for the Meiji era as well (Ishikawa, 1988).

An important aspect of intersectoral financial flows in Japan is that the flow of labour income from non-agricultural sectors into agriculture outweighs the outflow not only through land rents, but also through government taxation. Two factors explain the difference between the experiences of Japan and Taiwan, China, in this regard. First, unlike in Taiwan, China, Japanese landlords in this period mainly consisted of

Table 7.13. *Japan: financing of net agricultural resource outflow, 1918–22*
(annual averages, million current yen)

		1918–22
Net resource outflow	(R)	195 (5)[a]
Agriculture's sales	(X)	2 626 (62)
Agriculture's purchases	(M)	2 431 (58)
Financing items		
Net outflow of factor income[b]	$(F_a - Y_f)$	−318 (−9)
Net outflow of current transfers[c]	$(T_{fg} - T_{gf})$	288 (8)
Net outflow of capital transfers		225 (6)
Net private transfers	$(K_{fo} - K_{of})$	247 (18)
Government investment	$(K_{fg} - K_{gf})$	−22 (−1)

Notes:
[a] Figures in brackets are per cent share of agricultural income.
[b] Including current transfer of private sector.
[c] Refers only to government's net transfers.
Source: Ishikawa (1988, table 10.1, pp. 288–9).

cultivating landlords and their rent income did not constitute a net intersectoral outflow. Secondly, factor income in the form of wages of agricultural households from non-agricultural activities was virtually non-existent during the colonial period in Taiwan, China. The importance of this net factor income inflow in Japan stemmed from the rapid growth of non-agricultural sectors and the fast pace of structural change in the economy over the period. This type of wage income inflow from the non-agricultural activities of farm households could be regarded as part of the contribution of agriculture to economic growth through labour transfer, as mentioned earlier.[19] It has been argued that, as this wage income was supplementary to farm household income, it had a particularly important impact on industrial accumulation by keeping industrial wages low (see Shinohara, 1970).

Another important aspect of financial flows revealed by table 7.13 is the substantial capital outflow in the form of net private asset acquisition through the financial institutions. Taking this into account, the overall balance is a net outflow of finance from agriculture at current prices.[20] This, however, does not take into account the terms of trade effect.

As can be seen from table 7.14, there was an overall trend towards an improvement of agricultural terms of trade during the reference period, with the exception of the 1920s. The downward trend in the 1920s, however, was not sufficiently large to neutralise the gains made in the earlier period.

Table 7.14. *Japan: terms of trade of agriculture, 1888–1937*
(1888–92 = 100)

Year	Price indices of agricultural:		Net barter terms of trade (P_a/P_n)	Income terms of trade (million yen, 1888–92 prices)
	Sales (P_a)	Purchases (P_n)		
1888–92	100.00	100.00	100.00	0.0
1893–97	129.31	115.36	112.10	25.3
1898–1902	164.03	131.75	124.50	65.7
1903–07	195.45	151.87	128.70	84.4
1908–12	213.24	157.26	135.60	136.2
1913–17	228.26	184.08	124.00	93.6
1918–22	482.02	324.37	148.60	264.8
1923–27	452.70	305.88	148.00	280.1
1928–32	297.96	252.08	118.20	116.1
1933–37	331.75	248.13	133.70	230.7

Sources: Ohkawa and Shinohara (1979); Mody, Mundle and Raj (1985).

As a consequence, the income gains due to the terms of trade improvements, measured at 1888–92 prices, were more than sufficient to turn the direction of net resource flow towards agriculture. The movements in agricultural relative prices in this period were the combined result of government trade policy and the growth of productivity in manufacturing. During 1904–37, the Japanese government adopted a protectionist policy towards rice cultivation, with a nominal protection rate of between 20 and 80 per cent enforced in different years (Anderson, 1983). At the same time rice production policy in Taiwan, China, and other colonies was used to stem the inflationary pressures on food prices. The worsening of agricultural terms of trade over the 1920s was the result of the import of cheap rice from the colonies. Another important factor in the terms of trade equation was productivity growth in manufacturing which led to a relative cheapening of manufactured producer and consumer goods purchased by the agricultural sector over the period as a whole.

Given the cyclical behaviour of agricultural prices, the measurement of income gains from terms of trade changes depends crucially on the choice of base period. Measured in 1888–92 prices, the data in table 7.12 point to a flow of resources into agriculture over the 1888–1937 period. With a 1918–22 base, however, the direction of resource flow changes to an outflow from agriculture in the 1920s. A further relevant aspect of the resource flow process was the relatively large flow of funds into agriculture in the form of labour factor income, and the substantial savings outflow from farm households through the banking system. If the resource contribution of agriculture is thus redefined to include the sale of labour services by farm households to other sectors, then we would observe a relatively large positive savings outflow from agriculture at current prices. This definition of surplus, when measured at 1888–92 prices, indicates a moderate outflow of resources from agriculture in real terms. However, taking 1918–22 as the base period, it adds up to substantial real resource outflows from agriculture during the 1920s.

Apart from the contribution of 'part-time' labour as a supplementary source of farm household income, the agricultural sector also made a 'permanent' labour contribution to industrialisation by providing a constant supply of migrant labour to industry. It is estimated that between 1888 and 1937 more than 70 per cent of the increase in the non-agricultural labour force came from agriculture (Umemura, 1979).

A combination of favourable factors on the real side contributed to the reduction of the agricultural sector's demand for resources from the rest of the economy. The agricultural labour force in Japan declined over the period 1888–1937,[21] due to relatively moderate rates of population growth and rapid growth of non-agricultural employment.[22] The latter was important in reducing population pressure on land and maintaining the productivity of labour in agriculture in the face of the limited cultivable land available. Indeed, to satisfy the rising demand for agricultural products resulting from the growth of non-agricultural employment, labour productivity in agriculture had to be increased rapidly. The food balance was maintained by significant growth of agricultural labour productivity – 1.8 per cent per annum over the entire period. This achievement was due only to a limited extent to the increase in the land–labour ratio. Less than 40 per cent of labour productivity growth was attributable to this factor while more than 60 per cent was due to the increase in land productivity resulting from the spread of land-augmenting technical progress. Technical progress in Japanese agriculture took place through an efficient blend of fixed and variable capital, combined with land and labour resources, whereby only 25 per cent of the growth of output was due to increased inputs and 75 per cent resulted from the growth of input productivity (see Yamada and Hayami, 1979a). Fixed investment in irrigation and other land infrastructure paved the way for the spread of the land-augmenting seed-fertiliser technology which made the most efficient use of scarce land and relatively abundant supply of labour (see Ohkawa and Rosovsky, 1960; Johnston, 1966; Hayami et al., 1975; Yamada and Hayami, 1979b).

214   **Massoud Karshenas**

Table 7.15. *China: real intersectoral commodity flows, 1952–80* (billion yuan, 1952 prices)

Year	Real value of agricultural exports			Real value of agricultural purchases	Net balance
	Tax in kind	Market sales	Total		
1952	3.07	12.54	15.61	15.30	0.31
1953	2.80	12.93	15.73	18.26	− 2.53
1954	3.04	13.20	16.24	19.45	− 3.21
1955	3.00	14.04	17.04	23.54	− 6.50
1956	2.68	14.47	17.15	26.48	− 9.33
1957	2.93	15.50	18.43	25.97	− 7.54
1966	n.a.	n.a.	23.70	36.64	− 12.94
1980	n.a.	n.a.	46.71	124.18	− 77.47

Sources: Ishikawa (1967b), table 6, p. 39, for 1952–57 and Ishikawa (1988), for the remaining years.

China, 1952–80

Estimates of intersectoral resource flows in China for the period 1952–57 and for the years 1966 and 1980 are provided in Ishikawa (1967a, 1967b, 1988). The real value of commodity exchanges and their net balance for these years are shown in table 7.15. As can be seen, with the exception of 1952, there was a net inflow of resources into agriculture throughout the period, i.e., the financial contribution of agriculture to accumulation in the non-agricultural sector was negative.

Agricultural marketed surplus amounted to no more than about 30 per cent of gross output in the early 1950s. The limited degree of commercialisation of Chinese agriculture was indicative of the low productivity of labour and lack of specialisation. What is more noticeable is that the marketed surplus ratio remained fairly stable, with only a very slow upward trend until the 1970s. One reason for this was the mounting population pressure on land and the sluggish productivity of labour in agriculture. It is estimated that from 1957 to 1977, value added per agricultural worker actually declined by 0.5 per cent per annum (World Bank, 1983, p. 82). Another reason was the centralised planning of agricultural production and the policy of regional self-sufficiency in food production pursued by the government in the 1960s. In the late 1970s, with the introduction of price incentives and more commercial norms in agricultural production, there

Table 7.16. *China: terms of trade of agriculture, 1952–80* (1952 = 100)

Year	Price indices of agricultural:		Net barter terms of trade (P_a/P_n)	Income terms of trade (billion yuan, 1952 prices)
	Sales (P_a)	Purchases (P_n)		
1952	100.00	100.00	100.00	0.00
1953	108.33	101.10	107.15	1.13
1954	111.21	102.93	108.04	1.31
1955	110.86	104.76	105.82	0.99
1956	113.99	102.64	111.06	1.90
1957	118.83	106.70	111.37	2.09
1966	159.10	109.47	145.34	10.75
1980	231.12	105.40	219.28	55.72

Sources: Ishikawa (1967b), (1988).

was an acceleration in the growth of the marketed surplus ratio. By 1980, however, this marketed surplus ratio was still less than 40 per cent.

Commodity flows into agriculture showed more rapid growth in real terms, for a combination of reasons. As a result of terms of trade improvements, income and consumption in the agricultural sector, particularly of non-agricultural commodities, grew much faster than warranted by the rise in productivity. As table 7.16 shows, net barter terms of trade more than doubled in favour of agriculture between 1952 and 1980. The resulting income gains were about 74 per cent of the increase in gross agricultural output over the same period, in 1952 prices.

A further possible source of increase in demand for non-agricultural consumer goods in the farm sector, over and above that warranted by the growth of agricultural output, was the large inflow of wage income from non-agricultural activities of farm households. As table 7.17 shows, this was a major financing item in the intersectoral flow accounts. Indeed, if this item is regarded as a factor contribution of the farm sector and included in agricultural income, the net savings contribution of agriculture to non-agricultural accumulation in 1980 at current prices becomes positive[23] (table 7.17). This was due to the growing importance of commune-managed enterprises in rural areas as a non-agricultural income source. Compared to India, where factor incomes registered an outflow (based on Mundle's estimates) or a negligible inflow (based on our revised estimates), this

Table 7.17. *China: financing of net agricultural resource outflow, 1956 and 1980* (billion current yuan)

		1956	1980
Net resource outflow	(R)	−4.52	−22.93
Agriculture's sales	(X)	19.55	107.96
Agriculture's purchases	(M)	−24.07	−130.89
Financing items			
Net outflow of factor income[a]	$(F_a - Y_f)$	−3.74	−23.72
Labour income		−3.74	−23.72
Net outflow of current transfers[b]	$(T_{fg} - T_{gf})$	1.07	−1.54
Net outflow of capital transfers		−1.72	2.33
Errors and omissions		−1.03	—

Notes:
[a] Including current private sector transfers.
[b] Refers only to government's net transfers.
Sources: Ishikawa (1967b), (1988).

phenomenon highlights one of the important organisational achievements of the Chinese economy in making productive use of rural surplus labour.

The rapid inflow of manufactured producer goods was another important cause of the relatively fast increase of imports into the agricultural sector. Two periods could be distinguished with regard to the intensity of new manufactured input use in agriculture. During the 1950s remarkable output increases were achieved with moderate addition of new inputs. This was a period of recuperation when agriculture was recovering from the devastation of the war, while at the same time benefiting from institutional reforms and the expansion of cultivated land. With the crisis of agriculture in the early 1960s after the Great Leap Forward, acute food shortages led to policy changes and phenomenal increases in the inflow of mechanical and biochemical inputs to agriculture. Large price subsidies were introduced to encourage greater use of new manufactured inputs in agriculture. Investment allocations to fertiliser and agricultural machinery plants were increased to improve the supply of such products, particularly in the latter part of the 1970s.[24]

In the literature on Chinese agriculture, it is often claimed that in the sectoral allocation of investment by the government the agricultural sector was relatively neglected. This argument is often supported by the fact that agriculture received only about 10 per cent of the centralised investment funds in the government budget, which is disproportionately low compared with the sector's share in GDP (see, e.g., Lardy, 1983). There are, however, several flaws in this argument. First, it ignores the huge price subsidies on investment goods in agriculture. Taking these into account, the share of agriculture in centralised investment funds in real terms would rise by between 30 and 50 per cent. Second, it ignores investment financed by the internal funds of the communes and state farms. Finally, and perhaps most importantly, it neglects the use which was made of the internal resources of the farm sector, especially labour, in agricultural investment, particularly in construction and land infrastructure. To appreciate the magnitude of the investment effort in Chinese agriculture over this period, some comparisons with the experience of other developing countries (using World Bank estimates) would be helpful. For example, the use of chemical fertilisers (in nutrient units) in China amounted to 90 kg per hectare of arable land in 1978, while it was only 25 kg for other developing countries. The corresponding growth rates over the 1965–78 period were 11 and 9 per cent. Similarly, arable land per tractor in China in 1978 was 180 hectares with a trend rate of growth of 15 per cent, as compared with 270 hectares for other developing countries with a trend rate of growth of only 7 per cent. In terms of investment in land infrastructure too, China compares favourably with other countries. For example, the share of irrigated land in total arable land was 45 per cent in China in 1978, with a trend growth of over 3 per cent per annum in the 1960s and 1970s, whereas the corresponding figures for other developing countries were 17 per cent and 2 per cent respectively (World Bank, 1983, p. 25).

To sum up, the Chinese experience indicates a net resource inflow into agriculture throughout the three decades of centrally planned economic development. Contrary to the popular belief that central planning was a means of mobilisation of agricultural resources for industrial accumulation, the net finance contribution of agriculture to accumulation in other sectors was negative. Though mobilisation of surplus labour in agriculture appears to have made an important contribution to accumulation in the economy as a whole, the main beneficiary was in fact the agricultural sector itself. Even if we include the contribution of farm labour to the output of the non-agricultural sector as part of the agricultural savings contribution, the net resource inflow to agriculture in real terms would still remain positive and significant. More than 70 per cent of resource inflow into agriculture in 1980 was due to the favourable terms of trade gains (see tables 7.15 and 7.16).

An important explanatory factor on the real side in the Chinese experience of intersectoral commodity flows is the lack of commensurate response in agricultural output and marketed surplus to the growing amount of resources allocated to the sector during the 1960s and the early

Table 7.18. *China: growth of output, labour force and productivity in agriculture, 1952–79* (% per annum)

Period	Value added	Labour force	Value added per worker
1952–57	4.9	2.2	2.7
1957–77	1.6	2.1	−0.5
1977–79	9.4	1.0	8.4
1952–79	2.7	2.0	0.7

Source: World Bank (1983), table 3.8.

1970s. As can be seen from table 7.18, the rate of growth of agricultural value added during the 1957–77 period was below the growth of the agricultural labour force, leading to negative productivity growth of −0.5 per annum. This was a period of rapid growth in the inflow of new inputs into agriculture. The changing trends in output and productivity in different periods shown in table 7.18 should be viewed in the context of changing trends in the land–labour ratio. The 1950s were a period of expansion of cultivable land. Between 1952 and 1957 the total sown area increased by more than 35 million hectares, or close to 2.2 per cent per annum. During the 1957–77 period, however, due to the encroachment of residential dwellings and industrial sites and the exhaustion of new agricultural lands, the total sown area declined by 8.5 million hectares, or −0.3 per cent per annum.[25] In other words, the land–labour ratio which remained stable during the 1950s declined by about 2.5 per cent per annum between 1957 and 1979.[26] As far as growth in land productivity is concerned, therefore, the performance in the two sub-periods was not very different – 2.7 per cent annually in 1952–57 and about 2 per cent in 1957–77. Compared to the experience of other countries, these are quite respectable growth rates, particularly since they were sustained over a long period. But, despite the increased intensity of application of labour and other resources, the 1957–77 period still exhibits lower land productivity growth rates. The decline in the productivity of inputs over this period has been attributed to organisational problems such as overcentralisation of decision-making processes, inefficiencies arising from information asymmetries inherent in quantity planning, lack of incentives, lack of specialisation resulting from the government's policy of regional food self-sufficiency, etc. (see Lardy, 1983; World Bank, 1983). The great surge in agricultural production after the reforms of the late 1970s and the early 1980s is indicative of the extent to which organisational problems had previously hindered the realisation of the full productive potential of agriculture.[27]

A comparative overview

Comparison of the patterns and processes of intersectoral resource flows amongst the five countries and areas reviewed reveals interesting results which are sometimes strikingly at variance with what has hitherto been assumed, implicitly or explicitly, in the development literature. Particularly important is the finding that the 'net finance contribution' of agriculture to the growth of other sectors appears to have been negative in most of the economies in the sample and for much of the observation period. The intersectoral commodity exchanges in real terms showed a negative balance for the agricultural sector in India, Iran and China; the exceptions were Japan and Taiwan, China. This is particularly surprising in view of the fact that the first three countries have been following strong import-substituting industrialisation policies, in contrast to Taiwan, China. The popular notion that import-substitution industrialisation is tantamount to a resource squeeze on agriculture does not seem to hold for the sample of economies considered here; as we shall argue later, it may not hold for many other developing countries with similar initial conditions and development policies.

Other notable results relate to the mechanisms of resource transfer. Given that all the economies in the sample had large agricultural labour reserves at the beginning of their respective reference periods, their differences regarding the inflow of farm-labour factor income from non-agricultural activities are of special interest. These differences reflect the extent to which the various economies were successfully utilising surplus agricultural labour, when the option for a permanent transfer of labour out of the farm sector was not yet available. In Japan, the magnitude of this 'supplementary' wage income inflow to agriculture was so large that it overshadowed other intersectoral resource flows. The contribution of labour income was also important in Iran in the 1970s and in post-war Taiwan, China, both of which experienced rapid industrial growth in these periods. A comparison of the experience of the above three economies with India, where the inflow of factor income was negligible (according to some estimates even negative), shows that the rate of growth of the non-agricultural sector is a major determinant of factor income inflow in the market economies. This is not a surprising result, and probably not very novel. However, little research has been done on the type of activities which contribute most to such wage income flows into agriculture, and possible policy lessons which could be derived from the experience of economies such as Japan and Taiwan, China, in this respect.[28]

A further important result on factor income flows relates to the comparative experience of India and China. Like India, China experienced grave difficulties in absorbing its huge agricultural surplus labour in the non-agricultural sectors. Nevertheless, unlike India, the inflow of wage income from non-agricultural activities to the farm sector in China was substantial. This was a direct effect of the introduction of new organisational forms in Chinese agriculture over the reference period which, despite their shortcomings in other respects, were extremely effective in making productive use of agricultural surplus labour. Though the political circumstances in India may not allow such far-reaching agrarian reorganisation, there may still be lessons to be learned from China when daring organisational reforms are demanded by the gravity of the situation.

Another important source of surplus transfer was the terms of trade mechanism. In Iran and China, there was a continuous improvement in agricultural terms of trade throughout the period of investigation, and in India such an improvement was particularly visible from the mid-1960s. By the end of their respective reference periods, the three countries registered relatively large agricultural income gains as a result of the terms of trade improvement. In Japan too, there was an overall trend increase in agricultural relative prices which, despite a reversal in the 1920s, by the end of the period still produced substantial income gains in the agricultural sector measured in 1888–92 prices. In Taiwan, China, however, the terms of trade mechanism was yet another source of resource outflow from agriculture, particularly in the post-war period when government policies of taxation of agricultural inputs and compulsory rice exchanges led to a substantial worsening of the agricultural terms of trade. Once again, countries with import-substituting industrialisation policies were those which showed major surplus inflows to agriculture through terms of trade improvements.

Other financial mechanisms of surplus transfer (taxation, credit flows, rent payments, etc.) varied in significance between the economies depending on the institutional set-up, degree of commercialisation of agriculture and development of a market economy, and government policy. These have already been considered in detail and do not lend themselves to a brief summary here. What is important to note, however, is the extent to which the real side factors – population growth, labour absorption in non-agricultural sectors, choice of technique and, above all, technological progress – constrained the possibility of increasing agricultural resource outflow through the manipulation of financial and institutional factors. For example, amongst the economies surveyed, the institutional set-up of Chinese agriculture probably afforded the greatest discretion to the government in extracting resources from the agricultural sector. However, given the immense population pressure on land and the slow pace of labour productivity growth in agriculture, the possibilities for such resource extraction were limited. On the other hand, in Japan and Taiwan, China, where labour productivity in agriculture grew relatively fast as a result of land-augmenting technological progress and low capital expenditure requirements, there were larger possibilities for transfer of resources from agriculture through various policy measures. Under such favourable real side conditions, and with a fair degree of development of rural financial institutions, surplus transfer may take place through voluntary savings of agricultural households, as the experience of Japan shows.

Implications of intersectoral resource flows for industrial accumulation and growth

A central theme in the debate on intersectoral resource transfer has related to the savings contribution of agriculture to economic growth. It has been argued that, in a predominantly agrarian economy in the early stages of industrialisation, the agricultural sector must provide the initial funds for industrial investment. As we observed in the previous section, however, the net finance contribution of agriculture to industrial accumulation in most of the economies in the sample, and for much of the observation period, appears to be negative. We shall now examine the extent to which this phenomenon has retarded the pace of industrial accumulation in the economies concerned, and consider the plausibility of the central role often given to saving mobilisation in the study of intersectoral resource flows.

A remarkable fact about the economies in the sample is that they all achieved considerable success in raising the savings rate during their respective reference periods, as can be seen in table 7.19. Since the length of the reference period varies between countries, annualised figures may provide a better index of relative performance. The average annual growth rates of savings ratios for the different economies calculated over their respective reference periods were 1.4 per cent for China and Japan, 2.8 per cent for India, 7.1 per cent for Iran, and 1.6 per cent for Taiwan, China.[29] Clearly the performance of different economies in raising their savings ratio bears little relation to their experience regarding the direction and magnitude of agricultural surplus flows. It could even be argued that countries with a negative finance contribution of agriculture outperformed those with a positive contribution in the task of overall savings mobilisation.

It should be noted, however, that 'net finance contribution' of agriculture refers to the net resources made available by agriculture for non-agricultural investment, while the savings ratio is defined with reference to the

Table 7.19. *Rate of domestic savings and net agricultural surplus ratio* (%)

	Savings ratio[a]	Net agricultural surplus ratio[b]
China[c]		
1952	21.4	7.1
1957	24.9	1.4
1966	30.6	3.5
1980	31.5	−1.6
Japan		
1888–92	9.3	8.3
1908–12	15.0	8.5
1918–22	20.5	4.9
1933–37	18.6	2.6
India		
1951–53	9.4	n.a.
1960–63	13.6	2.7
1968–70	15.8	−0.1
Iran		
1963/64	13.5	3.6
1971/72	21.6	6.5
1976/77	35.2	3.4
Taiwan, China		
1911–15	9.8	16.8
1921–25	8.7	16.7
1931–35	10.8	13.5
1951–55	18.9	17.7
1956–60	21.3	14.2

Notes:
[a] Percentage of GDP at market prices, unless otherwise specified. For China, Japan, and Taiwan, China, figures refer to gross investment ratio.
[b] Agricultural value added minus the consumption of direct agricultural producers, as a percentage of GDP. Valued at current prices for all countries, except for Taiwan, China, which is valued at 1935–37 prices.
[c] For China ratios are expressed as percentage of net material product.
Sources: Lee (1971); Ohkawa and Shinohara (1979); China, Government of (1987); Karshenas (1990); Mundle and Ohkawa (1979); Mundle (1981).

economy as a whole. A more appropriate definition of the savings contribution of agriculture is the 'net agricultural surplus' as defined on p. 187 above. This refers to the income generated in agriculture minus the consumption of direct agricultural producers. Net agricultural surplus as a ratio of GDP is shown alongside the savings ratio in table 7.19. Two observations may be made in comparing these figures. First, the agricultural surplus ratio, in contrast to the overall savings rate, was almost negligible for all the economies over much of their reference period, with the exception of Meiji Japan and Taiwan, China. Second, and more importantly, the rate of increase in the savings ratio bore little resemblance to the change in the agricultural surplus ratio. While the overall rate of saving was increasing rapidly, the agricultural surplus ratio was either declining sharply, or remaining stable (in the case of Meiji Japan and Taiwan, China). This suggests that the explanation for the behaviour of the overall rates of saving and investment in these economies should be sought in factors other than those directly related to agricultural surplus mobilisation. With the exception of Meiji Japan and Taiwan, China, agriculture seems to have made little contribution to overall savings mobilisation, and in some cases it played a negative role. Nevertheless, this did not handicap these economies in achieving high overall rates of saving, even outperforming Meiji Japan and Taiwan, China.

The above result may seem paradoxical in view of the fact that the economies under consideration were predominantly agrarian economies with most of their labour force in agriculture and related activities. Nevertheless, they had all already achieved a certain degree of industrialisation at the beginning of their respective reference periods, largely in the food and textile industries, and it was the growth of the industrial sector which provided the funds for further accumulation. A comparison between data in tables 7.19 and 7.20 shows the high positive correlation between industrial growth and the increase in the savings ratio. It is now widely acknowledged, at least since the fact was highlighted in Lewis (1954), that the savings ratio tends to grow *pari passu* with the increase in the share of modern industry in national product. This is because in modern industrial enterprises retained profits form a major part of the accumulation funds; the higher the share of modern industry in national output, the higher the share of profits and thus *ceteris paribus* the savings ratio. There is, however, another important source of growth of savings in modern industry which arises from the increase in unit profits normally associated with major productivity gains in industry. An important attribute of modern manufacturing is that rapid growth of output is normally accompanied by high labour productivity growth. This may be seen in table 7.20 for the economies under consideration, where labour productivity growth

Table 7.20. *Growth of industrial output, productivity and real wages* (%)

| | Average annual growth rates of: | | |
	Output	Labour productivity	Real wages[a]
China			
1952–57	18.0	12.7	4.7
1957–70	10.0	} 3.0	−0.9
1970–79	9.2		1.9
Japan			
1885–1900	4.9	1.8	0.6
1900–20	5.1	2.4	2.5
1920–37	6.8	5.2	1.3
India			
1953–62	7.5	3.6	1.8
1962–70	4.7	3.7	−1.0
Iran[b]			
1966–70	13.2	4.6	4.1
1970–77	17.3	10.2	11.0
Taiwan, China			
1911–25	8.5	1.7	0.4
1925–40	7.2	4.9	−1.4
1951–60	10.8	6.2	0.8
1961–70	14.7	8.0	3.5
1970–80	14.0	8.0	8.1

Notes:
[a] Deflated by the consumer price index.
[b] For Iran the figures refer to the larger industrial enterprises (more than 50 employees).
Sources: Lee (1971); Ohkawa and Shinohara (1979); United Nations, *Yearbook of Industrial Statistics*, various issues; China, Government of, *Statistical Yearbook of China*, various issues; and World Bank (1983).

accounted for more than half the growth of industrial output in most periods. For any given level of industrial terms of trade and product wages in industry (i.e., industrial wages divided by the industrial price index), increases in labour productivity will be reflected in an equivalent increase in unit profits. This implies a higher saving ratio for any given share of industrial output in total national product. Increases in agricultural terms of trade and industrial product wages are mechanisms for redistributing productivity gains in industry amongst the industrial workers and agricultural producers. Comparing the data on productivity and real wage growth rates in the industrial sector, shown in table 7.20, it is evident that there were major gains in unit profits in all the economies over their respective reference periods, with the exception of Iran. Though the diverse terms of trade movements against the industrial sector in Japan, India and China to some extent reduced the growth of unit profits, this was not strong enough to wipe out the unit profit gains arising from the relatively large gap between the growth rates of productivity and real product wages.[30]

It appears, therefore, that the impressive increases in saving ratios in the countries and areas under study were mainly the consequence of the growth of the industrial sector – accounted for partly by the increase in the share of output of modern industry in national income and partly by the increase in unit profits in industry resulting from high productivity growth rates and relatively low real wage increases. In Iran the existence of oil revenues allowed an increase in the savings ratio alongside high rates of growth in real wages and consumption. This suggests that the emphasis on the savings contribution of agriculture, hitherto central in the debate on intersectoral resource transfer, may have been misplaced. It reflects a static view of the intersectoral resource allocation process which is not uncommon in the development literature – the sectoral allocation of a given amount of investible funds to maximise current total national output. However, viewed dynamically – considering the process of savings generation as an endogenous part of the process of intersectoral resource allocation – gives a totally different turn to the argument. This is not to deny the crucial role that agriculture plays in the growth process, particularly in the early stages of industrialisation, but it does point to the need for a shift of emphasis in assessing that role.

The role of agriculture becomes much more important when considered from the point of view of employment generation in non-agricultural sectors. A comparison between the experiences of China and India on the one hand, and Japan and Taiwan, China, on the other, brings this point into clear relief. As we saw earlier, the first two countries suffered from growing population pressure on land and an inadequate rate of absorption of labour in the non-agricultural sectors. Fast rates of population growth were only partially responsible for the growing population pressure on land; comparison with the experience of Taiwan, China, which had similar rates of population growth, shows that the low degree of labour absorption in the non-agricultural sectors is perhaps a more important cause.[31] This low absorption has traditionally been addressed in the development literature in terms of government industrial policies, technological possibilities of factor substitution in industry, factor price distortions, etc. These are clearly relevant issues, but their relevance is predicated upon procurement of an adequate 'wage fund' to sustain a larger non-agricultural labour force in the first place. As shown in table 7.20, even with apparently inadequate rates of labour absorption, real industrial wages in China and India declined during the 1960s as a result of the inadequate growth of agricultural marketed surplus.[32] Further increases in non-agricultural employment, which would have entailed a further decline in real wages under these circumstances, could have proved socially and even physiologically intolerable.[33]

The next question, therefore, concerns the extent to which intersectoral resource transfers affected the growth of agricultural output and marketed surplus in the economies under study. To begin with, no clear-cut correlation appears to exist between the growth of agriculture and the direction and magnitude of resource transfer over different reference periods. For example, Taiwan, China, showed a very rapid rate of growth in agricultural production despite a substantial net outflow of resources from the sector (agricultural output grew by 3.2 per cent per annum during 1911–20, 4.2 per cent during 1920–40, and 4.3 per cent during 1950–60). China showed relatively fast rates of growth of agricultural output (4.5 per cent per annum) between 1952 and 1957, which was a period of moderate resource inflow to agriculture, but the growth rate deteriorated to 2.2 per cent per annum during 1957–70, which was a period of heavy net resource inflow to agriculture. The growth rate recovered to 4.6 per cent per annum during 1970–80. In India agricultural output grew by 2.9 per cent per annum during 1951–65, but annual growth declined to 2.4 per cent from 1965 to 1970, which saw a greater net flow of resources into agriculture. In Iran, with a substantial flow of resources into agriculture, output grew at the relatively high rate of 4.3 per cent per annum during 1963–77, and in Japan, with an outflow of resources, agricultural output grew by 1.5 per cent between 1888 and 1937.[34]

The lack of any simple correlation between resource flows and agricultural growth indicates the significance in the growth process of the efficiency of resource use and mode of utilisation of resources allocated through intersectoral flows. Indeed, on the basis of the empirical evidence examined in the previous section, one may support the hypothesis that the degree to which resources are productively utilised in the agricultural sector is itself an important determinant of both agricultural growth and the magnitude and direction of net resource flows. The experiences of Japan and Taiwan, China, in this regard stand out in comparison to the other three countries. They were the only two economies where agriculture did not pose a constraint to the growth of industrial employment;[35] at the same time it made a net finance contribution to investment in other sectors. As argued in the previous section, the nature and pace of technological progress in agricultural production was the crucial factor in determining the contribution of agriculture to economic growth in both economies. The spread of land-augmenting technical progress, based on new seed-fertiliser technology, led to relatively fast growth of labour productivity with minimal fixed capital investment. The effectiveness of the new technology was bolstered by adequate and timely investment in irrigation and land infrastructure.[36] Basic investment in land infrastructure by the government was to a considerable extent complemented by private investment in small-scale labour-intensive projects making high use of the farm sector's own internal resources. The divisible nature of the seed-fertiliser technology made it accessible to small peasant holdings which formed the mainstay of farm organisation in both economies.[37] The improvements in irrigation and drainage systems induced the development and use of more fertiliser-responsive, high-yield variety seeds, which in turn were effective in counter-acting the rising cost of investment in land infrastructure and thus maintaining investment incentives (Yamada and Hayami, 1979b). The growth of productivity of resource use in agriculture resulting from technological progress accounted for more than 50 per cent of the growth of agricultural output in both economies throughout their respective reference periods. Without such high rates of technical progress, it is inconceivable that a net resource outflow from agriculture could have been maintained for so long without severely damaging the growth of agricultural output.

Similar technological packages consisting of new high-yield variety seeds and use of biochemical inputs were introduced in India and China during the 'Green Revolution'. As noted earlier, the substantial increases in the inflow of new producer goods inputs into agriculture in these two countries from the mid-1960s were aimed at bringing about a similar type of land-augmenting technical progress. These attempts, however, remained by and large unsuccessful, at least during the periods under study here; that is, agricultural growth was not commensurate with the cost of new inputs and the outcome was a growing net resource inflow to agriculture while the food supply constraint in the economy remained. If genuine technological progress is defined by the degree to which total factor productivity increases, then in contrast to Japan and Taiwan, China, the experiences of China and India do not constitute genuine technological progress.[38] The differences in the degree of success in achieving genuine technological progress amongst these countries derived from differences in agrarian institutions and government policies (see, e.g., Ishikawa, 1967a; Mody, Mundle and Raj, 1985; Hayami and Ruttan, 1985). Though there are valuable lessons in the experiences of Japan and Taiwan, China, concerning organisational factors which were conducive to genuine technological progress in agriculture, a few cautionary notes are in order on differences in initial conditions between economies. First, labour productivity in agriculture in Japan and Taiwan, China, at the beginning of their respective reference periods was well above levels prevailing in the other countries. As a consequence, the capacity of the private farm sector to make the necessary investments in adopting the new technology was that much greater. Secondly, the rate of growth of population in China and India was at least twice as high as in Japan. Though Taiwan, China, had a rate of population growth similar to China and India, the fact that it started from a base of much higher agricultural labour productivity put it in a different category, closer to Japanese initial conditions, than the other countries in the sample. The type of agrarian organisations which stimulate genuine technological progress, under these circumstances, may be very different from the historical cases of Japan and Taiwan, China. China, India and Iran have much to learn from each other, and from their own past experiences.

Concluding remarks

Despite the diversity of initial conditions and development paths followed in the different economies in our sample, a number of general conclusions with specific policy implications emerge from the study. It appears that the growth of agriculture, and in particular the nature of technological change in the sector, is of crucial importance for overall growth as well as for the pattern of structural change and intersectoral resource flows. In developing countries with limited cultivable land, growing population pressure and diminishing returns in agriculture, the possibilities for achieving significant land-augmenting technical progress offered by the 'Green Revolution' technology is of utmost importance. This no doubt requires a growing *gross* inflow of resources into agriculture in the form of new biochemical inputs, investment in irrigation and land infrastructure, investment in human capital, etc. Whether the final outcome is a *net* inflow to or outflow from agriculture depends on the efficiency of resource use and genuine technological progress in the sector. Net intersectoral resource flows, central to the savings-constrained models of growth, cannot be regarded as a policy instrument as such but rather as an intermediate target which helps in assessing the efficiency of resource use in agriculture. Successful technological progress which leads to growing productivity of labour in agriculture may automatically increase the sector's savings contribution to economic growth. This can take place through private financial institutions as in Japan, even without further enforcement through taxation policies, relative price changes, etc.[39] On the other hand, in a technologically stagnant agriculture, attempts to finance industrial investment through a forced extraction of resources from agriculture may be dissipated in inflationary spirals.

More importantly, the net finance contribution of agriculture, at least in the surplus-labour economies we have been studying, does not seem to matter significantly in generating savings in the economy as a whole when considered in a dynamic setting. Even in economies where agriculture made a negative finance contribution, great successes have been achieved in raising the overall savings ratio through a rise in the share of industrial output in national income and the relatively fast growth of productivity in manufacturing. The key contribution of technological progress in agriculture to economic growth seems to be through its effect in raising the productivity of agricultural labour. This is a crucial link in the process of growth and structural change in large agrarian economies, where sustained growth in the industrial 'wage fund' is essential for the maintenance of a growing non-agricultural labour force.

The degree of success in implementing land-augmenting technological progress in the agricultural sector of labour-surplus economies is important not only because of the contribution it makes to the removal of the wage constraint; it also plays a crucial role in the structural transformation of the economy as a whole and in the changing patterns of income distribution and poverty. A few observations in this connection may be made by way of further elaboration.[40]

The divisible nature of the new seed-fertiliser technology allows the benefits of technological progress to be spread amongst the small peasant holdings which constitute the core of the agricultural sector of developing countries. Of course, government policy directed towards the creation of an appropriate environment, such as the establishment of suitable agrarian institutions, clear definition of property rights, security of tenure and, above all, provision of infrastructural investments and supporting services, is an important pre-condition for reaping the distributional benefits of the new technology. In fact, such policies are essential for the successful diffusion of the new technology in the first place.

The growth of labour productivity in agriculture may lead to further beneficial distributional effects by increasing the demand for the products of labour-intensive industries, and particularly by encouraging the growth of such industries in the rural areas which may create an additional source of labour income for the farm sector.[41] The growth of labour productivity in agriculture is also a pre-condition for the alleviation of the worst types of poverty in large agrarian economies which face a food supply constraint. If such productivity growth is based on genuine technological progress which leads to cost reductions in agricultural production, it could be doubly beneficial to the eradication of poverty, on the one hand by reducing food prices, and on the other by generating new sources of employment for the poor.

The empirical evidence on intersectoral resource transfers, which is by and large confined to the countries and areas we have surveyed in this chapter, helps to highlight some of the most important factors in the process of economic growth and structural change. Further research which can shed light on the experience of other developing countries would certainly be valuable. The significance of intersectoral resource transfers, however, does not derive from the contribution they make to savings mobilisation, as emphasised by the savings-driven models of growth. It is rather the way the patterns and processes of intersectoral resource flows intertwine with the transformations in the structure of employment and income to bring about a sustained process of balanced growth. Factors which determine the efficiency of resource use in agriculture, the success or failure in the diffusion of new biochemical technologies, and the linkages between growth of agricultural productivity and the creation of non-farm employment, seem to be the key elements in this process.

Notes

I would like to thank Andrew McKay, Ahmad Ebrahimi, P.J.K. Kikuchi, Hassan Hakimian and Ajit Ghose for helpful comments on an earlier version of this study.

1 For a discussion of different rationales for the sectoral distinction, see Mundle (1981).
2 It also signifies the importance of the existence of an external source of finance, such as oil revenues in the case of Iran, in complementing national savings and, as we shall see, influencing the direction of net resource transfer.
3 See, e.g., Ishikawa (1967a) for estimates for the year 1951/52, Thamarajakshi (1969) for balance of trade estimates for 1950/51 and 1960/61, Krishna and Raychaudhuri (1980) and Mody (1981) for estimates of rural and agricultural savings respectively. Mody, Mundle and Raj (1985) give a useful summary of the existing studies.
4 Two other, less serious, shortcomings may also be mentioned. The first is that, while Mundle meticulously separates agricultural and non-agricultural popula-tions and estimates *per capita* consumption for each group, he does not account for the fact that agricultural households may be involved in non-agricultural activities. The second concerns the inclusion of food processing as part of the activities of agricultural households on the grounds that processing of food grains is partly done by them. Even if this argument were plausible, for the sake of consistency, the category of agricultural households would then have had to include households in the food processing industry.
5 According to Karshenas (1990), transport and traders' margins together

amounted to 23–25 per cent of agricultural sales in Iran. Since India is a much larger country, with a higher degree of regional specialisation in agricultural production, and possibly a lower degree of efficiency in transport and trade, the assumed margin of 20 per cent is likely to be on the low side.

6 As pointed out by Mundle (1981), the estimates for the first three years are based on different data definitions and thus are not comparable to the estimates for the other years.

7 The annual average rate of growth of real gross product in agriculture declined from 2.9 per cent during 1951–64 to 2.4 per cent during 1964–70. Though there has been some controversy over whether the agricultural growth rate actually declined, there is no claim that the rate increased (see Mody, Mundle and Raj, 1985).

8 The trend rate of increase in the input–output ratio of non-agricultural inputs in agricultural production increased from about 2 per cent during 1955–65 to about 11 per cent in the 1965–70 period (calculated from Mundle, 1981, table 4.7).

9 In fact, the land–labour ratio declined from 1.17 hectares in 1950 to 0.97 in 1960 and 0.84 in 1970 (see Chakravarty, 1987, table 15, p. 113).

10 Net agricultural imports from the rest of the world, which were less than 1 billion rupees (in 1960 prices) for the entire 1950–64 period, increased to 6.82 billion rupees (1960 prices) over the 1964–70 period, that is, by fifteen-fold on an annual average basis.

11 On the basis of the findings of other independent studies, this seems to be a more reasonable condition than that implied by Mundle's estimates. On the one hand, during this period India did not have a large and wealthy absentee landlord class. On the other, factor income through wage labour in non-agricultural activities seems to have formed a relatively large source of income for Indian agricultural households (see, e.g., Mellor *et al.*, 1968, pp. 309–29).

12 The agricultural labour force increased from about 1.1 million in 1911 to 1.4 million in 1940. During the 1940s, as a result of large-scale immigration, the agricultural labour force jumped by about 300,000, and remained at 1.7 million for the rest of the period.

13 Land taxes, constituting about 30 per cent of government tax revenue, were the main item in agricultural taxation up to the 1940s. With the reform of the tax system in the 1940s, which put greater emphasis on income taxes, land taxes declined to about 7 per cent of total tax revenue.

14 During the 1950s, the government collected more than 50 per cent of the rice sold and more than 30 per cent of rice production (see Lee, 1971, pp. 80–5).

15 In the 1953 land reform programme, about 60 per cent of private tenanted land was purchased by the government and resold to 200,000 tenant families who, as a result, became independent owner-operators (Lee, 1974).

16 For example, of the T$96 million annual net resource outflow from agriculture in 1956–60 (valued at 1935–37 prices as in table 7.6), more than 60 per cent was due to adverse terms of trade movements.

17 See, e.g., ILO (1972), Katouzian (1978), Shafaeddin (1980) and Ashraf (1982). According to the ILO report, 'large private capital (i.e., agro-industrial compa-

nies) is given the most assured supply of irrigation water, lands and government protection and subsidies (specially investment in infrastructure) most of which is denied to the smaller private individual entrepreneurs in agriculture'. For example, the bulk of development expenditure allocated to agriculture during the 1960s went on dam construction and the lands made available below the dams were handed over to mechanised agri-businesses. During the 1970s too more than 40 per cent of development expenditure in agriculture (excluding irrigation) was directly allocated to agri-businesses and farm corporations.

18 For example, in the latter half of the 1880s the tax burden on the agricultural sector was 20 per cent of agricultural value added compared with 2 per cent for the non-agricultural sector. In the early 1930s, however, the figures were 7 per cent and 4 per cent respectively – though by then the relative sizes of the two sectors had changed considerably, further increasing the share of non-agricultural taxes in total.

19 Mundle and Ohkawa (1979) refer to a concept of the savings contribution of agriculture to economic growth that includes net factor income inflows. On the basis of this definition, they show that there was a relatively large savings outflow from agriculture during 1888–1937. Their estimates, however, are subject to a number of qualifications. First, they do not take into account the terms of trade effect, their estimates being in current prices. Secondly, they do not take into account as part of agricultural investment the huge riparian investment of the government (see n.20 below). Taking these two factors into account, the net savings contribution of agriculture, even with their definition, becomes much smaller.

20 This is not strictly accurate. The estimates in table 7.13 do not take into account the large amount of government expenditure on riparian construction (mainly used for flood control and river improvement). Such expenditure in 1918–22 amounted to 290 million yen annually which, even if only partly included in agricultural investment, would tilt the balance towards an inflow of funds at current prices.

21 Average annual rates of growth of the agricultural labour force were 0.1 per in 1880–1900, − 0.6 per cent in 1900–20 and − 0.1 per cent in 1920–35.

22 The population growth rate rose from about 1 per cent in the late 1880s to 1.5 per cent in the 1930s. The share of the non-agricultural labour force in the total increased from 29 per cent in 1888 to 57 per cent in 1937.

23 Though, at constant prices, there would still be a substantial net savings inflow to agriculture due to the terms of trade effect.

24 For example, the total number of tractors in use increased from 1,300 in 1952 to 72,600 in 1965 and 745,000 in 1980. Hand tractors increased from 39,600 in 1965 to 1,874,000 in 1980. Accordingly, the machine-ploughed area increased from 0.1 million hectares in 1952 to 41 million hectares in 1980. The use of nitrogen fertilisers also increased from 0.19 million tons in 1952 to 4.94 million tons in 1965 and to 42 million tons in 1979.

25 These figures are based on the data in *Statistical Yearbook of China* (China, Government of, 1977).

26 This compares with a decline in the land–labour ratio of about 0.7 per cent per

annum in India over a similar period. By the end of the 1970s, there were more than three farm workers per hectare in China compared with one in India.

27 According to the *Statistical Yearbook of China* (China, Government of, 1987), gross agricultural output grew by more than 10 per cent a year in the first half of the 1980s.

28 The experience of Iran in this regard was very short-lived, and confined to a few years of the oil boom in the early 1970s (see Karshenas, 1990).

29 For China, the saving ratios in table 7.19 are shown as a percentage of net material product rather than GDP. This explains the high ratio compared to the other economies. The rates of increase in the savings ratio, however, are comparable.

30 This holds for all the countries except China. In China real product wages in industry grew by at least 2 percentage points faster than labour productivity over the 1952–80 period as a whole. The slow growth of real wages reported in table 7.20 was due to sluggish growth of agricultural marketed surplus and the increase in food prices. Between 1957 and 1970, for example, real product wages grew by 4.1 per cent per annum in Chinese manufacturing, while real wages (deflated by the consumer price index) declined by about 1 per cent per annum. This in a sense reflected the price paid by Chinese industrial workers for the flow of resources into agriculture through terms of trade changes. The experience of India in 1962–70 was to some extent similar: while real product wages in manufacturing grew by an annual average rate of 2.1 per cent, real industrial wages (deflated by the consumer price index) declined by 1 per cent per annum. In India, however, industrial productivity was growing by at least 1.5 percentage points above real product wages, reflecting a continuous growth in unit profits over this period. In Japan and Taiwan, China, too, real product wages growth was well below productivity growth in industry, reflecting rapid increases in unit profits over their respective reference periods.

31 The agricultural labour force in China increased by over 120 million or 72 per cent between 1952 and 1979, and in India by over 66 million or 65 per cent between 1951 and 1971. The share of the agricultural labour force in the total in India remained stable at around 70 per cent over this period, and in China it declined from 84 per cent to 74 per cent between 1952 and 1979. In Taiwan, China, this share declined from about 70 per cent in 1911 to 56 per cent in 1960. It further declined from 43.5 per cent in 1966 to only 21.5 per cent in 1979 (a change in the system of industrial classification reduced the share of agriculture by 10 per cent compared to the data for the earlier period).

32 In this regard it is important to note that the decline in real industrial wages in China and India in this period was not due to slow growth of money wages or real product wages. Real product wages in China during 1957–70 grew by an average annual rate of 4.1 per cent, well above labour productivity growth in industry. In India they increased by 2.1 per cent per annum, close to labour productivity growth, between 1962 and 1970. The decline in real wages was a result of the increase in agricultural terms of trade, symptomatic of the inadequate rate of growth of agricultural marketed surplus. In Taiwan, China, by contrast, the slow growth of real wages was the result of a slow increase in real

product wages, when agricultural terms of trade were declining in favour of industry.

33 Iran also experienced an inadequate rate of labour absorption in modern industry, although the causes are totally different from those in India and China. In Iran the low absorption was due to the government's industrial policies rather than to the inadequacy of the 'wage fund'. Because of easy availability of foreign exchange, urban food supplies could always be supplemented by imports. The combination of an abundant urban food supply and low labour absorption in modern industry meant that a substantial share of the increase in the labour force in Iran was absorbed in the urban informal sector with meagre productivity and low standards of living (see Radwan, 1975).

34 The output growth rates are taken from the following sources: Lee (1971) for Taiwan, China; Mody, Mundle and Raj (1985) for India; Karshenas (1990) for Iran; Ohkawa and Shinohara (1979) for Japan; and World Bank (1983) for China.

35 In pre-war Taiwan, China, certainly, there was ample room for expanding non-agricultural employment and at the same time supporting even higher rates of growth of industrial real wages than were actually experienced. This is evident from the substantial foreign trade surpluses in agricultural products and large capital outflows from the island over this period.

36 In Japan the basic investment in irrigation had to a large extent taken place in the pre-Meiji restoration period, and accordingly the burden of fixed investment in irrigation was less than in the other four countries (see Ishikawa, 1967a).

37 Modern mechanical-engineering technology, concerned with the application of mechanical power to field operations, was absent in both economies during their respective reference periods; this type of technology became prominent after the 1950s.

38 This also applies to Iran, though technical change in Iranian agriculture was of a different type, mainly directed towards extensive farming with a highly capital-intensive labour-saving technology.

39 This of course depends on the nature of agrarian institutions, and in particular the degree of development of rural financial institutions.

40 For a more comprehensive treatment of the implications of intersectoral resource transfers for income distribution and poverty see Karshenas (1989), from which the present chapter is adapted.

41 The existing empirical evidence suggests that increments in the income of poor peasant households are in fact largely spent on the products of such labour-intensive industries (see Mellor, 1989).

References

Adelman, I. and E. Thorbecke (eds.), 1966. *Theory and Design of Economic Development*, Baltimore: Johns Hopkins University Press.

Anderson, K., 1983. 'Growth of agricultural protection in East Asia', *Food Policy*, vol. 8, no. 4, November, pp. 327–36.

Ashraf, A., 1982. *Dehghanan, Zamin, va Enghelab* (Peasants, Land, and Revolution), Tehran: Amir Kabir Publishers, in Persian.

Ashraf, A. and A. Banuazizi, 1980. 'Policies and strategies of land reform in Iran', in Inayatulah (ed.) (1980).

Bagchi, A.K., 1975. 'Some characteristics of industrial growth in India', *Economic and Political Weekly*, Annual Number, February, pp. 157–64.

Bardhan, P.K., 1979. 'Wages and unemployment in a poor agrarian economy: A theoretical and empirical analysis', *Journal of Political Economy*, vol. 87, no. 3, June, pp. 479–500.

Chakravarty, S., 1987. *Development Planning: The Indian Experience*, Oxford: Oxford University Press.

Chenery, H. and T.N. Srinivasan (eds.), 1988. *Handbook of Development Economics*, vol. I, Amsterdam: Elsevier Science Publishers BV.

China, Government of, 1977. *Statistical Yearbook of China*. Beijing.

1987. *Statistical Yearbook of China*, Beijing.

Dobb, M., 1964. 'Some reflections on the theory of investment planning and economic growth', in M. Dobb (ed.), *Problems of Economic Dynamics and Planning: Essays in Honour of Michael Kalecki*, Warsaw: Polish Scientific Publishers.

Eicher, C. and L. Witt (eds.), 1964. *Agriculture in Economic Development*, New York: McGraw-Hill.

Ellman, M., 1975. 'Did the agricultural surplus provide the resources for the increase in investment in the USSR during the First Five Year Plan?', *Economic Journal*, vol. 85, no. 340, December, pp. 844–63.

Eltis, E. *et al.* (eds.), 1970. *Induction, Growth and Trade*, Oxford: Oxford University Press.

Fei, J.C.H. and G. Ranis, 1966. 'Agrarianism, dualism and economic development', in Adelman and Thorbecke (eds.) (1966).

Gutmann, P., 1981. 'The measurement of terms of trade effects', *Review of Income and Wealth*, series 27, no. 4, December, pp. 433–53.

Hayami, Y. and V.W. Ruttan, 1985. *Agricultural Development: An International Perspective*, Baltimore and London: Johns Hopkins University Press.

Hayami, Y., V. W. Ruttan and H.M. Southworth (eds.), 1979. *Agricultural Growth in Japan, Taiwan, Korea and the Philippines*. Honolulu: University Press of Hawaii.

Hayami, Y. *et al.*, 1975. *A Century of Agricultural Growth in Japan: Its Relevance to Asian Development*, Tokyo: University of Tokyo Press.

Hirschman, A.O., 1958. *The Strategy of Economic Development*, New Haven: Yale University Press.

ILO (International Labour Office), 1972. *Employment and Income Policies for Iran*, Geneva, Mimeo.

Inayatulah, B. (ed.), 1980. *Land Reform: Some Asian Experiences*, Kuala Lumpur, Malaysia: Asian and Pacific Development Administration Centre.

Ishikawa, S., 1967a. *Economic Development in Asian Perspective*. Tokyo: Kinokuniya Bookstore.

1967b. 'Resource flow between agriculture and industry: The Chinese experience', *Developing Economies*, vol. 5, no. 1, March, pp. 3–49.

1988. 'Patterns and processes of intersectoral resource flows: Comparison of cases in Asia', in Ranis and Schultz (eds.) (1988).

Islam, N. (ed.), 1974. *Agricultural Policy in Developing Countries*, London: Macmillan.

Johnston, B.F., 1966. 'Agriculture and economic development: The relevance of the Japanese experience', *Food Research Institute Studies*, vol. 6, no. 3, pp. 251–312.

Johnston, B.F. and J.W. Mellor, 1961. 'The role of agriculture in economic development', *American Economic Review*, vol. 51, no. 4, September, pp. 566–93.

Kaldor, N., 1967. *Strategic Factors in Economic Development*, New York: Cornell University Press.

Kalecki, M., 1970. 'Problems of financing development in a mixed economy', in Eltis *et al.* (eds.) (1970).

1976. *Essays on Developing Economies*, London: Harvester Press.

Karshenas, M., 1989. 'Intersectoral resource flows and development: Lessons of past experience', World Employment Programme, *Research Working Paper*, WEP 10–6/WP99, Geneva: ILO.

1990. *Oil, State and Industrialization in Iran*, Cambridge: Cambridge University Press.

Katouzian, H., 1978. 'Oil versus agriculture: A case of dual resource depletion in Iran', *Journal of Peasant Studies*, vol. 5, no. 3, April, pp. 347–69.

Kikuchi, M. and Y. Hayami, 1985. 'Agricultural growth against a land-resource constraint: Japan, Taiwan, Korea and the Philippines', in Ohkawa and Ranis (eds.) (1985).

Kravis, I. *et al.*, 1982. *World Product and Income: International Comparisons of Real Gross Product*, Baltimore: Johns Hopkins University Press.

Krishna, R. and G.S. Raychaudhuri, 1980. *Trends in Rural Savings and Private Capital Formation in India*, World Bank Staff, *Working Paper*, no. 382, Washington, DC: World Bank.

Kurabayashi, Y., 1971. 'The impact of changes in terms of trade on a system of national accounts: An attempted synthesis', *Review of Income and Wealth*, series 17, no. 3, September, pp. 285–97.

Kuznets, S., 1964. 'Economic growth and the contribution of agriculture: Notes on measurement', in Eicher and Witt (eds.) (1964).

Lardy, N.R., 1983. *Agriculture in China's Modern Economic Development*, Cambridge: Cambridge University Press.

Lee, T.H., 1971. *Intersectoral Capital Flows in the Economic Development of Taiwan 1895–1960*, Ithaca, New York: Cornell University Press.

1974. 'Food supply and population growth in developing countries: A case study of Taiwan', in Islam (ed.) (1974).

Lewis, W.A., 1954. 'Economic development with unlimited supplies of labour', *Manchester School of Economic and Social Studies*, vol. 22, no. 2, May, pp. 139–91.

Lipton, M., 1977. *Why Poor People Stay Poor: Urban Bias in World Development*, Cambridge, Mass.: Harvard University Press.

Mellor, J.W., 1989. 'Rural employment linkages through agricultural growth: Concepts, issues and questions', in Williamson and Panchamukhi (eds.) (1989).

Mellor, J.W. *et al.* 1968. *Developing Rural India*, Ithaca, New York: Cornell University Press.

Millar, J.R., 1970. 'Soviet rapid development and the agricultural surplus hypothesis', *Soviet Studies*, vol. 22, no. 1, July, pp. 77–93.

Mody, A., 1981. 'Resource flows between agriculture and non-agriculture in India, 1950–1970', *Economic and Political Weekly*, Annual Number, March, pp. 425–40.

Mody, A., S. Mundle and K.N. Raj, 1985. 'Resource flows from agriculture: Japan and India', in Ohkawa and Ranis (eds.) (1985).

Mundle, S., 1981. *Surplus Flows and Growth Imbalances: The Inter-Sectoral Flow of Real Resources in India: 1951–71*, New Delhi: Allied Publishers.

1985. 'The agrarian barrier to industrial growth', *Journal of Development Studies*, vol. 22, no. 1, October, pp. 49–80.

Mundle, S. and K. Ohkawa, 1979. 'Agricultural surplus flow in Japan, 1888–1937', *Developing Economies*, vol. 17, no. 3, September, pp. 247–65.

Nicholls, W.H., 1961. 'Industrialization, factor markets and agricultural development', *Journal of Political Economy*, vol. 69, no. 4, August, pp. 319–40.

1963. 'Agricultural surplus as a factor in economic development', *Journal of Political Economy*, vol. 71, no. 3, April, pp. 211–23.

Nowshirwani, V.F., 1976. 'Technology and employment programme: Agricultural mechanisation in Iran', World Employment Programme, *Research Working Paper*, WEP 2–22/WP 28, Geneva: ILO.

Nurkse, R., 1953. *Problems of Capital Formation in Under-developed Countries*, Oxford: Basil Blackwell.

Ohkawa, K. and G. Ranis (eds.), 1985. *Japan and the Developing Countries: A Comparative Analysis*, Oxford: Basil Blackwell.

Ohkawa, K. and H. Rosovsky, 1960. 'The role of agriculture in modern Japanese economic development', *Economic Development and Cultural Change*, vol. 9, no. 1, Part 2, October, pp. 43–67.

Ohkawa, K. and M. Shinohara (eds.), 1979. *Patterns of Japanese Economic Development: A Quantitative Appraisal*, New Haven: Yale University Press.

Owen, W.F., 1966. 'The double developmental squeeze on agriculture', *American Economic Review*, vol. 56, no. 1, March, pp. 43–70.

Rada, E.L. and T.H. Lee, 1963. 'Irrigation investment in Japan', Joint Commission on Rural Reconstruction, *Economic Digest Series*, no. 14.

Radwan, S., 1975. 'Employment implications of capital intensive industries in Iran', Report of an ILO Mission to Iran, Geneva: ILO, mimeo.

Raj, K.N., 1976. 'Growth and stagnation in Indian industrial development', *Economic and Political Weekly*, Annual Number, February, pp. 223–36.

Rangarajan, C., 1982. *Agricultural Growth and Industrial Performance in India*, Research Report, no. 33, Washington, DC: International Food Policy

Research Institute.

Ranis, G. and T.P. Schultz (eds.), 1988. *The State of Development Economics: Progress and Perspectives*, Oxford: Basil Blackwell.

Rosenstein-Rodan, P.N., 1943. 'Problems of industrialisation of Eastern and South-Eastern Europe', *Economic Journal*, vol. 53, no. 210, June–September, pp. 202–11.

Sen, A., 1981. 'The agricultural constraint to economic growth: The case of India', Ph.D. thesis, University of Cambridge.

Sen, A.K., 1957. 'Some notes on the choice of capital-intensity in development planning', *Quarterly Journal of Economics*, vol. 71, no. 4, November, pp. 561–84.

Shafaeddin, S.M., 1980. 'A critique of development policies based on oil revenues in recent years in Iran', Ph.D. thesis, University of Oxford.

Shetty, S.L., 1971. 'An inter-sectoral analysis of tax burden and taxable capacity', *Indian Journal of Agricultural Economics*, July–September.

Shinohara, M., 1970. *Structural Changes in Japan's Economic Development*, Tokyo: Kinokuniya Bookstore.

Streeten, P., 1959. 'Unbalanced growth', *Oxford Economic Papers*, vol. 11, June, pp. 167–90.

Stuvel, G., 1956. 'A new approach to the measurement of terms-of-trade effects', *Review of Economics and Statistics*, vol. 38, no. 3, August, pp. 294–307.

Taylor, L. and P. Arida, 1988. 'Long-run income distribution and growth', in Chenery and Srinivasan (eds.) (1988).

Thamarajakshi, R., 1969. 'Intersectoral terms of trade and marketed surplus of agricultural produces, 1951–52 to 1965–66', *Economic and Political Weekly*, vol. 4, no. 26, June.

Umemura, M., 1979. 'Population and labor force', in Ohkawa and Shinohara (eds.) (1979).

United Nations, 1968. 'A system of national accounts', *Studies in Methods*, series F, no. 2, rev. 3.

Various years. *Yearbook of Industrial Statistics*.

Williamson, J.G. and V.R. Panchamukhi (eds.), 1989. *The Balance between Industry and Agriculture in Economic Development: Sector Proportions*, vol. 2 of the Proceedings of the Eighth World Congress of the International Economic Association, 1–5 December 1986, Delhi, India: London: Macmillan.

World Bank, 1983. *China: Socialist Economic Development*, vols. I and II, World Bank Country Study, Washington, DC.

Yamada, S. and Y. Hayami, 1979a. 'Agriculture', in Ohkawa and Shinohara (eds) (1979).

1979b. 'Growth rates of Japanese agriculture, 1880–1970', in Hayami, Ruttan and Southworth (eds.) (1979).

Index

239